Performance Measurement for World Class Manufacturing

Performance Measurement for World Class Manufacturing

A Model for American Companies

Brian H. Maskell

Productivity Press, Inc.

CAMBRIDGE, MASSACHUSETTS

NORWALK, CONNECTICUT

Productivity Press
P.O. Box 3007
Cambridge, Massachusetts 02140
United States of America
Telephone: (617) 497-5146
Telefax: (617) 868-3524

Book and cover design: Joyce C. Weston
Printed and bound by: Maple-Vail Book Manufacturing Group
Printed in the United States of America

Library of Congress Cataloging-in-Publication Data

Maskell, Brian
    Performance measurement for world class manufacturing : a model for
American companies / by Brian H. Maskell.
        p.   cm.
    Includes bibliographical references and index.
    ISBN 0-915299-99-2
        1. United States—Manufactures—Management.   2. United States—Manufactures
—Labor productivity—Measurement.   I. Title.
HD9725.M367   1991   91-6855
658.5'036—dc20   CIP

91 92 93 10 9 8 7 6 5 4 3 2

To my mother and father,
Rose and Bill Maskell,
with much love.

They that live with Hope can dance without music.

George Herbert 1624

Contents

xi   Foreword

xv   Preface

xix   List of Illustrations

1   Chapter One • World Class Manufacturing and the Need for New Performance Measures

19   Chapter Two • Characteristics of the New Performance Measures

41   Chapter Three • Shortcomings of Traditional Management Accounting

75   Chapter Four • Measurement of Delivery Performance and Customer Service

123   Chapter Five • Measurement of Process Time

171   Chapter Six • Measurement of Production Flexibility

203   Chapter Seven • Measurement of Quality Performance

247   Chapter Eight • Financial Performance Measures

285   Chapter Nine • Measuring Social Issues

305   Chapter Ten • Establishing Performance Targets

331   Chapter Eleven • Producing the New Performance
       Measures

351   Chapter Twelve • Alternative Cost and Management
       Accounting Techniques

391   References
397   About the Author
399   Index

Foreword

With great enthusiasm, I present our readers with a timely book, as well-written as it is valuable. *Performance Measurement for World Class Manufacturing: A Model for American Companies*, by Brian H. Maskell explains, defines, and presents in detail the new performance measures currently setting the standards in successful world class manufacturing operations. Respected in Europe, Britain, and the United States, the author is both an engineer and a management accountant with broad experience in the manufacturing and distribution industries.

The new performance measures chosen by today's world class enterprises relate directly to successful manufacturing strategy. They utilize primarily nonfinancial measures. They vary by location, change over time, and are easy to use. Finally, they provide fast feedback to operators and managers and foster improvement instead of simply monitoring.

Mr. Maskell convincingly states that by replacing traditional management accounting and variance reports, these new measures can truly drive the production process. The troublesome nature of traditional management accounting is that the information is often irrelevant to manufacturing strategy. It distorts costs by assuming inaccurate cost patterns and apportioning overhead incorrectly. It is inflexible and impedes progress — and subjects everyone to the needs of the financial accounting systems. It summarily creates confusion throughout an organization — something we have all witnessed.

The book's twelve chapters address various issues including the shortcomings of traditional management accounting. They discuss and illustrate measures that are applicable specifically to delivery performance and customer service, process time, production flexibility, quality performance, and financial performance. Going beyond production operations, the author extends productivity measures to social issues such as morale, teamwork, employee involvement, leadership ability, training and education, and commitment to safety and environmental issues. He devotes a chapter to establishing useful performance targets (including competitive benchmarking, price targeting, and the half-life concept). Another chapter describes different software packages that can produce new performance measurement reports and assess a performance measurement system. Mr. Maskell closes his book with a full discussion of alternative cost and management accounting techniques being used.

To me, productivity should be a measure of a team, of a company, of a society. Individuals should not be the focus of productivity measurement because measures and rewards for individuals can work at cross purposes to what the organization is trying to achieve. Productivity improvement means the growth of the organization and of all its members. Therefore, our measures and rewards should focus individual efforts on what is best for the total situation.

That does not mean we can neglect individual champions. We should not neglect the quality of life in the workplace.

How can we focus on the productivity and quality of products and services and neglect the quality of life of those people producing the goods and services? In a productive world class business, the overall process is important. To achieve dramatic productivity growth, we must give people the opportunity to grow personally. They must feel enriched at work; challenged every day to continually improve and look at things from a fresh perspective. They should be free to look for problems, to investigate and to solve them — not to avoid them. This process of continuous improvement is the foundation of *Performance Measurement for World Class Manufacturing* — and is why I like it so much.

When America became the most productive society in the world following World War II, we shared our wealth by aiding other countries in rebuilding the world. We are a very generous and giving nation. But we were able to do it because our productivity, and hence our prosperity, had grown. You can't share what you don't have. The freedom of our society is unique. But if we lose our prosperity, it will put pressure on our freedom. The entire process requires us to change. And as we change, we encounter resistance. A law of physics holds that for every action there is an equal and opposite reaction. It is the same in our growth. The more energy we put into something, the more resistance comes back. This causes people to stop at the point of resistance. Productivity improvement comes from hard work. This should not be discouraging — it should be challenging and enriching.

Following that brief sermon, I urge you to read this book carefully. I also urge you to discuss it with others and apply the ideas to your own particular work environments. Many of the productivity measures presented here can and should be applied outside the manufacturing realm.

Lastly, while a book manuscript is the creation of an author's insight, the publishing process relies on many other people. In particular, I wish to thank acquisitions and project editor Cheryl Rosen; freelance editor Ron Bridenthal; production team members Susan Cobb, Jane Donovan, Gayle Joyce, David Lennon, Gary Ragaglia, Michele Saar, Kathlin Sweeney, and Karla Tolbert; book and jacket designer Joyce Weston; Northwind Editorial Services, indexers; and Maple-Vail Book Manufacturing Group, printer and binder.

Norman Bodek
Publisher

Preface

THIS BOOK IS WRITTEN for busy managers and production people who are involved in the implementation of world class manufacturing techniques. It addresses the issue of how to measure the effect of the multitude of changes required to bring a production plant up to the standards of a competitive 1990s company. The book is intended to be very practical — full of real examples and pragmatic approaches — while at the same time providing a framework around which the specific performance measurement needs of a company can be built.

Many good things have come out of the struggle of Western manufacturers to achieve world class competitiveness. The emphasis on quality, customer satisfaction, flexibility, just-in-time manufacturing, and changing management styles represents a quiet revolution being acted out in thousands of companies and production plants throughout the United States and Western Europe. But for many companies it has been, and continues to be, a herculean struggle — and some have not survived.

One outcome of this struggle has been the realization that many of the time-honored verities of our business culture are not only unhelpful in the productivity-conscious 1990s, but can be absolutely harmful to the future success of our businesses. One of these issues is performance measurement and management accounting. It is clear that the traditional methods no longer work and a new approach is required — an approach that is built upon the concepts and philosophy of world class manufacturing.

Another, more subtle, issue that needs to be faced is that of complexity. The traditional Western approach to the solution of management problems has been to create complex systems and mathematical solutions. This "operations research" approach to the solution of business problems has contributed to the development of highly sophisticated but poorly performing companies — reliant upon technicians and specialists — whose production personnel are alienated and unproductive. One thing we are learning from Japanese (and other Pacific rim) companies is the enormous value of simplicity and participation. Rather than approaching a complex problem by devising a complex solution, it is better to simplify the problem so that the solution is clear to everyone involved. It is not easy to simplify complex production problems; the genius of the pioneers of world class manufacturing has been their ability to cut through the surface problems so that the "real" issues are addressed and to apply the talents of the entire work force to the ongoing solution of these fundamental issues.

We are in danger of falling again into this "complexity trap." The inadequacy and irrelevance of traditional management accounting methods of performance measurement has gained much attention in recent years. However, the solution to these issues is not to devise more complex accounting models that fully reflect the complexity of modern industrial life. The world class approach is to focus in on the fundamental issues and develop performance measurement methods that address these issues — as they apply to your plant — in a way that is clear and straightforward.

This book is intended to provide practical guidelines that will enable manufacturing and distribution people to develop consistent, useful, and relevant measures of performance as they continue the struggle toward world class competitiveness.

The author recognizes that performance measurement is crucial to the success of many world class manufacturing endeavors and that this book is, by no means, the last word on the subject. He would welcome your comments and practical experience of performance measurement in world class manufacturing. Please address your comments to him in care of the publisher.

List of Illustrations

80	Figure 4-1	Vendor Delivery Performance Report
82	Figure 4-2	Vendor Delivery Performance Summary
83	Figure 4-3	Vendor Delivery Performance Graph
84	Figure 4-4	Vendor Delivery Performance Spread Chart
85	Figure 4-5	Manual Vendor Delivery Monitoring
86	Figure 4-6	Goods Receiving Put-away Tracking
90	Figure 4-7	Product Completions Report
92	Figure 4-8	Product Completions Summary
93	Figure 4-9	Schedule Adherence Charts
94	Figure 4-10	Completions by Cell Report
96	Figure 4-11	Work Order Completions Report
98	Figure 4-12	Past-due Parts Graph
100	Figure 4-13	Completions Schedule Table
101	Figure 4-14	Normalized Schedule Variance
103	Figure 4-15	Cell Performance Chart
104	Figure 4-16	Horizon of Stability
106	Figure 4-17	Order and Schedule Changes
107	Figure 4-18	Order Changes by Number of Days
108	Figure 4-19	Inventory Levels and Service Levels

110   Figure 4-20   Customer Service Level Report
112   Figure 4-21   Service Level by Dispatch Days
114   Figure 4-22   Service Level Report by Original Planned Date
118   Figure 4-23   Customer Survey Table
119   Figure 4-24   Customer Survey Chart
127   Figure 5-1   Economic Order Quantity
130   Figure 5-2   Detailed Cycle Time Report
131   Figure 5-3   Manual Cycle Time Analysis Report
134   Figure 5-4   Cycle Time Analysis from Routings
136   Figure 5-5   Production Cycle Time Board
137   Figure 5-6   Cycle Time Analysis Sheet
138   Figure 5-7   Spread of Cycle Times Chart
139   Figure 5-8   Cycle Time Upper Limit Chart
140   Figure 5-9   Production Completions Analysis Report
143   Figure 5-10   Production Lead Time
146   Figure 5-11   D:P Ratio Graph
149   Figure 5-12   Number of Setups by Time Class
150   Figure 5-13   Setups by Time Class Graph
151   Figure 5-14   Average Setup Times Analysis
153   Figure 5-15   Setup Times Summary
156   Figure 5-16   Material Availability Graph
158   Figure 5-17   Shop Floor Layout: Traditional and JIT
160   Figure 5-18   Distance Moved Report
161   Figure 5-19   Distance Moved Summary
164   Figure 5-20   Next Work Center Report
167   Figure 5-21   Production Up-time Graph
168   Figure 5-22   Down-time Reasons Chart
183   Figure 6-1   Circuit Breaker Bills of Material
185   Figure 6-2   Bills of Material with Differentiation at Last Level
187   Figure 6-3   Product Design Approaches
191   Figure 6-4   Bill of Material with Phantom Assemblies

193	Figure 6-5	Engineering and Manufacturing Bills
194	Figure 6-6	Three-level Production Layout
213	Figure 7-1	Incoming Quality Report
214	Figure 7-2	Vendor Performance Summary Report
216	Figure 7-3	Vendor Quality Chart
217	Figure 7-4	Total Supplier Quality Graph
218	Figure 7-5	Statistical Process Control Charts
222	Figure 7-6	Top Manager's Control Chart
223	Figure 7-7	Injection Molding Control Chart
224	Figure 7-8	Injection Molding Detail Chart
225	Figure 7-9	Demos Control Chart for Multi-variation Process
229	Figure 7-10	Customer Service Snake Chart
237	Figure 7-11	Inventory Accuracy Report
251	Figure 8-1	Scrap and Reject Report
254	Figure 8-2	Inventory Turns Report by ABC Class
255	Figure 8-3	Inventory Levels by Product Group
256	Figure 8-4	Graph of Stock Turns
262	Figure 8-5	Value-added Analysis Report
263	Figure 8-6	Value-added Analysis Summary
264	Figure 8-7	Value-added Hours per Person
267	Figure 8-8	Direct Labor Productivity Report
269	Figure 8-9	Production Completions Evaluation Report
279	Figure 8-10	Checkbook Accounting Report
281	Figure 8-11	System Complexity Analysis
316	Figure 10-1	Defect Time History
319	Figure 10-2	Observed Improvement Half Lives
324	Figure 10-3	Wang's Performance Pyramid
327	Figure 10-4	SMART System: Printed Circuit Board Manufacturing
336	Figure 11-1	Example Diagnostic Chart
347	Figure 11-2	Sample Screen from PRAXVU Report Writer
370	Figure 12-1	Hewlett-Packard UK Plant

Performance Measurement for World Class Manufacturing

CHAPTER ONE

World Class Manufacturing and the Need for New Performance Measures

*T*HERE ARE THREE primary reasons why new performance measures are required:

- Traditional management accounting is no longer relevant or useful to a company moving toward a world class manufacturing environment.
- Customers are requiring higher standards of quality, performance, and flexibility.
- Management techniques used in production plants are changing significantly.

As a beginning, let us examine these areas in more detail.

Traditional management accounting The techniques of management accounting were developed over a period from the late nineteenth century until the 1920s and 1930s. During this time theoretical and practical methods of management accounting became established, and these standard techniques were widely taught and applied. These traditional management accounting techniques became the accepted method of measuring the performance of a manufacturing plant or distribution operation.

Although there have been dramatic changes in manufacturing techniques and technology over the last 20 years, management accounting has stayed the same. Unfortunately this tradition leads to company managers being misled because the accounting system is measuring the wrong things in the wrong way; also, people are motivated to do the wrong things because they are endeavoring to achieve irrelevant targets.

Chapter 3 explores the problems of traditional management accounting in further depth. While the majority of this book will be dealing with nonfinancial performance measures, the book will later provide some insight into new approaches to cost and management accounting that are being proposed by academics, accounting firms, and industrial research consortia.

Customer requirements Although it was once acceptable to be less than prompt with deliveries, this is no longer the case. Customers specified standard reject rates when they placed orders; long lead times were considered a normal part of manufacturing business. Over the last 10 years, however, customers have become more and more demanding. On-time deliveries are a must, zero defects is an expected standard, and short lead times are becoming the norm in many industries.

In addition to these factors, there is a growing tendency toward single-sourcing (or limited sourcing). More orders go to fewer suppliers, and these suppliers are chosen for their quality and reliability. This aspect of just-in-time (JIT) manufacturing has forced many component manufacturers to rethink production philosophies.

In order to monitor how well a company is meeting the more stringent requirements of its customers, it has become necessary to introduce new methods of measuring production and distribution performance.

Management techniques The people aspects of world class manufacturing have had a profound effect on the way production plants are managed. Companies successful with the introduction of just-in-time production techniques give their shop floor operators much more authority and responsibility.

Much of decision making that was previously handled by middle managers is pushed down to the shop floor. This includes production scheduling, the control of quality, some preventive maintenance, and the introduction of new production methods.

The traditional reports that were used by the middle managers are no longer useful in this environment. New methods of reporting performance are needed, methods that are relevant and timely for the shop floor operators.

World Class Manufacturing

For the purpose of this book we will use the term *world class manufacturing* (WCM). This phrase was first publicized by Professor Richard Schonberger (as the title of his 1986 book) wherein he suggests that the term world class manufacturing "nicely captures the breadth and essence of the fundamental changes taking place in industrial enterprises."

In recent years the world has become a much smaller place than it was in previous generations. Marshall McLuhan's idea of the "global village" has come true. Manufacturers in almost every industry find themselves competing with companies from every corner of the globe — America, Europe, South America, Japan, and other Pacific Rim countries.

In the nineteenth century, Great Britain was the world's leading manufacturer; in the twentieth century, the United States became the most productive, efficient, and innovative country. Now that we are approaching the end of the twentieth century, there are many countries that have the potential to dominate world markets. The Japanese "miracle" is well-known; but countries such as West Germany, France, Korea, and Taiwan have also experienced a renaissance of industrial productivity and innovation.

The competition is fierce; the competitors are outstanding. The only way for a manufacturing company to succeed is to change. Old habits must be shed, and radical new approaches are needed in every aspect of the manufacturing process, from design to production to customer service.

The revolution taking place in Western manufacturing companies has many different aspects. One company's approach can be quite different from another's because there are differences in production processes, the needs of the market, product technology, and management styles. In addition, the problems and situations faced by manufacturing enterprises vary, and the areas requiring change can differ significantly.

The term world class manufacturing is a very broad one but will generally include the following:

- a new approach to product quality
- just-in-time production techniques
- change in the way the work force is managed
- a flexible approach to customer requirements

The world class manufacturing approach to quality is quite different from the traditional approach because the primary emphasis is placed on the resolution of the problems that cause poor quality, rather than merely detection of those problems. The purpose is to systematically expose and resolve the root causes of quality problems so that the company can ideally achieve zero defects, or 100-percent quality.

Traditional manufacturers have a large staff of inspectors whose job is to check the quality of everything that is brought into the plant and everything that is made within the plant. The concept holds that a high quality product is one that is studied and inspected at every step of the manufacturing process; inspection is performed by independent, trained inspectors rather than by the operators who are making the goods. Rejected materials are scrapped, repaired, or reworked, and suppliers whose products do not reach the acceptable quality levels are reprimanded.

This method is not only an expensive way of attempting to assure production quality standards, but is also ineffective. The experience of many companies is that the more inspectors there are on the floor, the worse the quality becomes. When everything is checked by others, the production personnel do not feel that they are responsible for doing a high quality job; they feel that quality is the inspector's responsibility.

The approach toward quality employed by successful world class manufacturers is quite different. First, a WCM company has a goal of zero defects, or 100-percent quality. A traditional manufacturer is content with a predetermined reject rate; a world class manufacturer is not satisfied until the reject rate is gradually and systematically reduced to zero.

A second aspect is that the quality control responsibility is placed on the shop floor with the production operators. The operators are responsible for doing their own quality control and a "pride of ownership" attitude is fostered. For this plan to work successfully the operators must have the tools and equipment necessary to inspect their own work, they must be well trained, and they must have the authority to stop the production line if they detect quality problems.

Many new techniques lend themselves to this style of production management. These techniques include statistical process control, the posting of quality results as they occur, the use of quality circles for devising long-term solutions to quality problems, and appropriate quality standards that reflect the importance of quality to each employee in a useful way.

This change in the approach toward quality has ramifications in other areas of the company. Changes are required in design and production engineering because products must be designed for quality. Products are not necessarily made from more expensive materials but are designed in such a way that they are easy to make, difficult to assemble incorrectly, and have common processes and common parts so that production personnel do not have to constantly learn new techniques.

Such changes to the process of design are radical. They require a much closer cooperation between design engineering and production. They need a new approach to design techniques with emphasis on quality, commonality, and ease of manufacture. The end result of all these changes to the design and manufacturing process is to build quality into the product, not to remove poor quality by final inspections.

Just-In-Time Manufacturing

A second element of world class manufacturing is a just-in-time (JIT) approach to the production process. JIT is another ill-defined term encompassing a multitude of techniques and ideas. The prime purpose of just-in-time is to eliminate wasteful activity. Waste is defined as any process that increases costs but does not add value to the product. These activities include inspection, unnecessary movement of materials, shop floor queues, rework or repair, storage of inventory (raw materials, work-in-process, or finished goods), and overhead personnel.

Just-in-time manufacturing aims to change the production process so that inventory not immediately required for production is eliminated. This goal is achieved by the following:

- Change the shop floor layout to reduce the movement of materials.
- Reduce production setup times so that products can be made in very small batches (ideally a lot size of one).
- Synchronize the manufacturing process so that subassemblies and components are available just when they are needed and not before (or after).
- Create mutually beneficial relationships with suppliers.

Shop floor layout A traditional manufacturing plant is not laid out for just-in-time manufacturing. The shop layout divides the factory into machine centers that group machines of a similar type together. Jobs are processed through the factory by moving the semi-completed material from one machine center to another according to the production routing for the product. In a typical traditional manufacturing plant the actual run time is frequently less than 10 percent of the total production time; the rest of the time is taken up by queuing.

This approach requires that the product physically be moved a considerable distance during the production process as it is transferred from one work center to another. Movement of materials is not only wasteful in itself, but also leads to material damage, high inventory investment, and longer production cycle times. A third problem is that this style of layout leads to complex control procedures. Where a particular job within the plant is not clear, complex planning and control systems are necessary to enable the managers and supervisors to keep track of the production schedules.

The preferred layout within a just-in-time production plant minimizes the movement of materials, people, and tooling.

This system usually involves laying out the shop floor as a series of manufacturing cells. In the cell system, dissimilar machines are grouped together based on the manufacturing process that is performed within the cell. Instead of a batch of material being moved between several work centers, a number of different machines are grouped into a cell so that all production tasks can be completed with virtually no movement of materials.

Such a grouping of activities into production cells assumes a degree of repetition in the process. The techniques of group technology are employed, where products being made in the plant are categorized according to production processes. Cells are dedicated to the production of a group of products and contain all the machines, assembly areas, and test equipment necessary to make a specific group of products.

In addition to eliminating the unnecessary movement of materials, this style of plant layout lends itself to flexibility of production. The rate of flow through a cell can be changed easily as customer orders change. The people within a cell are trained in multiple production tasks and can be assigned a wide range of activities based upon current needs. A cell can also become a responsibility center where the production personnel control their own quality.

Measurement of material movement throughout the production process can be an important performance measurement. This measure can be used to analyze the current layout and to aid in the design of better layouts. It also can be used for ongoing monitoring of production as products and product mix change.

Setup times Large production batches can cause high levels of inventory — both work-in-process and finished goods. Batch sizes (or lot sizes) frequently are determined by the setup times required to make an item. If eight hours are needed to set up a machine to make a product, then making a large quantity after doing all that setup work is generally desirable.

In contrast, a prime objective of just-in-time manufacturing is to reduce inventory. In fact, inventory is a passion in many JIT plants not only because inventory is costly and wasteful in itself, but also because high inventory levels traditionally have been used to cover a multitude of other shortcomings. High levels of buffer stocks are used to alleviate problems resulting from such situations as bad scheduling, poor vendor delivery, poor quality, and inaccurate record keeping.

An important tool for reducing inventory is the reduction of the aforementioned excessive production batch sizes. Reduction of batch sizes usually is necessary for reduction of setup times. A just-in-time manufacturer spends a great deal of time and effort studying setup times and devising methods of reducing them.

Setup time reductions cannot be achieved by one or two changes in the plant. They are achieved by a concerted and systematic effort throughout the entire production process. The chief offenders — those processes with the longest setup times and largest batch sizes — are identified first. Experience proves that setup times can be reduced by approximately 50 percent by merely studying the setup process and by establishing better procedures. Setup processes can be studied by examining current written procedures, by discussing setup with the people who do the tasks, and by videoing the process in action and analyzing the activities step-by-step. Once initial studies have been completed and the changes implemented, setup time can be still further reduced by modifying dies, tooling, and jigs. The techniques and innovative ideas associated with these programs have names like SMED (single-minute exchange of dies) and OTC (one-touch changeovers).

In some cases, achieving the level of setup time reduction that is required for just-in-time manufacturing while using the existing equipment just is not possible. New production equipment must be purchased specifically for the purpose of reducing setup times throughout the entire production process. Typical of obsolete or non-adaptive equipment are heat-treatment ovens, wave-soldering baths, extrusion or paint processes requiring lengthy wash-downs, and some specialized test equipment.

Setup time reduction can have a significant effect upon work-in-process (WIP) inventories, cycle times, and production flexibility. Benefits in these areas are achieved through many small improvements over an extended period, and meaningful analysis and monitoring tools are needed. The instituted improvements will provide a key performance measure in many just-in-time environments.

Synchronized manufacturing The ideal production plant will set the production capacity of each work cell so that each operation is synchronized with operations that come before and after. Unfortunately, there are no ideal production plants, but just-in-time manufacturers strive toward the goal of a totally synchronized production process in which each work center receives exactly what it needs when it needs it.

Several problems result from operations lacking in synchronization. Large work-in-process inventories are possible even when lot sizes are small and setup times are short. Shop floor queues are usually the result of bottleneck operations, poor production planning, and part shortages.

Bottleneck (or limiting) operations are those production operations with low capacity and large loads. These operations may be considered the weak link in the chain of production processes that go into making a finished product. For example, a bicycle manufacturer might be able to make 5,000 wheels per day, but can only make 2,000 frames; if the manufacturer continues to make 5,000 wheels each day, WIP inventories will build up because another stage in the process can only cope with 4,000 wheels (assuming there is no requirement for spare wheels).

Better synchronization can be achieved by approaching the problem from two different perspectives: production planning and shop floor execution. Production can be planned so that there is near-perfect synchronization between loads on each work cell. Such perfection can be achieved through careful master scheduling and detailed capacity planning through the limiting work centers. Some available software attempts to optimize production schedules by automatically finite scheduling of bottleneck work centers. This software is limited in its applicability and has not yet found general acceptance.

Most just-in-time manufacturers divorce production planning from shop floor execution and use some kind of "inventory pull" method on the shop floor. A shop floor pull system merely means that each supplying work center does not make anything until the next work center requests it to do so. The method is based upon the Japanese-developed *kanban* system. Subassemblies and components are supplied to a work center only when that work center issues kanban cards to the supplying work center. This approach can yield excellent synchronization, flexibility, and minimum inventories, providing each work center has a short setup time, small lot sizes, and short cycle times.

The closer a production plant comes to synchronized production control, the nearer it will be to genuine just-in-time manufacturing. Such an achievement requires excellence in every area of the production process.

Vendor relationships A traditional manufacturer tends to have an adversarial relationship with vendors. Procurement personnel are judged primarily on purchase price variance; in other words, they are rewarded for getting the lowest price.

The company will ensure that there are several suppliers for each part so that these vendors can be pitted against each other when contracts are negotiated and to ensure continuity of supply.

In contrast, world class manufacturers employ a variety of approaches to vendor relationships. Vendors are selected primarily on the basis of quality, delivery reliability, and flexibility. The theory is that the benefits of reliability, consistent quality, and just-in-time deliveries are far more valuable than a few pennies off the price.

The techniques required for a good vendor relationship include single sourcing, certification, and openness. The idea of single sourcing is to have just one supplier for any component or raw material that is purchased and to reduce the total number of vendors. The idea is simple; if a supplier does a large amount of business with your company, he will treat you with more care. If you have large orders going to fewer suppliers, then you are able to create closer, more cooperative relationships with each supplier. This approach has been used very successfully by companies such as Xerox, which reduced the vendor base from 5,000 to around 350 as a part of its successful JIT/Quality program.

Plunging into single-sourcing arrangements would be irresponsible if the vendor's performance record is not known. Performance is certified by a process that assesses every supplier's record of quality, delivery reliability, and flexibility. Deliveries from a certified vendor will be received without the need for incoming inspection and will often be delivered directly to the shop floor.

Vendors are certified to supply particular components when their performance in each aspect is up to standard. If a vendor does not match company standards, then the buyer will seek to resolve the problems. As the certification process develops, many vendors will be dropped and the total number will be reduced. Eventually the company will purchase components from only a small number of certified vendors.

Unfortunately, vendor certification has gained a negative connotation over the last few years because some larger companies have intimidated smaller suppliers into providing concessions on service and price. Many large companies have used their "clout" to force smaller vendors to hold large inventories of finished components in order to support their customer's just-in-time requirements. Such practices only push wasteful safety stocks back onto the vendor rather than allow the vendor to move into world class manufacturing. This approach runs contrary to vendor relationships within WCM where mutually beneficial long-term relationships are the primary aim.

A good starting point for improving relationships is openness. World class manufacturers have an open-door policy with their vendors. There is a free exchange of technical information, clear communication of needs, expectations, and performance, and a sharing of financial data about the products being supplied. This open communication provides a basis upon which trust can be built. As these relationships progress, further cooperation can develop. Many companies find that suppliers are able to assist with the design of components and subassemblies and that their contribution often results in better design and lower costs.

World class manufacturers need unprecedented levels of quality and reliability, just-in-time deliveries, and short lead times and often require additional services such as deliveries in sequence or special point-of-use packaging. In return, the vendor receives large orders, longer-term contracts, and fair prices. A vendor will often require just-in-time payment for just-in-time deliveries. Thus, a "happy circle" frequently develops as suppliers themselves move into world class manufacturing. The WCM techniques required to provide the superior levels of quality and service have the effect of making the supplier much more productive, and the price of their products can be reduced. In fact, many companies are paying less for components and raw materials while receiving just-in-time deliveries and zero defects.

People Management

Frequently, the most difficult problems to solve when introducing world class manufacturing techniques are related to the management of people. A company committed to world class manufacturing must be prepared for fundamental changes in management style and philosophy. After years of mutual distrust and poor relationships, both managers and production personnel often find making the required changes difficult.

The experience of many plants has been that the shop floor operators, appropriately managed, can make the largest contribution to the attainment of world class manufacturing goals. Technology changes and automation have taken much of the physical work out of the production process; world class manufacturers attempt to make full use of their work force's hands-on knowledge of how to make the products better, faster, and safer.

New approaches to the management of people can take several years to introduce. What is required is trust, honesty, and success. It takes time and experience to develop trusting relationships between people and their managers.

Transfer of responsibility A traditional manufacturer tends to treat production personnel as suppliers of labor, not thought. Middle managers and supervisors are employed to make day-to-day decisions, resolve problems, and take responsibility for production. A world class manufacturer will take steps to give operators greater control of their daily work. They will have prime responsibility for product quality, scheduling some preventive maintenance, and for attaining production targets.

This change does not mean that middle managers, engineers, and specialists are no longer required; however, their roles change. Instead of being the primary decision makers, they become expert advisors, coaches, and mentors to the shop floor operators and are the people who become the champions of change to senior managers.

If the operators are to have responsibility for production quality in their areas, then they need to have the authority to stop the production line when quality problems arise. They need to have expert assistance readily available to them. They need to have the equipment and training to enable them to perform these new tasks. The end result is better managed and better controlled plants because, instead of having just a few inspectors and planners trying to look after the entire operation, there are now hundreds of people who now see their responsibilities including quality, delivery to schedule, and customer service.

Education and cross-training World class manufacturers dedicate a great deal of time and money to educating their employees. Some of this education is devoted to on-going training in just-in-time manufacturing, quality control, and customer service. Another important area is the training of operators to do a wide range of tasks within the production plant.

This cross-training of people allows world class manufacturers to have greater flexibility because operators can be moved between tasks. If the customer demand is high in one product group and lower in another, then people can be moved to an area of the plant where they are most needed. If the product mix is such that the production rate on different work centers has to change so that synchronization is maintained, then the number of people in each work center can be changed.

Problem solving and quality circles The introduction of quality circles within world class manufacturing has been received with mixed opinions by Western manufacturing industry. In the early days of JIT there were many experiments with quality circles that did not work well, often because they were not accompanied by other important aspects of world class manufacturing.

The purpose of a quality circle approach is to have every employee involved in solving production (and other) problems. No matter how this participation is organized, whether quality circles as such or other methods are used, the goal is to have the active participation of *all* the employees, each of whom can contribute his or her own individual skills and experiences.

In the past, problems were solved by middle managers, engineers, and specialists. In a world class manufacturing plant, the entire work force is involved in one or more projects aimed at continually improving products, processes, and services. These programs have found spectacular success in many companies because an atmosphere of team involvement and common cause has enabled people who previously had very little opportunity to contribute to become innovative and resourceful problem solvers. In addition, the people involved in these efforts enjoy their work more because they have a wider variety of tasks and because their ideas are treated with respect.

Flexibility

While many Western manufacturers are working hard to attain world class status in terms of quality, delivery performance, and customer service, many top Japanese companies are building upon existing excellence. The next challenge facing Western manufacturers in the near future will be one of flexibility.

At one time, the belief was that the techniques of just-in-time manufacturing were suited only to repetitive production processes with highly predictable schedules. While it is true that JIT is easier in such an environment, many companies are now extending just-in-time concepts into more complicated production situations where product quantities and production mix change frequently.

In their 1988 report "Flexibility: The Next Competitive Battle,"[1] Professors Miller and Nakane show that many leading Japanese manufacturers emphasize production flexibility and price. They are striving to make products at a low cost and with a high degree of flexibility to meet the needs of their customers.

There are two aspects of flexibility that are important — (1) production flexibility and (2) design flexibility. Production flexibility is achieved when the company can offer short lead times, when the product mix within the plant can be changed significantly from day to day, and when people within the plant are cross-trained to manufacture a wider range of products. A company that can offer this level of flexibility to its customers (without a price penalty) has a significant competitive advantage.

Design flexibility is related to the company's ability to introduce new products and modifications to current products. Market needs change quickly. A company must be able to understand the current and future need of its customers, to develop innovative products, and to get those products to the marketplace quickly. Once, seven to ten years were needed to bring a new automobile from conception to production; today, Nissan can introduce an entirely new car in less than three years. In 1988, in less than nine months, Suzuki replaced its Samurai all-terrain vehicle (which had been criticized in the press for its instability) with the Sidekick throughout the U.S. market. This level of flexibility to meet customer needs in both the short and longer term is the mark of a company truly committed to world class manufacturing.

Summary

As companies introduce world class manufacturing techniques, they need new methods of performance measurement to control production plants. These new methods are needed because:

- Traditional management accounting is not relevant to world class manufacturing.
- Customers are requiring higher standards of quality, performance, and flexibility.
- New management methods employed by world class manufacturers require different kinds of performance measures.

While different companies introduce world class manufacturing in different ways, the following attributes are always included:

- a new approach to quality
- JIT manufacturing techniques
- changes in management of the work force
- a more flexible approach to meeting customer needs

CHAPTER TWO

Characteristics of the New Performance Measures

*I*N RECENT YEARS, many companies have been experimenting with performance measurement systems that seem suited to world class manufacturing. Most of these performance measures are not new; they have been used by companies for a long time. What is new, however, is the importance attached to them. These measures truly drive the production and distribution processes, replacing the traditional accounting and variance reports.

Although the new performance measures being used by world class manufacturers vary considerably, they have seven common characteristics:

- They are directly related to the manufacturing strategy.
- They primarily use nonfinancial measures.
- They vary between locations.
- They change over time as needs change.
- They are simple and easy to use.
- They provide fast feedback to operators and managers.
- They are intended to foster improvement rather than just monitor.

A Direct Relationship to Manufacturing Strategy

A world class manufacturer invariably will have a clearly defined manufacturing strategy. The strategy may differ from one company to another, but will center around such issues as quality, reliability, short lead times, flexibility, or customer satisfaction. Performance measures must directly measure the success or failure of each of the manufacturing strategies.

Establishing a manufacturing strategy Although the manufacturing strategy does not have to be formally established, many firms put their approach to manufacturing into a concise statement. The manufacturing strategy, which must be congruent with the overall business strategy, usually can be stated succinctly. For example:

- XYZ Company will manufacture a complete range of domestic electronics at the lowest possible cost.
- ABC Company will provide the shortest lead times for the manufacture of innovative, custom-designed fluid pumping equipment.
- The Sav-U range of automotive safety products will continue to be known for reliability and high quality of manufacture.

These examples are very short. In practice, a company's manufacturing strategy, probably two or three paragraphs of text, will cover the range of issues that company managers consider to be of importance. If the strategy cannot be printed on one page, it is too long. If it is not readily understandable to every production employee, then it is too complicated. It should be short, cover the key issues, and be a guideline to all employees. The type of manufacturing strategy chosen for a company will have a large bearing on the kind of performance measures required. If a company strategy includes innovation as a primary goal, then it will measure the number of new product launches, the time to market of new products, and the flexibility of the production plants. Companies involved in competitive mass marketing will be interested in market share, quality, customer satisfaction, and margins. A company that stresses employee involvement will be interested in turnover, participation in quality circles, the number of improvement suggestions, and the level of cross-training.

Relating performance measures to the manufacturing strategy
There are two reasons for keeping performance measures in line with the manufacturing strategy. The first is obvious — a company needs to know how well it is achieving the goals laid down in the strategy. It is important to choose a small number of pertinent performance measures that enable the company managers to assess progress constantly.

The second reason is that people concentrate on whatever is measured. If a firm measures and reports the results of someone's work, the person will be motivated to improve. In a very real sense, the choice of performance measures can steer company direction. Appropriately selected performance measures give a clear signal to all people in the company about the priorities that are important to senior managers.

This approach has been used successfully in companies that have many divisions or many production plants and wish to control these plants without stifling the authority of local managers. Local managers can be given as much power and influence as they wish to take, but their success is measured in terms that assure adherence to overall manufacturing strategy.

Key elements of manufacturing strategy There are six elements around which a manufacturing strategy can be built.

The amount of emphasis that a company places on each of these areas will define the strategy.

1. quality
2. cost
3. delivery reliability
4. lead time
5. flexibility
6. employee relationships

There is room for some optimism here. Recent surveys of Western manufacturers have shown considerable improvement in all six of these areas. The bad news is that many manufacturers in Japan and other Pacific Rim countries still have a significant advantage. Worse news is that some of the very best Japanese companies now have a clearly defined manufacturing strategy that will enable them to become highly flexible and very low cost producers, while maintaining present levels of quality and reliability. The challenge to Western manufacturers is to have a strategy that is truly world class in scope and to implement performance measures that are congruent with that strategy.

Many companies have added a new dimension to their manufacturing strategies — that of service to the community. The community includes their own employees, their immediate neighbors, the local area, and the world in general. A manufacturing strategy document often will contain reference to providing a safe, profitable, and enriching lifestyle for employees, will stress the need for environmental responsibility, and/or incorporate specific services to the community such as educational opportunities, facility use, and so forth.

Nonfinancial Measures

For traditional manufacturers, financial results are of paramount importance for measuring company performance.

Within world class manufacturing, other performance measures now are at least equal if not more important to the financial results and are the only measures used by the operational staff.

Financial measures remain important for external reporting, and there is still a need to have cost accounts and the financial accounts integrated and consistent. But the day-to-day control of manufacturing and distribution operations is handled better with nonfinancial measures.

The fundamental flaw in the use of management accounting reports for operational performance measurement is the assumption that financial reports are valid and relevant to the control of daily business operations. This assumption is wrong. Not only are financial reports irrelevant to daily operations, they are generally confusing, misleading, and in some cases positively harmful to the business.

Performance Measures Must Be Relevant

If production personnel, supervisors, and managers are to use performance measures to help achieve the manufacturing strategy, the performance measures must directly inform them of success or failure. Reports must present the results of their efforts in terms that are relevant to their work and must not be disguised in financial figures.

For example, a company wishing to reduce work-in-process inventories and increase production flexibility will implement a program of setup time reductions so that production batch sizes can be reduced. The appropriate measure to assist operational personnel with this task is a report showing the setup times actually achieved within each work center. Traditional financial reports will show WIP inventory values, setup labor costs, tooling costs, and overhead burdens — none of which are of any significant value to the industrial engineers, supervisors, managers, and operators who are working each day to get the setups as fast, smooth, and efficient as possible.

A parent wishing to improve a child's school grades could devise a scheme whereby the child's allowance is based upon the previous week's grades. If the child were told only how much the week's allowance amounted to, and not given information about the grades in each subject, then he or she would not know what action would be required to increase the weekly income. Similarly, production personnel must be given measures that are directly relevant to their tasks. If the strategy is right and the production personnel are continuously achieving and improving upon clearly defined goals, then the financial aspects will take care of themselves.

Performance Measures Must Lead in the Right Direction

Many financial performance measures currently in widespread use are not only irrelevant, but make people do the wrong things. In most traditional manufacturing plants, the actual labor content of a production step is measured and then overheads are apportioned based upon labor costs. In most industries today, however, the labor content of the product is relatively small. A traditional approach assigns a disproportionate emphasis to labor costs, thus forcing managers to concentrate too much effort on reducing labor content. In reality, there are other far more significant issues they should be tackling — issues like quality, inventory levels, employee participation, production synchronization, on-time deliveries, and customer satisfaction. Traditional financial performance measures were not designed to address such aspects of a company's business, but yet remain the primary (and usually obsolete) method of performance measurement in most companies.

There is a well-documented story concerning the plant manager at one of Northern Telecom's larger plants. This plant, a leader in world class manufacturing, had instituted new performance measures to support production policies.

One day the management accountant met with the plant manager to discuss budgets. The accountant had spent many months preparing a detailed budget for the plant and wished to have the budget distributed to the managers and supervisors in the usual way. To the accountant's astonishment, the plant manager threw the neatly bound budget proposal straight into the trash can and declared he never wanted to see a budget again.

This is an extreme example, and the plant manager's point was not that budgets were unimportant, but that he did not want his operational managers and supervisors subjected to using budgets to control their production activities. The budgets were irrelevant and misleading, running counter to the world class manufacturing ideas being implemented within the plant.

Performance measures used to control production plants and warehouses must be directly relevant and applicable to the jobs being done. Financial reports are rarely relevant to production control; nonfinancial reports are more useful.

Variation Among Locations

One notable aspect of world class manufacturing is that the implementation of these radical changes varies considerably from one company to another and from one location to another within the same company. Performance measures may differ significantly between locations because different aspects of WCM may be more important in one location than another. Alternatively, the requirement may be to measure the same aspects of WCM, but to measure them in different ways. These differences must be taken into account by the performance measurement systems that are put in place.

Differences in WCM Implementation

World class manufacturing cannot be implemented by merely setting policies and expecting people to put those policies into practice. The changes required are so radical that each production plant needs at least one senior manager with the vision, determination, and skill to see the task through to completion. In their book *In Search of Excellence,* Peters and Waterman describe this kind of leader as a champion and show that all innovative companies require people like this — people with the drive to be the champions of change. Each champion approaches the tasks in a different way; each has his or her own priorities and methods of implementing world class manufacturing techniques in each plant, warehouse, or factory.

In addition to differences in style and priorities, there are significant differences among other needs of manufacturing plants. These differences derive from the products manufactured, the production processes required, the people employed within the plant, the age and suitability of the equipment, and the existing strengths and weaknesses of the plant.

Differences in Performance Measures Between Plants

There are many aspects of world class manufacturing and there are performance measurement methods that can be used to monitor each aspect. It is not possible to give equal importance to all measures; if too many measures are used, they become misleading and confusing instead of helpful. A company making progress with world class manufacturing will identify the key issues that must be tracked in detail at each location.

Some larger companies that have embarked upon a world class manufacturing approach across many plants have chosen deliberately to concentrate only on certain aspects of WCM in each location. Manufacturing policies include all aspects of WCM, but each plant focuses on a limited number of key issues. The performance measurement requirements at each location reflect the importance of each aspect in that plant. Performance measurement reports that are to be applied in each location, therefore, cannot be defined centrally. A better approach is to give the local managers, project team, and champions the authority to define the required measures for themselves so that the reports and reporting techniques can be tailored to the needs of their individual locations.

Problems Caused by Different Performance Measures

One of the most useful aspects of traditional cost and management accounting techniques is that the same reports can be used by everybody in the company, thus enabling a consistency of reporting that simplifies the comparison of one plant with another. This standardization is not the case when new methods of WCM performance measurement are introduced.

Chapter 10 addresses some methods used by leading companies in attempting to overcome this problem. There are no clear-cut solutions because diversity is inherent within the ideas of world class manufacturing. If standard reporting is required from each location, then that reporting will not be relevant from most of the plants because the plants are, in fact, different. The old management accounting reports gave consistency of reporting, but the information being reported was misleading and irrelevant.

This aspect, like many other facets of world class manufacturing, requires a change in outlook on the part of senior managers. The control of the company will focus on the achievement of a range of strategic and tactical goals that will vary from division to division and from plant to plant. If the goals have been set correctly and the measurement methods are relevant, then the financial results will take care of themselves. It makes no sense to chastise a plant manager for not achieving corporate financial objectives if his goals have been set in terms of quality, customer service, and cycle times.

Changes Over Time

The concept of continuous improvement is an important aspect of just-in-time and world class manufacturing. The basic idea is that nothing is ever perfect and no matter how much improvement has been made, there is still room for more. Performance measures must be flexible. Throughout the implementation of a world class approach to manufacturing — and beyond, needs and priorities will change; the performance measurement system must be able to accommodate these changes.

World class manufacturing is not a project started on one date and completed on another. Companies successful with world class manufacturing recognize that a cultural change is required in the way their business is run. There are no "quick fixes" here. The journey to world class status is made up of thousands of small steps in which each improvement opens up the possibility of more improvement.

Continuous Improvement

This book seeks to provide practical answers to the problems of performance measurement. It deliberately steers clear of the philosophical and cultural aspects of world class manufacturing because it is more important for managers to put ideas into practice than to philosophize about them. However, merely to implement a few new techniques is not good enough; the company approach must change fundamentally.

At the heart of this basic change is the concept of continuous improvement. At first sight, the idea makes good old-fashioned common sense. Everyone in the company strives to improve productivity and effectiveness, day in and day out. In fact, more profound than that is the change in the way everyone in the company views themselves and their work. It is an atmosphere of consistent analysis, innovation, and improvement.

A striking example of this attitude occurred recently when Nissan recognized the need to reduce production costs because exchange rate changes between the dollar and the yen were undermining profits. As a part of redesign efforts aimed at cutting the manufacturing costs of products, the work force was asked to submit ideas. The result was 28,000 suggestions from one plant alone, more than three suggestions per person! The Nissan work force is so instilled with the idea of continuous improvement that it was bursting with ideas, suggestions, and innovation. When such an atmosphere prevails, it is impossible not to get better and better.

Continuous Improvement and Performance Measurement

When world class manufacturing is first introduced into a plant, the project team will concentrate on specific aspects that are important at that time. Such issues as quality, customer service level, lead times, and inventory investment are often the highest priorities. Performance measures are established to address these issues.

Once the introduction of WCM techniques begins to be successful and positive results are seen, the emphasis of the plant changes to other issues. The original aspects are still important, but the improvements seen in these areas enable the company managers to move on to new areas of improvement. At this point, the performance measures need to change and emphasize new issues. The previous issues will continue to be reported, but summarized information is usually sufficient. Thus, old issues can be monitored for continuing improvement and any problems highlighted, but new issues can receive primary attention. The performance measurement systems must have enough flexibility to adapt the reporting emphasis as changes occur within the company over time.

Simplicity and Ease of Use

The most effective performance measurements are ones people readily understand. The tendency in the past has been to devise complex measures that relate more than one aspect of performance and then to produce an index or a ratio. These complex measures tend to be unsuccessful within world class manufacturing.

For people to be successfully motivated by performance reports, they must clearly understand the reports and be able to see the relevance to their jobs and to the company's manufacturing objectives.

Measure the Issues Directly

Plain and simple measures of the most important elements of the business are better than subtle and complex measures. If an issue is measured directly and presented in straightforward terms, then people find the results easier to use and the performance measure is more effective.

For example, because there are many ways to measure customer service level, a company will often invent a composite measure that incorporates several aspects of customer service. The elements of measurement will include order lines delivered late, order lines partially shipped, customer returns, age of the outstanding back orders, and so on. Each element of service level is significant and can be combined and weighted into a single service level factor or ratio that shows the company's effectiveness in this area.

There are two problems with this approach, the first being that the ratio does not have any tangible meaning. In order to understand the importance of the ratio and to analyze changes in the ratio over time, the user is required to have a full grasp of the way the ratio has been constructed and weighted and to know precisely what the managers had in mind when the measure was devised. The result is frequent confusion and misunderstanding of the findings of the performance measure.

The second problem is that changes and trends in performance can be hidden by the ratio. In the assessment of customer service level, for example, a marked increase in customer returns can be offset by an increase in on-time deliveries; the net result may be no change in the reported ratio when, in fact, the performance of the company has changed significantly.

Managers judged by the results of these kinds of measures are sometimes forced to make decisions that are bad for the company but which make the ratio look good. One company measured the cost of sales in the traditional way, but the repair of returned parts was credited to cost of sales when the repair was completed. If an area of the company had a poor cost-of-sales result one month, the region manager would put a number of people to work repairing returned subassemblies. The cost-of-sales figure would go down, but valuable time had been wasted and spare part inventory needlessly increased.

These composite measures are difficult for people to understand, can be misleading, and can result in poor decisions by managers. It is much better to select performance issues that are significant to the company operations and measure them directly.

Objections to the direct approach There is an important objection to the direct approach. A company's business frequently is complex and subtle, and the complexity of the performance measures merely reflect the complexity of the business. A composite ratio can conceivably provide a more complete picture of the company's performance because it takes account of the diverse issues involved in business.

There is, of course, some truth in this viewpoint. But the fact remains that no matter how subtly the measure has been

devised and no matter how thoroughly it reflects the conflicting parameters of the business, it will not be effective if the
people using it do not have a clear picture of what that performance measure means.

Some analysts have suggested that simpler performance
measures are required within world class manufacturing
because more responsibility is now being given to shop floor
operators and to people who do not have the training and
educational background to grasp the subtle and complex
issues involved. This allegation is untrue and patronizing.
Many times — when world class manufacturing is introduced, with its emphasis on moving authority and responsibility to the shop floor — the shop floor operators,
supervisors, and clerical staff are able to contribute enormously to the operational improvement. The people are far
from being ignorant and incapable; they frequently demonstrate a clearer understanding of the business and its needs
than do their managers. Anyone who can raise a family, educate their children, purchase a house, and plan for their retire-
ment on shop floor wages is more than capable of
understanding the subtleties of a manufacturing business.

What is true, however, is that the performance measures
are now used by more people. As the shop floor operators
assume responsibility for quality, scheduling, preventive
maintenance, customer service, and so forth, they will need to
use the performance measures that were previously only of
interest to the middle managers and analysts. Because performance measurement reporting is thus used by a wider range
of people, there must be a common understanding of the
meaning of the measures. If the measures are simple and
straightforward, there will be no misunderstanding.

Report the Measurements Directly

Traditional performance measurement techniques rely on
reports that are distributed to the managers who need to use

the information. These reports are usually produced weekly or monthly and contain a complete analysis of the issues being measured.

In contrast, the results of performance measurement can be shown by more immediate and direct methods. These methods include the use of charts, graphs, signals, and bulletin boards. World class manufacturing plants often display the results of the performance measures continuously throughout the day on boards, charts, or graphs located adjacent to the production cells or lines. There are many examples of performance reports that lend themselves to direct presentation including, among others:

- statistical process control charts (X-bar and R charts)
- inventory accuracy levels in a warehouse
- reject rates
- production rates and adherence to schedule
- customer service levels
- absenteeism
- safety records
- average setup times

The advantage of this kind of presentation is that information is being shown clearly, directly, and in a way that everyone can understand. Direct reporting methods can be useful motivators because shop floor personnel are able to monitor their own performance on a continuous basis and the results are displayed clearly for all to see.

The media used for this kind of reporting varies. Simple chalkboards showing schedules and the actual production are often used. Electronic display screens are particularly useful if the results are being monitored automatically. Hand-drawn charts and graphs are favored for the display of information like SPC data because operators (and others) can easily observe trends and deviations.

Manual signals are useful when the information being measured is simple. For example, colored lights are often used to indicate if a machine or cell is meeting quality standards. The light is green when all is well, orange (or yellow) when there is a problem that requires attention, and red when the operator has stopped the line because of a quality deviation.

A New England toy maker uses an ingenious technique on the final assembly packing operation. The complex operation requires sophisticated machines that count the quantity of each component being packed into the boxes as they travel down the line. The process is controlled by a dedicated computer system that reports the current situation on a monitor. The monitor screen has a colored border, and the tracking system displays a different color according to the situation on the line. These colored borders are clearly visible from a considerable distance and the operators can see at a glance the status of each line. When a warning color shows, the operator goes to the monitor where the full details are displayed. Thus, one operator can monitor many lines simultaneously.

In another example, a pharmaceutical company uses a method of random surveys of each work cell to ensure that safety procedures are being carried out fastidiously. A colored sticker is attached to each work cell notice board showing green, orange, or red. A work cell with a red sticker has seriously violated safety procedures, orange signifies minor violations, and a green sticker designates complete adherence to all safety issues. There is great competition between the work cells to ensure that a green sticker is obtained. This system is an excellent method of monitoring adherence to important company policies.

Another use of direct display methods is for the reporting of quality problems. It is common within world class manufacturing plants to write the cause of a quality problem on a board within the work cell. This information can then be used to analyze quality problems, determine the most frequent causes, and develop plans to prevent problems from occurring in the future.

An optical fiber manufacturer in Pennsylvania uses a "fishbone" chart to display quality problems that occur each day on the fiber manufacture line. The nature of the problem is written on a yellow self-adhesive sheet and fixed to the appropriate section of the fishbone chart. The chart is displayed prominently within the plant, and production personnel are encouraged to read the chart and review the problems. When someone has a suggestion for solving a quality problem, they affix a pink sheet onto the chart. The chart is used both to report problems and as a communications medium for the resolution of problems.

Direct display methods are not always feasible, but they can be a very powerful way of using performance measurement for day-to-day management and improvement of the production process.

Provide Fast Feedback

In most companies, cost accounting reports are available weekly or monthly and show the variances in such things as material costs, material usage, labor productivity, labor rates, overhead allocation, and others. By the time the reports reach the people, little can be done about the problem. Either the problem occurred so long ago that it is not possible to investigate the cause, or the problem has already been identified and corrected by other means.

With a world class manufacturing approach it is important to be able to detect and resolve problems as they occur — not several days later, when the reports are produced. Many problems can be detected on the spot by the operators if they are provided with the training and equipment that enable them to continuously monitor quality, rate of flow, setup times, and other aspects.

World class manufacturing emphasizes the elimination of anything that causes waste within the production process. Any measurement of quality seeks to detect production deviations so that the root cause of a deviation can be eliminated. These deviations must be discovered immediately as they occur, because a production deviation that is allowed to persist will result in a large quantity of product being manufactured incorrectly, which in turn results in scrap, rework, and waste.

Within a traditional manufacturing environment, such problems are overcome by holding safety stocks of components and subassemblies so that materials requiring rework or scrap do not delay production or delivery. Most material planning and control systems establish standard scrap quantities for components and assemblies. The system automatically calculates a need for additional supplies of material to overcome problems in the process.

This approach is anathema to a world class manufacturer. To hold additional safety stock in anticipation of future quality problems is the opposite of a just-in-time philosophy. Inventory levels must be kept low and, if possible, holding inventory must be eliminated. Fast feedback of quality deviations facilitates problem resolution, continuous improvement, and accomplishing low inventory levels.

How To Provide Fast Feedback Reporting

The most common method of providing fast feedback is the use of visual signals, as described in the previous section. If a quality problem is identified, the production line can be stopped by the operator and a red signal posted. These actions communicate the presence of a quality problem to the technicians, supervisors, and operators who are able to solve the problem. These line stops or serious quality deviations are monitored to detect any recurring patterns and to provide information to the participation groups (quality circles) who can devise ways to prevent future problems.

Information that must be provided through printed reports can be fed back quickly if the report is made available more frequently. A customer service report, for example, can be made available daily, by shift, or as required. Ready availability is particularly advantageous if the supervisor or operator can request the report to be printed whenever it is needed, instead of having to request it through an overnight computer run.

Fostering Rather Than Monitoring Improvement

This last characteristic of performance measurement for world class manufacturing has to do with motivation. Performance measures need to show clearly where improvement has been made and where more improvement is possible, rather than merely to monitor people's work. Traditional performance measures are based very much upon the concept of monitoring people's work so that they can be assessed, rather than upon providing information that will help the people to improve. This subtle but important distinction underlines the change in approach to the management of people in a WCM company.

Fostering Improvement Through
Positive Performance Measurement

There are a number of aspects within the new approach to performance measurement that help foster improvement, some of which have been touched upon already. Fast feedback of information enables people to better understand their work and to resolve problems quickly as they arise. Simple, well-designed performance measures give clear and concise pictures of the current situation, provide a common understanding among the operators, supervisors, and managers of the plant's strengths and weaknesses, and focus attention on the key issues of the manufacturing strategy.

Performance measures should focus on the positive aspects as well as the problems. As a rule, all performance measures should point up what has been done right, rather than emphasize the negative. For example, it is better to express production efficiency as a yield of good product rather than as a reject rate. It is better to show the percentage of orders shipped to customers on time than to show the number of late orders.

Some of this is merely cosmetic, but does betray an underlying attitude: that everyone in the company is going to concentrate on getting better and better. There is a winning streak and as time goes by these measures of performance will go up and up. Psychologically, people are motivated more by seeing the results of their improvement as an increase in the measurements, a graph going upward, rather than by seeing a reduction of their errors.

There is significant emphasis within world class manufacturing plants on the discovery and resolution of problems. There also needs to be an emphasis on discovering what is being done well and why it is being done well. Everyone who is concerned with quality must study what they do right so that these strengths can be built upon and so that the same approaches can be applied in problem areas. All performance measures must concentrate on the positive aspects of the plant's performance and be used to provide a direction toward improvement; therefore, a fundamental change of emphasis is required.

Traditionally, performance measurement has been used to monitor people's work, often with a view assessing their pay and promotion. This practice leads to fear and nervousness, rather than to innovation and improvement. People make comments like: "You're only as good as your last mistake in this company," or "Successes are soon forgotten, but failures are remembered forever." Attitudes like this are harmful to a world class manufacturing approach. The right approach is for people to feel encouraged to be innovative, to be problem solvers rather than just to keep out of trouble.

Performance measures must be used in a nonthreatening manner. The measures themselves are, of course, impartial; the important issue is how they are interpreted and used. Using them in the traditional way will be contrary to the objectives of world class manufacturing; using them to encourage innovation and problem solving promotes continuous improvement.

Inter-plant Issues

One characteristic of traditional performance measurement is that measures are the same for all plants and locations within the company and, therefore, lend themselves to inter-plant comparisons. These inter-plant comparisons are not normally possible within the new methods of measuring performance.

Two key aspects are that new performance measures (1) vary between plants and (2) vary over time. Comparing one plant with another does not make sense in this environment because like is not always compared with like. Measures vary from location to location because of differences between these locations, and to make blanket comparisons one with another is not productive or meaningful toward improvement. In fact, these same issues are present with the traditional performance measures. To think that these measures give a useful comparison between plants is an illusion.

In the use of new performance measures, absolute values of the results are less important than the trends that are occurring. The primary purpose of performance measures is to assess changes taking place within the organization. Where two plants stand in relation to each other does not matter; what does matter is that each plant improves its performance. The changes over time are of most importance and should be emphasized by the performance measurement system so that continuous improvement is fostered within each location.

Summary

Although the performance measurements being used by successful world class manufacturers vary considerably, seven common characteristics can be identified. These new performance measures:

- directly relate to the manufacturing strategy
- primarily use nonfinancial measures
- vary among locations
- change over time
- are simple and easy to use
- provide fast feedback to operators and managers
- foster improvement instead of simply monitoring

The majority of performance measures chosen by world class manufacturers are not new. As stated at the beginning of this chapter, many of them have been used for many years. What is new, however, is the importance attached to them. By replacing the traditional management accounting and variance reports, these new measures truly drive the production process.

CHAPTER THREE

Shortcomings of Traditional Management Accounting*

*T*RADITIONAL CONCEPTS of cost and management accounting were developed in the late nineteenth and early twentieth centuries to meet the dynamic needs of expanding manufacturing industries in Europe and America. The concepts were fully formalized by the 1930s and have since been the basis of manufacturing performance measurement, inventory valuation, product pricing, and capital investment analysis. In the last 15 to 20 years, however, the climate of Western manufacturing industry has changed enormously, while the techniques of management accounting have changed very little.

History of Management Accounting

The historical development of management accounting is fascinating. Contrary to the popular myths depicting accountants as humorless men in gray suits, the people

---

* This chapter explains why traditional management accounting is unsuited for the needs of world class manufacturers. Readers anxious to get into the practical use of the new concepts of performance measurement may wish to proceed directly to Chapter 4.

responsible for introducing the concepts of cost accounting were dynamic and innovative leaders. These business people were among the pioneers of the nineteenth-century industrial explosion.

Although double-entry bookkeeping was first formalized in Venice during the fourteenth century as a method of tracking commercial transactions, management accounting was not required by the merchants and owners of small businesses in the years prior to the industrial revolution. The advent of large industrial organizations in the nineteenth century created a need to provide information about the financial transactions occurring within these companies.

New accounting methods were required because entrepreneurs were beginning to hire workers on a long-term basis, make long-range capital investments, establish hierarchical company structures, and introduce more intricate production technologies. The highly involved decision making within these more complex organizations required better internal financial information.

Early costing systems concentrated on conversion costs for the calculation of cost-per-ton or cost-per-unit of straightforward manufacturing processes like steel making. These costs included materials and labor and occasionally some allocation of overheads. As communications and transportation improved in the mid-nineteenth century, new management accounting techniques were required to control more far-flung enterprises like the railroads, retail stores, and services. These needs brought about the development of cost and profit centers, and new performance measures for the individual branches.

The influence of the scientific management movement, with its emphasis on a standard method for each production task, led to the introduction of standard costs for manufactured products. The diversified corporations that first developed in the early twentieth century required the use of budgeting, capital investment analysis, performance measurement ratios, and divisionalized accounting.

All of the essential elements of modern management accounting had been established and codified by 1930. These elements included forecasting, budgeting, standard costing, overhead absorption, variance analysis, transfer pricing, return-on-investment (ROI) calculations, and so forth. In addition, the integration of cost accounts with the financial accounts had by that time become accepted practice and was required by auditors.

Since the 1930s, there have not been any significant changes in the techniques of management accounting. There have been many refinements introduced, there has been a great deal of academic research, but the fundamental principles have not changed.

In contrast to this stable picture, manufacturing industry has changed enormously. Products have changed dramatically. Production technology has been transformed and automation has changed the cost distributions. Research and development cycles in some industries are much longer and more costly, and employee needs and aspirations are very different. In short, a revolution has occurred in the manufacturing industry and the rate of change is increasing each year. Traditional methods of management accounting have simply not kept pace with these dynamic changes.

Function of Management Accounting

The purpose of financial accounting is to report the company's activities to interested parties *outside* the company. The purpose of management accounting is to supply information to people *inside* the company. This information is used for planning and controlling the operations of the business. Management accounting can be divided into five areas:

1. pricing
2. budgeting
3. performance measurement
4. integration with financial accounts
5. investment analysis

Pricing decisions traditionally have required detailed, accurate information about the costs of the products and the relative costs of changing volumes and product mixes. This fact is particularly applicable to companies that make specialty products with prices not governed by market forces.

The development of departmental budgets is a significant part of the management accountant's job in most companies. Budget development provides the tactics through which company strategy will be achieved. Budgets are also used as a primary performance measure; monthly reports are produced showing each department's actual expenditure in comparison to the budgeted expenses.

Most manufacturers use a standard costing system. Standard costs are assigned to each manufactured product, and these standards can be broken down for each individual step in the production process. The standards are used as the primary measure of performance when the actual costs are entered into the costing system. Any variances between the standard and actual costs can be analyzed to highlight production problems and to monitor each department's productivity.

The integration of the financial accounts with the management accounts revolves around the valuation of inventories. Inventory valuation is required for balance sheet reporting and is usually split between raw materials, work-in-process, and finished goods inventories. The determination of inventory values for partially completed products and subassemblies is a complex task, governed by standard accounting practice, and frequently leads to a distortion of the cost picture.

The management accountant can assist company managers in decisions relating to investment. Investment can be the purchase of new plants, equipment, and facilities; it can also be the process of deciding when and how new products should be launched and old products discontinued. There are a series of techniques including return-on-investment (ROI) and net-present-value (NPV) calculations that can be employed for these kinds of strategic decisions. The analysis of investment projects always involves making choices between conflicting priorities. Management accounting, in this area, must provide a detailed financial analysis so that these decisions can be made knowledgeably and objectively.

Problems with Management Accounting

The root cause of problems that many companies have with traditional management accounting is that management accounting techniques have not kept pace with the changes taking place in manufacturing industry. These problems fall into the following five categories:

1. *Lack of relevance*
   - Management accounting reports are not directly related to the manufacturing strategy.
   - Financial measures are not meaningful for the control of production and distribution operations.
   - The application of cost accounting to pricing decisions is frequently irrelevant and misleading.

2. *Cost distortion*
   - Traditional cost accounting is concerned with cost elements. The pattern of cost elements has changed

in recent years, and this detailed analysis is less important.
- The distinction between direct and indirect costs is not as rigid as it used to be. The same is true of variable and fixed costs.
- Traditional methods of apportioning overheads can significantly distort product costs.

3. *Inflexibility*
- Traditional management accounting reports do not vary from plant to plant within an organization. Similarly, they usually do not change over time as needs of the business change.
- Cost accounting reports frequently are received too late to be of value.
- Cost accounting reports frequently are viewed with disdain by operations managers because they do not help them with their job and because they are often used to censure the operations manager when variances are unfavorable.

4. *Impediment to progress in world class manufacturing*
- Traditional methods of assessing the pay-back on capital projects can impede the introduction of world class manufacturing.
- Cost accounting often causes managers to do wasteful and unnecessary tasks in order to make the figures look good.
- Concentrating on machine and labor efficiency rates encourages the production of large batch quantities.
- Overhead absorption variances encourage large batch sizes and overproduction.
- Cost accounting requires much detailed data that is costly to obtain.
- Cost accounting reinforces the entrenched ideas and outmoded methods that need to be replaced.

5. *Subjection to the needs of financial accounting*
  • Too often cost accounts are regarded as a subsidiary ledger of financial accounts. To be of value, management accounting systems must be based on different methods and assumptions than on the financial accounts. These methods apply to such issues as inventory valuation, overhead absorption, and accounting periods.

Each of these five problem categories will be examined now in detail.

Lack of Relevance

When the techniques of management accounting were developed, the best method of automating calculations was the slide rule. Today anyone using a slide rule would be regarded as eccentric because recent changes in technology have rendered it obsolete. In the same way, changes in product and production technology have rendered traditional management accounting techniques irrelevant and wasteful.

Management Accounting and Manufacturing Strategy

As noted in Chapter 2, the performance measurement system must support the company manufacturing strategy. Within a world class environment the manufacturing strategy will be established in primarily nonfinancial terms. The strategy will often make reference to such financial goals as lowering costs, achieving margins, realizing returns on assets, or contributing to stock value; but the majority of strategic factors will be nonfinancial.

There is a wide diversity in the manufacturing strategies employed by different companies because there are important differences between companies. These differences center around the products, the market, the location, and the management philosophy. Issues addressed by the manufacturing strategy include quality, reliability, flexibility, innovation, lead times, customer satisfaction, and social issues. None of these factors can be monitored using traditional cost and management accounting techniques.

Management Accounting and Operational Control

Financial measures are not meaningful for the control of production or distribution operations. Most people in a factory do not think in terms of the financial aspects of their work; they concentrate on such issues as production rates, yield quantities, on-time deliveries, reject rates, schedule changes, and stock-outs.

When a manager or supervisor in the plant receives a cost accounting report, he or she has to spend considerable time analyzing the figures presented so that the information can become meaningful and then must translate the data from financial information to the practical daily issues of the shop floor. This cumbersome task is, at best, wasteful activity and, at worst, can result in significant misunderstandings that result in damage to the company's operations. For performance measurement reports to be meaningful and useful to the managers, supervisors, and operators, they must directly measure the important issues facing the production plant. They must not be camouflaged in financial figures.

Management Accounting and Pricing

Management accounting techniques have become of less significance to pricing decisions in recent years. The reason for this is that world-wide competition has made the prices of a wider range of products more market-driven than cost-driven. Few companies have the luxury of setting prices according to an acceptable margin above the product costs.

Consequently, there is now significant change in the way that products are marketed. Many companies, predominantly

Japanese companies, are much more concerned about market share and long-term viability than about the markup on an individual product. This change in emphasis has led to significant competitive pressure for Western manufacturers. The new requirement is to establish a price based upon the needs of the market in order to give the company a competitive edge; account must be taken not only of the product itself but also of any other aspects related to a customer's purchase decision.

For the majority of manufacturers (other than some defense suppliers), prices are established by marketing decision rather than by analysis of costs. There is still a need to analyze production costs in comparison to prices so that the managers can assess which products are most profitable. The trend is to establish acceptable manufacturing costs based on the required market price. This trend results in an analysis of the production process and inevitably leads to the introduction of world class manufacturing techniques and the application of continuous improvement. A prime example of this was discussed in Chapter 2 when Nissan saw a loss of profitability as a result of exchange rate changes between the yen and the dollar. The requirement was to introduce more improvements in their already world class operations so that increased productivity would offset the changes in the exchange rate.

Cost Distortion

During the early days, management accounting emphasized the detailed analysis of a product's cost elements. At that time, cost elements were usually quite clear; labor was by far the largest cost, followed by materials and overhead. Many underlying principles of traditional cost accounting are based on these cost patterns. Typically, the labor content of a product would be in the 75- to 95-percent range of the total product cost.

Cost patterns have, however, changed significantly in the last 50 years. New technologies and new production techniques have given rise to a marked reduction in the amount of labor required to manufacture a product — the labor content of the "average" product manufactured in the United States in 1988 was 7 percent of the total cost. In addition to the three primary cost elements, new elements are becoming more significant, including technology costs, engineering costs, and other costs traditionally regarded as overheads. The traditional system, with its concentration on the reporting of labor, material, and overhead costs, does not emphasize the right issues. Too much time and effort is expended measuring and evaluating elements that are increasingly less important. As other aspects of production costing become more significant, sometimes the right aspects are not addressed by the traditional systems.

Direct and Variable Costs — Indirect and Fixed Costs

The distinction between direct and indirect costs was once clearer than it is today. When the overhead was small in comparison to the labor content of the product, there was no need to analyze overhead costs in great detail; they did not materially affect product-costing calculations. Any function costs within the plant not directly attributable to specific products were lumped into the overhead and absorbed in the usual way. Indirect costs included all management and supervisory costs; all sales, marketing, and distribution costs; product development costs; and administration activities. Now that the overhead costs of a production facility tend to be a more significant element of total production costs, they need to be analyzed more closely.

Frequently, overhead costs can be subdivided into fixed and variable portions, as there are many overhead costs that do vary with the amount of product manufactured. For example, in many companies electricity costs vary according to the amount of goods produced, particularly when a large amount of electricity is used in the production process or where an increased volume requires moving to substantial overtime or additional production shifts. Other costs, like the company president's private plane, are entirely fixed and unrelated to production volumes. Many cost accounting systems divide the overhead apportionment calculations into fixed and variable elements and allocate a little of the fixed costs to each production job and allocate the variable costs in the traditional manner.

Some of the new approaches to cost accounting introduced in recent years insist that almost all costs are direct costs and that it is possible to assign a cost driver with which to apportion these costs to individual products or product groups. This approach (of which activity-based costing is the most well known) does not rely on traditional factors for the application of overhead. Most costs within the plant do not vary directly with labor hours, labor costs, material costs, or machine hours. However, many do vary in proportion to other factors — or cost drivers. If these cost drivers can be identified and overhead apportionment rates applied to them, then costs previously regarded as indirect costs now can be applied as direct costs. The key to this issue is that overheads are such a large amount of the *total* product cost that it is important to analyze these overhead costs and develop methods for applying them as direct costs.

Overhead Apportionment Distorts Costs

Whenever a company manufactures and sells multiple products and services, the product costs assessed by a traditional costing system will be distorted. As an example, consider two factories that manufacture electric light bulbs. The two factories are similar in size, equipment, and production facilities; but they have very different types of output. The first factory produces 10 million 100-watt 120-volt clear bulbs each year. The second factory makes the same product, but in much smaller quantities; it also manufactures a wide range of other bulbs including a variety of colors, four different wattages, and two different voltages. In all, the second plant manufactures 64 different kinds of bulbs, some in small quantities and some in large quantities ranging from batches of 1,000 to 500,000.

Despite the fact that they make similar products, the two plants are very different inside. The second plant has more people because of the need to schedule production, do changeovers, receive materials, expedite orders, inspect goods, move materials, and so on. Owing to the complexity of planning and scheduling the high degree of product variation and product-mix change, the second plant experiences higher inventory levels (raw material, WIP, and finished goods), more down time, and more rejects. In addition, the second plant has a complex computerized production planning and control system.

Overhead costs required to manufacture products in the second plant are considerably higher than those of the first plant. These overhead costs are traditionally apportioned to each production batch based upon an absorption factor that is related to labor hours, labor cost, material costs, machine time, or machine costs, despite the fact that labor is becoming an increasingly smaller element of production costs in most industries.

When overhead costs are allocated for bulbs manufactured in the second plant, the standard 100-watt clear bulb will show a much higher cost than the same bulb made in the first plant. If this bulb represents 30 percent of the second plant's output, then 30 percent of the overhead costs will be allocated to that type of bulb. In a similar way, a 220-volt blue bulb which represents only 0.5 percent of the plant's output, will have just 0.5 percent of the overhead costs allocated. In fact, however, the amounts of labor, machine time, and materials are the same for the two different kinds of bulb, so the actual overhead will be the same for each of the bulbs irrespective of their style or production volume. In reality, the 220-volt blue bulb consumes much more overhead per bulb than the 100-watt clear bulb because it is produced infrequently in small batches and small quantities.

The management accountant, when reviewing the two plants, will see the production costs of the 100-watt clear bulb to be higher in the second plant than in the first. Similarly, the margins on the higher-priced 220-volt blue bulbs will be considered more advantageous than the margins on the standard bulbs. The management accounting system will show the standard 100-watt bulb to be less profitable than the 220-volt blue bulb, and the logical result will be to reduce production of the standard bulb and make larger quantities of the less popular bulbs available for sale at higher prices.

This policy could lead to disaster. In truth, the cost of manufacturing the 100-watt clear bulb is significantly lower than the cost of making the more unusual bulbs, but the costing system will give the opposite opinion. This method of allocating overheads (which is used by virtually every manufacturer) significantly distorts the costs of individual products when a production plant manufactures a range of products.

Further Distortions of Product Costs

To make matters worse, the method of calculating overhead absorption rates can introduce further confusion and distortion. Assessment of overhead absorption rates is calculated annually based upon estimated production volumes, production mixes, and indirect costs. As the year progresses and the production volumes and mixes change, the overhead that is "absorbed" will likely be different from that estimated by the accountants at the start of the year. This situation leads to the complex concept of over- and under-absorption variances.

As noted earlier, a further source of distortion derives from decisions made concerning which costs are fixed and which are variable. In some cases, it is clear which costs are directly variable — material costs, labor costs, machine time, and others usually are considered variable direct costs. Other costs like building maintenance, the factory restaurant, and so forth clearly are fixed indirect costs. There are other costs that cannot be classified so clearly, including such items as the cost of the procurement department, the computer systems, and the machine and tooling maintenance personnel. These costs are volume related and can vary according to the type of product being manufactured — they are variable costs. However, to find a simple method with which these costs can be correctly applied to specific products is difficult. These costs frequently are considered to be fixed overhead and are apportioned in the usual way.

Inflexibility

One attribute of traditional management accounting is that the reports are consistent. They have been developed over many years into a science that ensures their completeness and correctness companywide. Unfortunately, this completeness is a disadvantage to a world class manufacturer, particularly when the company has a multi-plant manufacturing and distribution network.

Management Accounting Reports Do Not Vary Across Plants

An important aspect in the implementation of world class manufacturing is that each production plant is different, with different products, different processes, different strengths and weaknesses, different problems, and different people. Performance measurement within these plants will need to be different. Traditional systems do not take these different needs into account.

In addition to the performance measurement needs varying from plant to plant, the needs of each individual plant also change as time passes. Continuous improvement brings with it a requirement to measure effectiveness in different ways as changes and improvements are introduced. Far greater flexibility is required in the performance measurement techniques than is available within a traditional management accounting system. The management accounting reports used by the senior managers to judge the performance of each plant may show that the plants are performing poorly when in fact they are doing marvelously well. It is the reports that are wrong; they are measuring the wrong things, and a lack of flexibility can become a serious problem when the managers of a manufacturing or distribution facility are working to bring their plant up to world class status.

Cost Accounting Reports Are Too Late To Be Valuable

Chapter 2 emphasized the need for fast feedback within the performance measurement system. Management accounting reports in most companies are distributed once a month, usually several days after the close of the financial period. By the time the managers and supervisors get the reports, the information may be six weeks or more out of date. The intention within a world class manufacturing environment is to be immediately responsive to changes and problems within the production process. It is just not useful to have the primary performance reports produced on a monthly or even a weekly basis.

Impediment to Progress in World Class Manufacturing

There are two primary aspects where traditional management accounting techniques of capital investment assessment conflict with the needs of world class manufacturing. The first area is the need to view implementation of world class manufacturing techniques in their entirety, not to look at each project individually. The second is that the criteria for capital investment within WCM differ from those of a traditional environment.

General Problems with Traditional Capital Investment Methods

The classic textbook method for assessing the viability of a capital project is to calculate certain key factors related to the project. These usually include such aspects as the discounted cash flow (DCF), the return on investment (ROI), the internal rate of return, and the payback period. The calculation of these factors is based upon forecasts and estimates of the project costs and benefits in question. The investigation occasionally is enhanced by the use of sensitivity analysis, which seeks to assess how dependent the factors are on the accuracy of the primary assumptions and estimates. The calculated factors are then used to stack up the various proposed capital projects in sequence of their expected benefit to the company. Projects with the highest potential benefits are then initiated.

The problem with this approach has always been that the analysis is frequently based upon ill-defined assumptions and projections. Often the more politically astute managers can thus adjust the figures in favor of the projects in which they are interested.

A senior manager in one company commented that, owing to the successful implementation of six inventory reduction projects during his ten years on the job, the company should now have *negative* inventory. Each project claimed significant inventory reduction; all six added together would have reduced the inventory to less than nothing. Clearly, the figures used to justify the projects were not realistic.

How Traditional Capital Investment Methods
Affect World Class Manufacturing

In the implementation of projects related to world class manufacturing, none of the traditional factors takes account of the issues that really matter. Quality is not accounted for within these factors; nor is flexibility, short lead times, and customer satisfaction. These so-called intangibles are ignored by the traditional management accounting methods.

In addition, classic methods do not take account of implementation of world class manufacturing as a management philosophy. World class manufacturing is not a set of projects — it is total change in the way the company approaches the design, production, and distribution of products and services. An individual project may not be cost-justified on its own merits in traditional terms, yet it may be pivotal to the success of a world class manufacturing approach. Such projects cannot be seen as isolated events; they must be seen within the context of an overall change in production methodology.

New Elements in the Capital Project Evaluation

World class manufacturing introduces new aspects into the decision-making process for capital projects. These aspects include the need for flexibility, matching output to demand, and changing machine usage assumptions.

One objective for an ideal world class manufacturer is to make today what the customer requires today — no more and no less. This approach will ensure low inventory levels and high service levels. As customers do not place orders according to the production plan, the manufacturing plant must be flexible to meet the customer demand. Very few manufacturers have achieved such a high degree of flexibility and customer service, but a world class manufacturer would be working toward this goal.

Flexibility of this kind requires small lot sizes or production runs, short cycle times, and the ability to quickly change production mix and volumes. These features need to be considered when reviewing capital purchase decisions, because financial analysis alone does not adequately assess the situation when these decisions are being made.

On some occasions, flexibility can be achieved by buying very sophisticated machines, such as robots or numerical control machines; but very often a less sophisticated and specialized machine will provide greater flexibility. A sophisticated machine usually requires highly trained technicians to assist with setup, changeover, or reprogramming. This need can introduce delays into the setup process and result in longer lead times and larger batch sizes. In contrast, a machine that can be set up by the operator will provide shorter changeovers than a more specialized machine. Simplicity of setup can be achieved by using either a less sophisticated machine (often at a lower cost) or a machine whose sophistication has made it easier to operate and change over.

There is another important wider aspect of flexibility. Many companies have one or more very large machines that are central to their manufacturing operation, for example, heat-treatment ovens or wave-soldering machines. These machines can be a hindrance to a just-in-time manufacturer because many subassemblies have to be routed through this work center, thus negating any substantial attempt to reorganize the shop floor into production cells, to reduce material movements, and to create an efficient manufacturing flow. In addition, the physical size of these machines and such special installation requirements as high voltage, special ventilation and noise reduction systems, reinforced floors, and so forth, make it very difficult to move the machine when the shop floor is being reorganized.

A company using just-in-time techniques will reorganize its shop floor layouts frequently so as to match output to customer demand and maintain a minimum of material movements, and the machines favored by world class manufacturers facilitate fast setups and changeovers by the operator. The equipment should be able to manufacture a wide range of the products and be readily moved when production requirements change. These aspects of the capital purchase decision are not considered in traditional methods of analysis.

Matching Output to Demand

When a company launches a new product and needs to buy new machinery (and/or a plant), the traditional approach to capital purchases is to buy a machine that will not only meet current capacity requirements but will meet the needs of at least three to five years of projected growth. This approach is taken because the long-term cost savings of the purchase of a large, high-volume machine appears to be substantial.

In reality, this analysis can be misleading. During the first two or three years, usage is lower than capacity; frequently the growth forecasts are too optimistic, the machine never reaches full potential, and the expected benefits do not accrue. Conversely, if the new product is a huge success, the machine is over-utilized (perhaps on a three-shift, seven-day-week basis) and quality may be sacrificed in order to achieve higher production volumes. Such a high-risk approach to the acquisition of production equipment requires that a great deal of money must be spent at an early stage in anticipation of future demands, which may or may not materialize.

The world class manufacturing approach is the opposite of the traditional approach. The capacity to manufacture is made available just in time, in the same way that materials are made available. When a new product is launched, new machines are bought with enough capacity to meet immediate needs for six to 12 months. This approach may require machines that are smaller and, perhaps, slower than before. The machines chosen will be flexible so that, in the event of the new product failing to meet planned sales, the equipment can be diverted to another use. When the product takes off, additional machines can be purchased to meet the increasing demand. The advantages of this approach are:

- It is low risk because capital outlay is low in the early stages of production.
- As demand for the new product increases, the production capability can be increased in convenient stages.
- It lends itself to the WCM techniques of cellular production and flexible plant layout.
- There is additional flexibility because these machines can be used for other products, should that be required.

There are a number of critical factors involved in capital purchase decisions within a world class manufacturing plant that are not accounted for in the traditional methods of assessing capital projects.

Machine and Labor Efficiencies and Batch Size

Key measures widely used by companies with traditional management accounting systems are the labor and machine efficiencies. A company that invests a large amount of money in a production plant wants to make sure that machines are being used effectively and that the company is getting the maximum possible return on its investment. Similarly, the company wants to monitor the productivity of operators who are a large proportion of the payroll and who have been trained by the company at great expense. Thus, the labor and machine efficiency reports show good figures when people and machines are producing large quantities of product. A machine slowed down or stopped for any reason will show a poor result. If small production batches are introduced, with a proportionally larger number of setups, the efficiency reports will also show a poor performance.

Assessing production effectiveness in this way runs counter to the tenets of world class manufacturing. World class manufacturers are striving for small batch sizes and fast changeovers; their aim is zero inventory and synchronized production flow throughout the plant. Consequently, machines will be deliberately idle when there is no immediate need for the component, subassemblies, and products they make. In traditional plants where machine and labor efficiencies are closely monitored, the plant manager must keep machines running irrespective of whether the products being made are needed. These plants will also make production runs as long as possible in order to reflect well in the efficiency reports.

This difference highlights the conflict between world class manufacturing and traditional management accounting. The results of this kind of efficiency reporting are not only inconvenient for the plant moving toward world class methods, but also are specifically harmful to that effort.

Why Efficiency Reports Are Harmful

Traditional machine and labor efficiency reporting is concerned only with the measure of efficiency at an individual production work center. The assumption is that if you monitor the efficiency of each individual work center, the total efficiency of the plant will be maximized automatically. The efficiency of the plant is the sum of the efficiencies of the work centers.

This view is too simplistic. There are many more issues involved with the efficient and productive management of a manufacturing plant which world class manufacturers consider the keys to competitiveness. They include quality, zero inventories, small batches, fast setups, short cycle times, customer satisfaction, flexibility, production cells, and synchronized production flows.

A platoon of soldiers can march effectively only if every individual marches in time with the others. Some soldiers may be able to march more quickly and efficiently, but if they did so the whole platoon would be stumbling over each other and no progress would be made. The same is true within a production plant where the highest efficiencies are obtained by synchronizing production flow throughout the entire plant. The majority of machines may be operating below their peak efficiency because they are limited by the overall production flow rate. Either production flow will be limited by a small number of bottleneck operations, or the flow will have been deliberately varied so that output of finished products matches the varying needs of the customers.

The control and optimization of bottleneck work centers is a significant aspect of synchronized manufacturing. In the short term, bottleneck work centers will be carefully scheduled to maximize their throughput because the overall productivity of the plant is significantly affected by the throughput of these work centers. In the longer term, these work centers will be modified and upgraded so that their throughputs can be increased and the efficiency of the whole process increased. Performance measures used by world class manufacturers need to be concerned with the entire production process, not with the individual steps within the process.

Overhead Absorption Variances Favor Large Batches

One of the many variance reports produced regularly by traditional management accounting systems is the overhead absorption variance report. Its purpose is to show how much of the budgeted overhead has been allocated as a result of the actual production within the plant.

Overhead absorption rates generally are calculated annually when budgets are established. Absorption rates are determined using the same assumptions that are built into the budgets, including product mix, production volume, batch sizes, and overhead expenses. If production proves that these assumptions are 100-percent correct, then the application of overhead amounts will be precisely in line with the budget. This, of course, is virtually never the case in reality because production rates, mix, batch size, and expenses can vary considerably from plan.

Small variations in the absorption of overheads are generally written off at the end of each accounting period. Large variations can cause considerable accounting problems because they affect inventory valuations and, therefore, the company's balance sheet and income statement. These differences are investigated rigorously so that the cause of the variance can be established. If a substantial over- or under-absorption of overhead exists at the financial year end, the accountants are required to prorate the differences across the year-end inventory and cost-of-sales figures.

Introduction of world class manufacturing techniques requires production personnel to have smaller batch sizes and more setups; as a result, there is often under-absorption of overheads. In addition, synchronized and levelized production scheduling requires that some (perhaps most) machines run at a slower than maximum rate so that inventories do not build up at bottleneck work centers. Again, the effect of this approach is to under-absorb the overheads established in a traditional cost accounting system.

The way to ensure that overhead absorption variances are always positive is to run large batches through each machine center. The objective within world class manufacturing is just the opposite. It is difficult for a plant manager to introduce world class manufacturing techniques when old accounting systems continue to show negatives on variance reports that have traditionally been considered of importance.

Encourages Wasteful Activities

Many wasteful activities within a production plant are caused by the managers' and operators' attempts to satisfy the management accounting system. It is common for production supervisors to rush a large amount of product out of the plant in the last few days of the financial period. Production targets have been set and managers and supervisors are judged by their adherence to those targets. Thus, products are released that are below quality standard, the flow of production is disrupted, a lot of time is wasted in expediting jobs, and an illusion of productivity covers up flawed production processes that should be improved.

The budget in many companies (and government agencies) is developed by allocating next year's budget based upon the money spent in the current year by each department. If a department fails to spend all allocated resources in a year, then its budget is cut in the following year. Thus, managers of the departments may spend money (often at the last minute) on items that are not needed so that they will not experience budget cuts in the following year.

Inventory targets can cause managers and supervisors to go to extraordinary lengths to ensure compliance. When there is an imbalance of inventory between plants and warehouses, products (particularly slow-moving items) are moved from one warehouse to another so that the inventory figures look good. Sometimes it is not necessary to physically move the goods — it is sufficient for the costing system that the material be on order by a warehouse. At the end of the period, the inventory manager also often releases purchase or transfer orders, which are then promptly cancelled when the new period is opened.

This inventive nonsense intended for "bucking the system" can be elevated to an art form by the use of special codes and order numbers that are understood by everybody to be "dummy" transfers, and so forth. This devious activity is especially effective when moving products across country borders because of dealing not only with transfer costs but also with varying exchange rates, which can totally obscure the nature of the transaction.

Do these practices add value to the product? Is the customer better served as a result? Is product quality improved? Hardly. All of these ludicrous activities are unadulterated waste. Everybody knows they are stupid and pointless; yet such activities are very common in manufacturing and distribution plants throughout the world.

Entrenched Ideas and Systems

A common notion holds that accountants in general, and management accountants in particular, are conservative by nature, reluctant to innovate, and obstructive of progress. Such is not necessarily the case. When a company implements a world class manufacturing or just-in-time approach to production, the management accountants are often the people who immediately appreciate the benefits of the new approaches and participate fully in their implementation.

It is true, however, that in many companies that have been successful with world class manufacturing techniques, the accounting systems have not changed as quickly as the production techniques and have become a hindrance to the progress of improvement. There are some good reasons for this slower change.

Accountants have a responsibility to maintain independence to a certain extent; the accountant as the internal watchdog is a valuable counterbalance to rampant innovation! In addition, cost and management accounting systems are frequently complex and thorough, and it is not easy to modify or dismantle systems of this kind.

Another area of difficulty for management accountants, who have been trained to observe clearly defined accounting practices, is that there are no industry-wide guidelines on the role of management accounting within a world class manufacturing environment. Accounting bodies themselves have been slow to provide education and training in the new concepts. At a time when production personnel have been going through significant retraining in the ideas of just-in-time, total quality control, and world class manufacturing techniques, there has been little opportunity for management accountants to be retrained in their disciplines.

Cost Accounting Systems Are Wasteful

The primary emphasis of world class manufacturing — the elimination of waste from the production process — has resulted in significant changes in material flow, quality control, product design, personnel training and employment, and production planning. The use of the cost accounting systems is an area of considerable waste, and these systems frequently impede the progress of world class manufacturing.

Many production plants track costs by production job, by assigning a work order number to each job, and by tracking the labor, material, outside processes, and overhead costs against the job. This detailed tracking requires considerable effort on the part of production personnel. Any material issued to each individual job must be recorded in detail; actual hours worked on each job must be tracked; any scrap or rework must be assigned to the specific work order number where the problem originated. As the work order moves through the plant, each step in the production process is recorded in terms of labor/machine hours, quantity completed, and quantity scrapped. This detailed recording is done so that work-in-process inventory valuation can be accurate.

This is the question that must be continuously asked: "Is this activity beneficial to the company?" In some cases, detail is essential; in most plants, it is wasteful and unnecessary. Detailed tracking of labor costs is usually a waste of time; labor costs are not significant enough in comparison to warrant the effort required to gain the information. Valuation of WIP inventories is frequently unnecessary because the improved cycle times resulting from world class manufacturing mean that the value of work-in-process is quite low.

Tracking of completions by individual job step is sometimes justified on the basis that it is required for production planning and control of the shop floor. In contrast, the world class manufacturing techniques of cellular manufacturing, inventory pull, and reduced cycle times no longer require detailed tracking of completion quantities at each step in the process. It is sufficient to record completions at each cell or when the goods become a finished product.

Costing systems employed within a world class manufacturing environment are much simpler than in a traditional production plant. Work orders are usually eliminated and the detailed collection of production cost data is not required.

Integration with Financial Accounts

It is an unchallenged assumption that a company's management accounts should be integrated with — perhaps even subject to — the financial accounts. In reality, this aspect of management accounting can be harmful to a company seeking to move into world class manufacturing. The role of management accounting is very different from that of financial accounting.

There is no requirement that the financial and management accounts be integrated, yet it is a well established tradition that the management accounts should be *driven* by the needs of the financial accounts. Financial accounts, as noted earlier, are primarily used to report the company's financial situation to people outside of the company, like stockholders, government agencies, and other interested parties. The management accounts provide financial information for people inside the company and are used by managers to control activities and set policy.

Why Management Accounts Are Integrated

Management accounts traditionally are integrated with financial accounts because there is information required for the balance sheet and income statement that is obtained from the management accounting systems. The most important of this information is the inventory valuation and the related costs of sales.

In addition to this requirement there is also a long-accepted expectation that the accounting systems within a company should all balance out together and "cross-foot." If a manager has two reports showing the same information and the valuation is different between the two, he or she will want to know which one is "right" and which one is "wrong."

The fact is, as every accountant knows, there is really no such thing as a "correct" cost accounting transaction because there are assumptions and standards built into the system which slant the information. The purpose of these assumptions is to provide a conservative consistency to the accounting process. Such consistency is an important criteria for the financial accounting reports.

While this approach is valuable and necessary within the financial accounting arena, within management accounting it is often more useful to have different assumptions and methods. A problem with traditional cost accounting is that the information is seen primarily as a subsidiary ledger of the financial accounts; as a result, much of the usefulness of the cost accounting information is lost.

Inventory Valuation with Full-absorption Costing

Methods of valuing inventory for the financial accounts are laid down by the professional bodies in each country in the form of accounting standards. Invariably these standards require the full absorption of overheads into the balance sheet inventories. As discussed earlier in this chapter, conventional methods of absorbing overheads can cause significant cost distortion, thus giving erroneous information and leading to poor decisions by managers.

Additional problems are caused when product (or partially completed product) is moved from one plant to another within the same company. Thus, product is often moved at "transfer prices" which reflect a certain amount of internal profit margin back to the plant that made the items. Cost and management accounts should not include artificial cost uplifts because real changes in the value or cost of the products are quite obscured.

Application of overhead burdens on partially completed products, for the purpose of reporting work-in-process inventory values, can also cause difficulties as production methods change. Many production plants have products made up of similar components and subassemblies; the finished products are differentiated at the final stage of manufacture. As these firms move into world class manufacturing, they may wish to plan and schedule production only of subassemblies and components and to manufacture finished products to customer orders on a just-in-time, assemble-to-order basis. If inventory must be held at all, it will be held at the subassembly level.

Decisions relating to production style must be made entirely on the implications for customer service, quality, flexibility, and actual cost. The method and timing of overhead apportionments should not affect this decision. In reality, a move to this style of production can show any significant change in WIP inventories owing to the method of apportioning overhead burdens. The cost and management accounts should be able to show this information more clearly, without being required to present the data in the form dictated by the financial accounts.

Inventory Valuation for World Class Manufacturing

An important aspect of world class manufacturing is the elimination of inventories at all production levels. Significant reductions in cycle time, reductions in production batch sizes (ideally to a size of one), synchronized manufacturing that eliminates shop floor queues, and just-in-time deliveries from vendors help achieve inventory reduction. As inventory levels fall, the importance of inventory valuation diminishes and valuation becomes easier to calculate. For example, if cycle times are reduced to the point where WIP inventories are negligible, then only raw materials and finished products need to be valued.

In most traditional manufacturers, inventory value is an important part of the financial situation. A significant rise or fall of inventory levels can have great impact on the company's financial position, and it is necessary to record these values in detail. The radical reductions in inventory levels experienced by world class manufacturers, however, not only provide enormous benefits to the company, but also make inventory valuation a far less significant part of the financial accounts. Less detailed, simpler methods of valuing inventory can be employed. Cost accounting is no longer integrated with financial accounts for inventory valuation purposes. The absorption of overheads into inventory accounts can be done as a mass adjustment rather than in detail according to each individual product. The objective of the elimination of inventory is to reduce the amount of work to be done, reduce the number of transactions to be recorded, simplify the systems, and make the management accounts more useful to company managers.

The monthly cycle As noted earlier, typical monthly management accounting reports are not useful in a world class manufacturing environment. Reports are produced monthly because they are tied to the financial accounting systems, which are usually monthly based. There is no reason for management accounts to be produced in the same time scale as financial accounts.

Indeed, there is nothing magical about the monthly cycle. There are 365 days in the year because that is the way the earth moves around the sun. The first calendars were large circles drawn by Babylonian mathematicians and divided into 360 segments. These segments were then divided into ten months by pious pagans who named some of the months after their gods. July and August were added by Julius Caesar in honor of himself and his adopted son Augustus; Augustus moved one day out of February and into August so that his month would be the same length as his father's. The year was set at 365 days by Pope Gregory in 1582; it was adjusted in England in 1752 with the introduction of leap years.

None of this has any bearing whatsoever on when management accounting information should be presented; all it does is cause confusion. This confusion is exacerbated by the use of 4:4:5 week accounting cycles and by the introduction of different calendars for production, forecasting, sales and marketing, and accounting. World class manufacturing looks for simplicity of operations; tying the management accounts to the financial accounting cycles has no value.

Short-term view An incisive criticism leveled at Western managers is the accusation of short-term thinking. Financial accounting underpins this short-term approach. The monthly, quarterly, annual reports are used by stockholders, market analysts, and company executives to judge the state of the company. The problem is not so much with the reported information, but the short-term view of the people using it. World class manufacturers are typically long term in their approach to design, production, and marketing.

There is no reason why management accounts should be governed by the short-term approach of financial accounting. Within world class manufacturing, management accounting information is used to track trends and changes, not to cause concern about the results on a specific date or period-end. "Short-termism" has no place in world class manufacturing; WCM is looking for continuous improvement and the gradual introduction of radically new approaches to production. The major Japanese companies took 30 or 40 years to achieve their current levels of productivity, and they are still dissatisfied and moving on. In general, the benefits of world class manufacturing are not seen in the company's balance sheet and income statement for some time; often there may be negative short-term results. It is a strategy that is looking to the long term.

Summary

Traditional management accounting was developed during the industrial revolution and the early part of the twentieth century. The techniques of management accounting have not significantly changed since the 1930s when industry-wide standards were adopted. Enormous changes have taken place in technology and production techniques, and the old style of management accounting is no longer useful. It is at best irrelevant and at worst positively harmful.

The primary problems with traditional management accounting include:

- *lack of relevance* to manufacturing strategy, the daily control of production, and product pricing decisions

- *cost distortion* caused by assuming inaccurate cost patterns, by not correctly distinguishing direct and indirect costs, and by apportioning overheads incorrectly
- *inflexibility* because reports do not vary from plant to plant and from time to time, and because the reports are too late to be of value
- *impediment to progress* in WCM by assessing capital projects incorrectly, concentrating on machine and labor efficiencies, encouraging large batch sizes, causing managers to do wasteful activities, and maintaining wasteful and obsolete systems
- *subjection to the needs of the financial accounting systems,* which causes confusion and makes the cost accounting information much less useful

CHAPTER FOUR

Measurement of Delivery Performance and Customer Service

*T*HE NEXT SIX chapters present practical examples of the performance measures being used by world class manufacturing companies. It must be understood that no one uses *all* of these measures; they are given to show the kinds of measures that make sense in a world class manufacturing environment and are not intended to be used as a blueprint for any particular company. The performance measurement needs of companies moving into world class manufacturing will vary considerably and will change as time goes by and as the concept of continuous improvement becomes a daily reality. The ideas and examples in these chapters provide guidelines that can be used to develop effective measures within a given company.

In reality, a company will select a small number of key measures with which to monitor the progress of the business. Individual departments and plants will often have several additional measures giving managers, supervisors, and operators a more detailed analysis of the factors affecting production. Too many measures can confuse people and obscure the company's strategic direction; there must be few enough measures so that the people can understand them and use them effectively.

These Performance Measures Are Not New

Very few performance measures used by world class manufacturers are entirely new; most have been in use for many years. The difference is that these are the primary methods used by these companies to monitor and control the business. Traditional reports may still be produced for external reporting, but are not used by the plant or departmental managers for operational decision making.

A further consideration is that the inclusion of a performance measure does not necessarily mean that all companies must aim at 100-percent achievement of these measures in order to be considered "world class." The setting of performance goals will be discussed in some detail in Chapter 10; the targets established (if they are established at all) will vary according to the stage the company has reached with WCM, the kinds of product manufactured, and the needs of the market. For example, a semiconductor chip manufacturer will measure product yields in great detail using statistical process control (SPC). However, the limitations of many processes (at the present time) make a 100-percent yield an impossibility; for many companies a 20-percent yield is considered very good. In addition, there are limitations to the control of these yields in some of the processes. The reasons for high or low yields may not be clearly understood, and the yield levels have more to do with probability than process control.

Reports, Charts, Pictures, and Signals

There are several different ways of presenting performance measurement information. The traditional way is through the use of printed reports, often computer produced.

In these chapters, many examples of computer-produced performance measurement reports will be shown.

In many instances the performance information can be better presented using charts or pictures. These graphical views can show the situation clearly and succinctly; the current performance can be seen at a glance without the need to interpret a page of figures, particularly when statistical information is being used. A bell-shaped curve is more meaningful to the non-specialist than are columns of figures showing means and standard deviations.

A further extension of this approach is the use of signals. When there is a clearly defined standard that can be measured, then a signal can show if the process is meeting the standard or is deviating from it. These methods are most often useful when measuring quality issues.

Delivery Performance Measures

Delivering goods on time is the essence of just-in-time manufacturing. In a company making anything other than a very simple product, the delivery of the finished product on time to the customer is the culmination of a long series of steps being done right. These stages include correct scheduling; ensuring high quality; on-time deliveries of raw materials and components; manufacturing at the right time in the right quantity; and shipping the finished product when it is needed.

Doing many things right in a manufacturing plant is not easy. Traditionally most companies have done many things wrong most of the time and have been compensated for problems by holding large inventories, by panic expediting, and by continuous fire-fighting. All these activities are highly wasteful and are the opposite of world class manufacturing goals. A just-in-time environment follows these sequence of events:

1. Place orders with vendors for the right raw materials and components in the right quantities.

2. Deliver orders on time and in the correct quantities.
3. Schedule the shop floor correctly in accordance with customer needs.
4. Maintain the schedule of each production cell.
5. Deliver the correct products and quantities to the customers on time.

Each of these areas of activity can be assessed with an appropriate performance measure. For example:

- Placing an incorrect order with vendors and then modifying the orders is an expensive and wasteful activity both for the company and the vendor. *Measuring the number of changes in a time period* can give a good idea of the effectiveness of the planning process.
- *Vendor delivery performance* is a key measure used by most world class manufacturers.
- The *effectiveness of the shop floor schedules* can also be measured by the number of changes over time.
- *On-time schedules* and *schedule adherence by work cell* are common measures in world class manufacturing plants.
- *Customer service level, past-due orders,* and *lost sales reports* (in their various guises) are used by most companies.

Vendor Delivery Performance

There are two key issues related to vendor deliveries — delivery performance and vendor quality. Although these issues are very much related, this chapter will deal with delivery performance alone; vendor quality will be discussed in Chapter 7.

On-time deliveries from vendors are key to a just-in-time approach to manufacturing. On-time deliveries have always been important because early deliveries build inventory and late deliveries cause production disruption and wasteful expediting activities; but it is only with the introduction of just-in-time manufacturing that this problem has been taken seriously.

Some companies embark on just-in-time by immediately trying to lure suppliers into providing JIT deliveries. The right place to start with a just-in-time program is to get one's own house in order before attempting to apply leverage to vendors. Whatever stage a company is at with regard to just-in-time, it is valuable to have an effective measure of vendor delivery performance.

Vendor Delivery Performance Detail Report

Figure 4-1 shows an example of a vendor delivery performance report, which is produced by date range and sorted by vendor number (or alphabetically by vendor name). The first line shows the vendor number, vendor name, and vendor type code followed by some summary figures relating to that vendor. These year-to-date summaries include the value of orders placed on the vendor, the number of purchase order lines placed, number of lines received, number of those lines received early, and the number of lines received late.

The second line shows the buyer code, part number and description, and the certification information. Certification (see Chapter 1) is a method widely used by world class manufacturers to pre-examine a vendor's quality and delivery performance so that inspection procedures can be avoided and on-time deliveries ensured. The certification information shown on this report is the certification code (describing the type of certification applicable to this part from this vendor) and the certification reference, which cross refers the certification to its originating document.

Detailed information is shown on the third line. Each individual delivery of the part during the time frame of the report

```
UNITRONIX CORPORATION – PRAXA SYSTEMS                                    PAGE 1
VENDOR DELIVERY PERFORMANCE REPORT                                  25-NOV-1990

CO BR   VENDOR              TYPE  YTD-PO-VALUE  YTD-LINES  YTD-REC'D  YTD-EARLY  YTD-LATE  YTD-REJECT

BUYER        PRODUCT NO

PO NUMBER  ITEM  LOT NO.  QTY      UM  QTY       UM  DATE         DATE        LATE  VARIANCE   VAR %   SHIP  TO
                          DUE          REC'D         DUE          REC'D                                      LOC

01 01 00300   ARKLAND COMPANY         B   495,988.70      23         11        6        5             0.00

100  3P2         PCB #1                     CERT. CODE 7 REF.: A1 S3245-A1

32456-P  001  1034  3000.00 EA  2900.00      12-NOV-1990  10-NOV-1990   2    -100.00   0.03-   01 01  1

100  4P2         PCB #3                     CERT. CODE 7 REF.: A2 S2341-A2

32456-P  002  1031  1200.00 EA  1000.00      17-OCT-1990  27-NOV-1990  41-   -200.00   0.17-   01 01  1
32456-P  003  1034   125.00 EA   100.00       1-NOV-1990  10-NOV-1990   9-    -25.00   0.20-   01 01  1
32456-P  004  1036  1200.00 EA  1000.00      21-NOV-1990  24-NOV-1990   3-   -200.00   0.17-   01 01  1
32456-P  005  1036  2000.00 EA  2500.00      28-NOV-1990  24-NOV-1990   4     500.00   0.25    01 01  1

TOTAL FOR VENDOR = 00300  7525.00   7500.00

                           AVERAGE LATE:      9.40-      AV. VAR %:   0.0500
                           LINES LATE:        3          %-LATE:     60.00
                           LINES EARLY:       2          %-EARLY:    40.00
                           LINES-ONE-TIME:    0          %-ON-TIME:   0.00
```

Figure 4-1. Vendor Delivery Performance Report

is listed giving the purchase order number, P.O. line number, and the delivery lot number. The quantity due, quantity received, and their units of measure are shown along with the due date and the delivery date. This information is analyzed by calculating the number of days late (negative = late), the quantity variance, and the percentage variance.

Detailed information is presented for every product received from the vendor over the date range of the report, and summaries are given for each vendor. The summaries show the total quantity of parts due, the total quantity received, the average lateness, the number of lines late, number of lines early, and the number of lines on time. The number of lines information is also shown as a percentage, and the average quantity variance percentage is calculated.

This report gives a detailed breakdown of the delivery record for each vendor over the date range of the report. The units of measurement are delivery lots and days late. Units, dollars, or tons may be appropriate denominators in some companies. Pick units that make sense for your plant and do not spend a lot of time arguing about the most appropriate units; providing you are consistent, the real information will become apparent.

Vendor Performance Summary Report

Although detail is important, particularly when negotiating with vendors, it is the trends that are more important. How is the vendor's performance changing over time? Is the vendor's performance consistently different for different products or locations? Are lateness and quantity variances related?

As in Figure 4-2, a summary report can be produced across a date range and can summarize the performance of each vendor. This summary data can be plotted for several vendors (see Figure 4-3) and the trends analyzed.

Another method of presenting summarized information is by the use of bar charts. These charts can show not only the

UNITRONIX CORP – PRAXA SYSTEMS
VENDOR DELIVERY PERFORMANCE SUMMARY

PAGE 2
30-NOV-1990

CO	BR	VENDOR		AV. VARIANCE	%-LATE	%-EARLY	%-ON-TIME	LNES REC'D	LNES LATE	LNES EARLY
01	01	00100	FRANKLIN SUPPLY	0.1200	65.15	31.82	3.03	132	86	42
01	01	00200	GREENLEY & STUBBS	0.0720	3.33	51.67	45.00	120	4	62
01	01	00300	ARKLAND COMPANY	0.0500	60.20	39.80	0.00	98	59	39
01	01	00400	SETTLESON INC	0.3500	43.23	37.41	19.36	155	67	58
01	01	00750	BEST-TECH	0.1100	21.95	17.07	60.98	82	18	14
01	01	00850	EECI	0.0667	13.00	13.90	73.10	223	28	31
01	01		EAST BANK PLANT	0.2618	32.34	29.14	38.52	810	262	236

Figure 4-2. Vendor Delivery Performance Summary

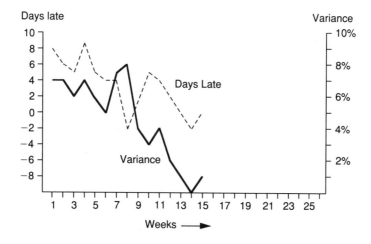

Figure 4-3. Vendor Delivery Performance Graph

average information, but also the spread of delivery lateness. A vendor who is consistently late can actually be preferable to a vendor whose deliveries are erratic. Figure 4-4 gives an example of a bar chart presenting this kind of comparative information.

Vendors	No. of Deliveries	Week Ending: April 24
Briant & May	18	
Carlington	26	
Dunlevy & Co	21	
EG & F	44	
Milnthorpe	12	
O.C.A.C.	32	
Power-Rite	21	
Rochester's	18	

Figure 4-4. Vendor Delivery Performance Spread Chart

Manual Charts for Vendor Performance Measurement

A simple manual chart that can be used in a plant which receives regular deliveries from the same suppliers each week (day or month) is shown in Figure 4-5. Whenever an on-time delivery is received from a supplier, the goods receiving personnel shade the first available box in the vendor's row. If the delivery is late, an "L" is put in the box; if it is early, an "E" is put in the box. As the weeks go by, a clear pattern will build up showing the vendor's performance and any trends in that performance.

Week ending: September 28

Vendor	1	2	3	4	5	6	7	8	9	10	11
Bradford	■	■	■	L	■						
Bundey Bros.	E	■	E	L	L	■					
California Ind.	■	E	■								
Danneman Co											
Donozelli	■	■	■	■	E	E	■				
Mandrake & G	■	E	■	E	L	■					
NDF	L	E	L	L	L						
Shipley	E	■	■	L	E	■	■	■			
Watfordby	■										

Figure 4-5. Manual Vendor Delivery Monitoring

This same simple technique can be extended to show rejects by marking the squares with reject quantities or a reject symbol. The chart then shows both the delivery and the quality aspects of vendor performance.

Unpack and Put-away

Measurement of the vendor delivery performance is valuable, but on-time deliveries are beneficial only if the receiving department can get the parts unpacked and delivered on time to the right place. In an advanced just-in-time operation, most of the parts will be prepacked into containers that can be delivered straight to the shop floor. In addition, the facilities are organized so that the vendor can deliver to the production cell instead of going via a goods receiving operation.

The use of standard containers with standard container quantities is a valuable tool of just-in-time manufacturing and can be implemented quite easily in most production plants. Deliveries directly from the supplier to the shop floor are more difficult to organize. Thus, an efficient goods receiving operation is an essential element of any world class manufacturer.

A visual measure of goods receiving efficiency is shown in Figure 4-6. Every time a delivery is received, the left-hand column is incremented by one; every time goods are successfully delivered to the work station or stock point, the right-hand column is incremented. The backlog of deliveries can then be clearly seen and the supervisor can allocate additional people to work in the receiving area if the backlog becomes too big. The put-away data can be transferred to a summary chart at the end of each day so that trends can be observed, problem areas analyzed, and capacity requirements forecast.

Schedule Adherence

Just-in-time manufacturing relies on all production tasks being completed on time and on schedule. The concept of synchronized manufacturing assumes strict adherence to schedules so that there is no queuing or unplanned waiting at each work center or cell. A traditional manufacturer typically will extend planned lead times to take account of shop floor

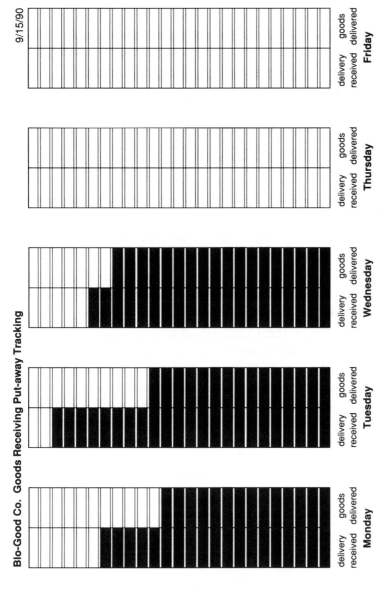

Figure 4-6. Goods Receiving Put-away Tracking

slippage and will hold additional safety stock to buffer these kinds of problems.

A world class manufacturer stresses the continuous reduction of cycle times and inventories. As these objectives begin to be achieved, the issue of schedule adherence becomes important. The broad definition of quality within a world class manufacturing environment is the elimination of variation in the product and in the process; schedule adherence is a method of measuring one aspect of quality in the production process.

Operators establish schedules As with many aspects of world class manufacturing, schedule adherence cannot be considered on its own; it must be seen in the broader context of the implementation of just-in-time approaches to the management of production personnel. It is reasonable to strictly monitor the schedule adherence of a person, cell, or plant only if that individual has had the opportunity to establish the schedule in the first place.

Within WCM the responsibility for detailed plant scheduling rests with the shop floor operators. As with production planners and schedulers in a traditional plant, operators need the necessary training and detailed information to perform these tasks effectively. When the scheduling is done by the people who are also responsible for completing the schedule, there is a greater degree of commitment to that schedule, more practicality built into it, and a better chance of achievement.

In some WCM plants the schedule is always achieved; if there is any slippage, then (assuming a major disaster has not occurred) the operators just continue to work until that day's schedule is completed. There is no question about adherence to schedule; the question is how long will it take to complete it. Schedule achievement on this basis requires close teamwork between managers and operators, a fundamental understanding of the concepts of world class manufacturing, and a widespread commitment to the company's goals. This kind of commitment takes time to develop. It cannot be instituted by policy and relies on the development of trust and respect between managers, supervisors, operators, and staff personnel.

Most companies setting out on the road to world class manufacturing are not able to introduce this kind of commitment and flexibility in the short term. Nevertheless, it is possible and desirable to have the operators and supervisors who are responsible for the achievement of the schedule also to be responsible for establishing the schedule.

Product Completions Report

Most production plants need a detailed report of daily production. The product completions report (Figure 4-7) shows the scheduled and completed quantities for each product over a range of dates. The report is sorted and summarized by product group and then summarizes schedule adherence for the whole plant.

The first line of the product completions report shows the plant number (in this example, the plant number is designated by the corporation and branch numbers — CO/BR), the product group, product number, description, and standard (or target) cost. The second line shows the date of the production schedule, the production cell group code, the cell number, and the cell description. The completion information includes the quantity scheduled for that date, the quantity completed, and the quantity over or under schedule (which are also given as a percentage of the original schedule). Scheduled and completed quantities are also shown valued at standard (or target or average) cost. (The production schedules shown on the production completion report are the daily, rate-based schedules. Figure 4-11 shows a similar report for plants using work orders to plan and control production.) The total lines for each product give the total quantities scheduled, completed, over/under schedules, and the total value of the schedules and completions. In addition, the lower total lines provide the number of schedules and the number of over schedules and under schedules over the time period of the report. These totals are then summarized for all the products within the product group.

The production completions report shows the details of production on each individual schedule over the time period requested, and this information is required so that the detailed picture can be seen. For performance measurement, it would be more useful to have a summarized report of the schedules and completions.

Product Completions Summary

The summary report shown in Figure 4-8 provides total schedule and completion information for each product. If this report is run daily or weekly showing the cumulative figures for each product, it can be used to show the period-to-date or year-to-date production trends. This year- or period-to-date information may be presented using graphs or bar charts (see Figure 4-9), which more clearly show trends and comparisons between product groups.

The product completions summary report lists each product and shows the total quantity scheduled over the date range, the total completed, and the quantities and percentages of over schedules and under schedules. The total scheduled and completion values are shown, together with the number of schedules placed over the time period and the number of these that were completed over or under schedule.

UNITRONIX CORP
PRODUCT COMPLETIONS/SCHEDULES REPORT
BY PRODUCT GROUP & PRODUCT NUMBER

PAGE 2
6-JAN-1990

CO BR PROD.GROUP
01 01 EXCEL

PRODUCT NO
CELL   1030   MECHANICAL PENCIL – RED

PRODUCT COST   3.5000

GROUP DATE		SCHEDULE	COMPLETED	UNDER	UNDER-%	OVER	OVER-%	SCHED-VALUE	COMPL-VALUE
10-AUG-1990 100	F101 FINAL ASSY LINE 1 DEPT 100	1875	1875	0	0.00	0	0.00	6,563	6,563
	F102 FINAL ASSY 2 DEPT 100	550	550	0	0.00	0	0.00	1,925	1,925
13-AUG-1990	F101 FINAL ASSY LINE 1 DEPT 100	1750	1750	0	0.00	0	0.00	6,125	6,125
	F102 FINAL ASSY 2 DEPT 100	600	600	0	0.00	0	0.00	2,100	2,100
14-AUG-1990	F101 FINAL ASSY LINE 1 DEPT 100	1750	1750	0	0.00	0	0.00	6,125	6,125
	F102 FINAL ASSY 2 DEPT 100	600	600	0	0.00	0	0.00	2,100	2,100
15-AUG-1990	F101 FINAL ASSY LINE 1 DEPT 100	1750	1750	0	0.00	0	0.00	6,125	6,125
	F102 FINAL ASSY 2 DEPT 100	600	600	0	0.00	0	0.00	2,100	2,100
16-AUG-1990	F101 FINAL ASSY LINE 1 DEPT 100	1750	625	1125	64.29	0	0.00	6,125	2,188
	F102 FINAL ASSY 2 DEPT 100	600	750	0	0.00	150	25.00	2,100	2,625
TOTAL FOR PRODUCT NO = 1030		16675	15700	1125	6.75	150	0.90	58,363	54,950

NO. OF SCHEDULES   14
NO. UNDER SCHEDULE   1
NO. OVER SCHEDULE   1

```
01 01 EXCEL     2030      PENCIL ASSEMBLY — RED              8.7500

200 L202 FLOW LINE 2 DEPT 200

 9-AUG-1990     1000   1000      0     0.00      0    0.00    8,750    8,750
10-AUG-1990     1000   1000      0     0.00      0    0.00    8,750    8,750
13-AUG-1990     1000   1000      0     0.00      0    0.00    8,750    8,750
14-AUG-1990     1000   1000      0     0.00      0    0.00    8,750    8,750
15-AUG-1990     1000   1000      0     0.00      0    0.00    8,750    8,750
16-AUG-1990     1000   1000      0     0.00      0    0.00    8,750    8,750
17-AUG-1990     1000      0   1000   100.00      0    0.00        0        0

TOTAL FOR PRODUCT NO = 2030
                7000   6000   1000    14.29      0    0.00   61,250   52,500

                      NO. OF SCHEDULES       7
                      NO. UNDER SCHEDULE     1
                      NO. OVER SCHEDULE      0

TOTAL FOR PRODUCT NO = EXCEL
               44963  38550   6623    14.73    210    0.47  211,095  179,217

                      NO. OF SCHEDULES      51
                      NO. UNDER SCHEDULE     8
                      NO. OVER SCHEDULE      2
```

Figure 4-7. Product Completions Report

UNITRONIX CORP
PRODUCT COMPLETIONS SUMMARY REPORT
BY PRODUCT GROUP & PRODUCT NUMBER

PAGE1
6-JAN

	SCHEDULE	COMPLETED	UNDER	UNDER-%	OVER	OVER-%	SCHED-VALUE	COMP-VALUE	TOTAL NUMBER	NUMBER UNDER	NUMBER OVER
PRODUCT = 1010	14648	10800	3848	26.27	0	0.00	66648	49140	13	4	0
PRODUCT = 1020	6640	6050	650	9.79	60	0.90	24834	22267	17	2	1
PRODUCT = 1030	16675	15700	1125	6.75	150	0.90	58363	54950	14	1	1
PRODUCT = 2030	7000	6000	1000	14.29	0	0.00	61250	52500	7	1	0
PRODUCT GROUP = EXCEL	44963	38550	6623	14.73	210	0.47	211095	179217	51	8	2
TOTAL FOR BRANCH = 01	44963	38550	6623	14.73	210	0.47	211095	179217	51	8	2
TOTAL FOR CORP = 01	44963	38550	6623	14.73	210	0.47	211095	179217	51	8	2

Figure 4-8. Product Completions Summary

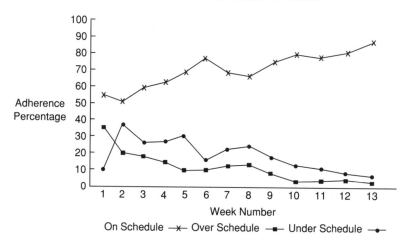

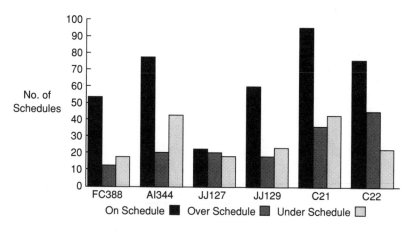

Figure 4-9. Schedule Adherence Chart

Cell Completions Report

Operators and supervisors are interested in the production performance of their cell or cells. This detailed information can be assessed using the completions by cell report shown in Figure 4-10.

UNITRONIX CORP
PRODUCTION CELL COMPLETIONS/SCHEDULES REPORT
BY CELL GROUP & CELL

PAGE 8
6-JAN-1991

CO BR GROUP CELL PRODUCT	GROUP	SCHEDULE	COMPLETED	VARIANCE	VAR-%	SCHED-VALUE	COMPL-VALUE
01 01 100 F101 FINAL ASSY LINE 1 DEPT 100							
15-AUG-1990 1010 MECHANICAL PENCIL - BLACK	EXCEL	2000	1052	948	47.40	9,100	4,787
1020 MECHANICAL PENCIL - BLUE		400	250	150	37.50	1,496	935
1030 MECHANICAL PENCIL - RED		1750	1750	0	0.00	6,125	6,125
TOTAL FOR DATE = 15-AUG-1990		4150	3052	1098	73.54	16,721	11,847
01 01 100 F101 FINAL ASSY LINE 1 DEPT 100							
16-Aug-1990 1010 MECHANICAL PENCIL - BLACK	EXCEL	2000	0	2000	100.0	9,100	0
1030 MECHANICAL PENCIL - RED		1750	625	1125	64.29	6,125	2,188
TOTAL FOR DATE = 16-AUG-1990		3750	625	3125	16.67	15,225	2,188
TOTAL FOR MONTH = 8							

Figure 4-10. Completions by Cell Report

The report is sorted and totaled by production cell number (or name) and the schedule date. The first line shows the plant number (CO/BR), the production cell group, and the cell number and description. The second line shows the schedule date, the product number manufactured by the cell that day, its description, and the product group for that product. The schedule information is given quite simply as the quantity and value scheduled, the quantity and value completed, and the variance between the schedule and the completion expressed as quantity and percentage. This detailed information is summarized for the whole day's activities within each cell, and then summarized up to the month number for month-to-date and year-to-date analysis.

For performance measurement purposes, this information is better shown in summary form. The summary report would show the schedule and completion quantities, their values, and the total variance in quantity and percentage. This information is totalled for each day at each cell and then totalled for the period-to-date. Report summary and trend data can be plotted on graphs and bar charts.

Work Order Completions Report

A report showing detailed completions for a work order driven production control system is shown in Figure 4-11. The first line shows the plant number (CO/BR), the work order number, product number, and description. In a make-to-order environment, this line also could list the customer number, sales order, and order line number from which the work order is derived. If this work order is one of a series of work orders that are all required for one project or activity, then the project information could be shown and the completion information could be summarized by project number.

The second line of the report provides the schedule and completion information for each job step within the work

UNITRONIX CORP
WORK ORDER COMPLETIONS BOARD

CO	BR	WORK-ORDER STP	WORK OPER CNTR	PRODUCT START-DATE	END-DATE	COMPL-DATE	AUTHORIZED QTY	COMPLETE QTY	SCRAP QTY	STAT	VAR-%	VAR.	SCHED. VALUE	COMPL. VALUE
01	01	0115		M1A1		CATHODE RAY TUBE (CRT)								
		10	0600	26-JUL-1990	30-JUL-1990	22-JUL-1990	115	115	0	C	0.00	0	34,156.15	34,156.15
		20	0700	30-JUL-1990	2-AUG-1990	30-JUL-1990	115	113	2	C	0.00	0	34,156.15	33,562.13
		30	0700	2-AUG-1990	6-AUG-1990	2-AUG-1990	115	112	1	C	1.74	2	34,156.15	33,265.12
		40	0700	6-AUG-1990	7-AUG-1990	4-AUG-1990	115	110	0	C	4.35	5	34,156.15	32,671.10
		50	0500	7-AUG-1990	13-AUG-1990	00-XXX-0000	115	52	0	Y	54.78	63	34,156.15	15,444.52
		60	0500	13-AUG-1990	15-AUG-1990	00-XXX-0000	115	0	0		100.00	115	34,156.15	0.00
WORK ORDER = 0115							690	502	3		26.81	185		
01	01	14053		M1A1		CATHODE RAY TUBE (CRT)								
		10	0600	16-JUL-1990	19-JUL-1990	25-JUL-1990	200	200	0	C	00.0	0	59,402.00	59,402.00
		20	0700	19-JUL-1990	25-JUL-1990	30-JUL-1990	200	198	0	C	1.00	2	59,402.00	58,807.98
		30	0700	25-JUL-1990	27-JUL-1990	4-AUG-1990	200	190	0	C	5.00	10	59,402.00	56,431.90
		40	0700	27-JUL-1990	31-JUL-1990	2-AUG-1990	200	190	9	C	0.50	1	59,402.00	56,431.90
		50	0500	31-JUL-1990	7-AUG-1990	00-XXX-0000	200	123	0	Y	38.50	77	59,402.00	36,532.23
		60	0500	7-AUG-1990	12-AUG-1990	00-XXX-0000	200	0	0		100.00	200	59,402.00	0
WORK ORDER = 14053							1200	901	9		24.17	290		
01	01	59633A		M1A1		CATHODE RAY TUBE (CRT)								
		10	0600	18-MAY-1990	4-JUN-1990	2-JUN-1990	1250	1200	46	C	0.32	4	371,262.50	356,412.00
		20	0700	4-JUN-1990	3-JUL-1990	5-JUL-1990	1250	1200	0	C	4.00	50	371,262.50	356,412.00
		30	0700	3-JUL-1990	12-JUL-1990	11-JUL-1990	1250	1192	8	C	4.00	50	371,262.50	354,035.92
		40	0700	12-JUL-1990	26-JUL-1990	26-JUL-1990	1250	1190	0	C	4.80	60	371,262.50	353,441.90
		50	0500	26-JUL-1990	30-AUG-1990	00-XXX-0000	1250	220	11	Y	81.52	1019	371,262.50	65,342.20
		60	0500	30-AUG-1990	15-SEP-1990	00-XXX-0000	1250	0	0		100.00	1250	371,262.50	0.00
WORK ORDER = 59633A							7500	5002	65		32.44	2433		
TOTAL FOR PRODUCT = M1A1							31962	9706	77		69.39	22179		

Figure 4-11. Work Order Completions Report

order. This information includes the job step number, work center number, scheduled start date, scheduled end date, and actual completion date. The quantity information gives the authorized quantity, completed quantity, any scrap/rejects, variance quantity and percentage, and the status of the job step (C = complete, Y = in process). The second line also shows the value of the scheduled and completed product.

The report is selected by date range and includes only those job steps which should have been completed by the date of the report. The report is sorted by work order number within product number and is totalled for the product number, product group, and plant number.

A summary version of this report is used to show the information at product, product family, and plant level. A similar report and summary sorted by work center is used to present the work order completions information at a work center level. In some production plants, where similar operations are performed in different work centers, it can be useful to report and summarize the completion information by operation code rather than by work order or work center.

In some companies, a report of this kind also includes information about whether the completion of a job step was late, early, or on-time. This data can be derived easily from the end-date and completion-date on the report. A composite factor could be calculated which combines the quantity completed with the days late or early information and which attempts to give a single measure of the work center's effectiveness.

Past-due Products Graph

A simple and effective method of recording schedule adherence that is popular in just-in-time plants is to count the number of production schedules that are past due at the end of each week or day. This statistic can be easily obtained either manually or from the production control system and can be presented in graph form either on paper or on a board within the shop floor. An example is shown in Figure 4-12.

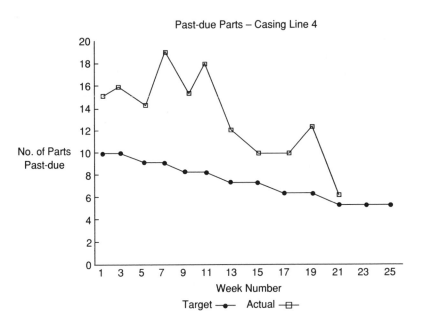

Figure 4-12. Past-due Parts Graph

The number of products past due can be the number of different products, the number of different schedules, the number of released orders, or the number of kanbans left over at the end of the day. The particular factor that is counted will vary from one plant to another. Select the count that is most relevant and easiest to obtain; do not spend a lot of time wrangling over which measure is the "right one," and do not measure more than one factor. Keep it simple.

The past-due products graph can be maintained by each production cell, production line, group of cells, product, product group, or for the entire plant. If possible, it is best for the shop floor operators or supervisors to track these numbers and post them on the graph or board. Targets then can be established with the operators as part of the continuous improvement process.

Another variation of this idea is to keep track of the average age of the schedules or work orders. The age can be calculated from the schedule date or the work order start date, and the average can be calculated and plotted on a graph or bar chart. This information can be shown for each cell, work center, product, product group, or for the entire plant.

Completions and Schedules Table

Another simple approach is just to keep track of how many schedules at a cell are completed on time and full quantity. This information can be monitored at each cell and posted on boards or charts at the cell.

Some companies find it helpful to set a target amount for the completion quantities; in other words, to allow for an acceptable variance when determining if a schedule is complete. Figure 4-13 shows a table where the schedule for each product is given together with a target completion quantity. The schedule is considered complete and on time if the quantity completed is greater than the target quantity. In the example, the target quantity is 97.5 percent of the full quantity in each case. In reality, this allowed variance may change for different products or shifts, and it will be reduced over time as an element of the continuous improvement process.

Normalized Schedule Variance

A measure that is popular with some companies is the normalized variance (see Figure 4-14). This average is calculated by adding up the absolute variances (that is, ignoring whether the variance is positive or negative) between schedules and completions for all the schedules at a production cell

```
BRANDLEY & PARRY INC.

                   PRODUCTION SCHEDULE REPORTING

     CELL:  FAB-62 PRE WELD FORMING
----------------------------------------------------------------
    ITEM:| 12-1A 12-1B 12-2A 13-1F AB16  AB17  BB16  BB17  DEF1

WEEK RATE:| 1000  1200  1000   650   45    45    90    90   150
95% ALLOWED:| 950 1,140   950   618   43    43    86    86   143
----------|-----------------------------------------------------
WEEK NUMBER |
          |
        1 | ***** *****             ***** ***** ***** ***** ***** *****
          |             892
        2 | ***** ***** ***** ***** *****                   ***** *****
          |                                     40    75
        3 | ***** *****             ***** ***** *****        ***** *****
          |             933                           75
        4 | ***** ***** *****       455 ***** *****          ***** *****
          |                                           75
        5 | ***** *****             ***** ***** ***** ***** ***** *****
          |             928
        6 | ***** *****             ***** *****       ***** ***** *****
          |             922                     40
        7 | ***** ***** ***** ***** ***** ***** *****              *****
          |                                                 85
        8 |
          |
        9 |
          |
       10 |
          |
       11 |
          |
       12 |
          |
       13 |
```

Figure 4-13. Completions Schedule Table

and then dividing that total by the total quantity scheduled on that cell. The disadvantage of this measure is that it presents a factor which is not immediately understandable to the user. The advantage is that it enables comparisons between

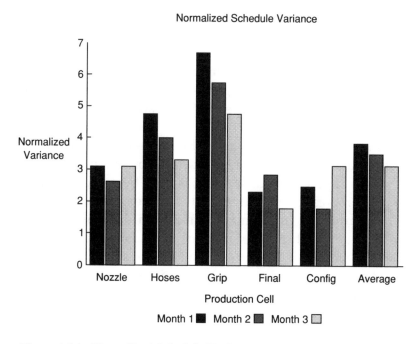

Figure 4-14. Normalized Schedule Variance

different kinds of production cells making different volumes of product, and it gives equal importance to an overrun and an underrun.

Boards, signals, and manual schedule reporting As with all aspects of performance measurement within a world class manufacturing site, it is frequently advantageous to report performance in simple, visual, manual ways. Boards, graphs, or tables at each work center show the schedule for that day and the amount completed. The completion quantity can be posted periodically (each hour, twice per day, daily, and so forth) and the operators can monitor their own progress.

It can be helpful to automate some of this activity by having the completions recorded by a process control or reporting system which then reports the latest data back to the cell via a video display unit (VDU) or terminal. The technology used is not important; what is important is that the information is readily available to the operators and supervisors in a form that makes sense to them.

A spreadsheet is often helpful because it can quickly and easily translate a lot of data into useful information. Figure 4-15 shows a simple spreadsheet that is used by one company to report progress on their five production cells within a factory. The completion information is reported daily and entered into the spreadsheet. The summary spreadsheet (as shown in the illustration) is produced giving the results for previous weeks and giving the period-to-date information averaged and summarized across the whole production time period for the cell.

Analysis tools like this can be valuable because they are simple, can be produced locally by the shop floor supervisor or production control group, can be changed over time as circumstances change, and can be the basis for further analysis at a later stage. In addition, most spreadsheet programs can print graphs, bar charts, and pie charts which can be useful for presenting information clearly and succinctly.

Order Changes and Schedule Changes

The effectiveness of production planning and control can be assessed by addressing the number of changes required in the orders placed by the system. There are three basic kinds of orders: purchase orders, production orders, and customer orders. Each of these orders defines when to buy or make a product and how much of the product is needed. A customer order will result in a production schedule or work order on the shop floor. These final assembly orders spawn production

CELL PERFORMANCE CHART
APRIL 1991

	NOZZLE	HOSE	GRIP	FINAL	CONFIG	TOTAL
WEEK 1						
QTY ON TIME	7564	576	3500	4856	3956	20452
% ON TIME	92.3	95.3	87.5	83.2	95.2	89.7
NO ON TIME	15	4	7	10	16	52
% NO ON TIME	93.8	80	87.5	83.3	94.1	89.7
WEEK 2						
QTY ON TIME	8657	465	4000	5842	4821	23785
% ON TIME	87.1	92.3	80	88.5	96.3	87.9
NO ON TIME	12	3	8	12	21	56
% NO ON TIME	85.7	75	80	80	95.5	86.2
WEEK 3						
QTY ON TIME	9844	421	3500	6251	3866	23882
% ON TIME	96	82.2	87.5	92.3	97.1	93.6
NO ON TIME	18	5	7	15	17	62
% NO ON TIME	94.7	83.3	87.5	88.2	94.4	91.1
WEEK 4						
QTY ON TIME	5748	822	4500	4521	3442	19033
% ON TIME	91.1	72.2	100	93.3	94.5	93.1
NO ON TIME	13	8	9	13	17	60
% NO ON TIME	86.7	80	100	92.9	94.4	90.9
PERIOD TO DATE						
AV. ON TIME	7953	571	3875	5368	4021	21788
% ON TIME	93.2	93.5	88.6	90.5	97	92.3
AV.NO ON TIME	15	5	8	13	18	58
% NO ON TIME	91.8	82.5	86.1	86.1	94.6	91.2

Figure 4-15. Cell Performance Chart

orders for subassemblies and components, in turn creating a requirement for purchase orders of raw materials and components. If the production planning and control system requires a large number of changes to these orders, in addition to the wasted activity of processing the changes in the plant, quite likely there is considerable waste in terms of inventory, production queues, and unfulfilled completions.

It can be argued that the number of changes in the customer's orders cannot be attributed to shortcomings in the supplier's manufacturing process. On the contrary, significant changes in customer orders indicate that the lead times offered to customers are too long. Empirical analysis done in this area shows that there is a "horizon of stability" for orders (see Figure 4-16). If the lead time offered to the customer is less than the horizon of stability, there is a low occurrence of order change. As the lead time gets longer, the chances of customers changing their orders increase dramatically. The objective is to reduce the customer lead time to the point where there is a greater stability in the order quantity and requirement date.

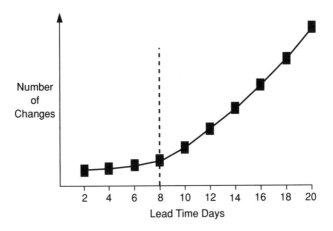

Figure 4-16. Horizon of Stability

Reports tracking the order and schedule changes are designed to determine the reasons why product is delivered late. The number of changes to customer orders, purchase orders, and the production schedule is a leading indicator of future delivery problems.

The basic data required to monitor these factors can be obtained from the people responsible for making these changes. It is unusual for order entry, purchasing, and production control systems to keep track of the number of changes in detail, but data can be recorded manually by using simple procedures like a count of the order change documents each day or by having the people entering the orders keep a checklist where they mark a chart every time a change order is processed.

This information can be presented graphically (as in Figure 4-17) showing the number of changes in each of the three categories for each product group. Often it is not easy to keep track of which product group for which a purchase order is required, particularly when there is significant commonality of components between products. The purchase order information may have to be presented by the plant as a whole rather than by product group.

A more detailed way of presenting this information is to record not only the number of occurrences but also the number of days out from today the change is required. This data can again be shown on a bar chart for each product group or for the entire plant (see Figure 4-18).

As with most of the performance measurement reports in a world class manufacturing environment, it is the trend of these order and schedule changes that is significant. The true cost of making order changes is very high, and the entire process is always a non-value-added activity. Many of the improvements that are introduced as a part of just-in-time and world class manufacturing will result in a reduction of the number of order changes. The measurement of how these order and schedule changes reduce is a good way to monitor the success of different continuous improvement activities.

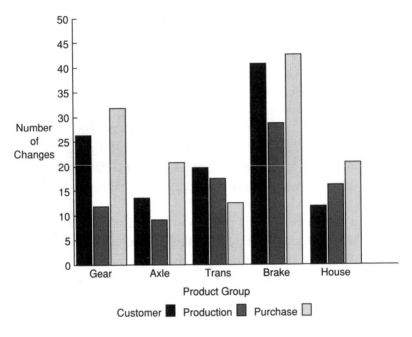

Figure 4-17. Order and Schedule Changes

Customer Service Level

A world class manufacturer puts customers' needs at the top of the agenda. The idea of being "close to the customer" is an important one for any company attempting to compete against global competition. There are two primary methods of looking at customer service — the first is a quantitative approach, the second is qualitative. The *quantitative approach* is the more traditional method of calculating customer service level by comparing the orders placed by customers with the shipments to those customers. The *qualitative* approach is concerned with the customer's perception of the service they are receiving. Because this information is not readily available, it must be obtained from the customers themselves and is by necessity a subjective judgment.

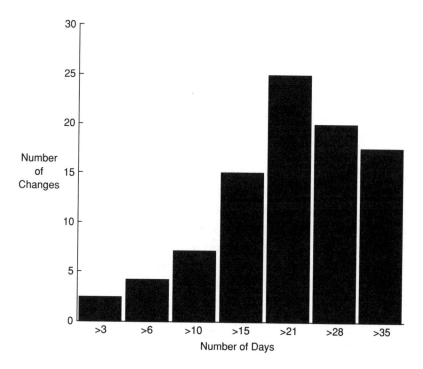

Figure 4-18. Order Changes by Number of Days

Quantitative Service Level Measures

Two elements of quantitative customer service level need to be discussed: (1) delivery performance and (2) quality. This section deals mainly with delivery performance; the quality aspects of customer service are dealt with also in detail in Chapter 7.

The key question that needs to be answered by any company seeking to serve its customers is: "Are we delivering the right products, the right quantities, and on the right date?" Very few companies can affirm that they always deliver the full quantity on time every time. In previous years, it has been strongly argued that most companies should not try to achieve this status because the level of inventory investment required to meet this objective would be pro-hibitively expensive. The traditional approach to this problem has been to calculate statistically the amount of inventory required to meet prescribed levels of service.

Figure 4-19 shows a graph of the relationship between ser-vice level and inventory costs. The Y-axis shows the amount of safety stock (over and above forecasted demand) that is required to provide the service level percentage given on the X-axis. The graph shows that as the desired level of customer service increases, the required safety stock increases expo-nentially. Traditional wisdom would say that it is therefore sensible to assign a desired level of service that is compatible with customer expectations and affordable in terms of inven-tory levels.

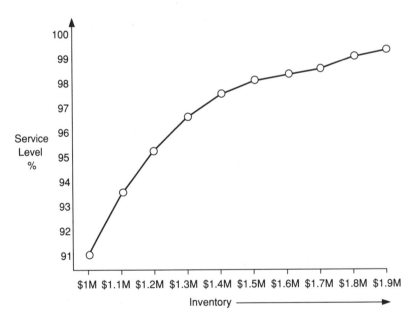

Figure 4-19. Inventory Levels and Service Levels

A world class manufacturer would view this issue differently. Customers deserve a 100-percent level of service, and if they do not get it from one company — they will go to another. Although the graph in Figure 4-19 is statistically sound, it does not take account of the fact that in reality poor service level has many causes, and the statistical variations of demand are usually not a primary problem. The primary problems are long lead times (manufacturing, administrative, and distribution), poor quality, unreliable deliveries, and poor logistics. These issues are addressed by a world class manufacturing approach and are prime targets for a continuous improvement endeavor.

The traditional approach to measuring customer service level can be readily adapted to world class manufacturing. Reports are produced showing the customer orders, their required dates, and quantities. These reports are compared with the shipping dates and quantities intended to fulfill these orders; a percentage is calculated for the product, product group, customer, and so forth. An example of this kind of customer service level report is given in Figure 4-20.

There are many questions that need to be asked when designing or using a customer service level report. These questions hinge around the method of calculating the service level percentage. The total quantity shipped can be divided by the total quantity ordered and a percentage calculated. This method is used in Figure 4-20 and is adequate for most companies, but it does not take into account how much of each order line was satisfied. A 90-percent service level may be calculated because all order lines were shipped 10 percent short, in a situation that is quite different from shipping nine lines complete and not shipping one line at all.

Another approach is to measure the percentage of order lines that were shipped complete. This method will give a

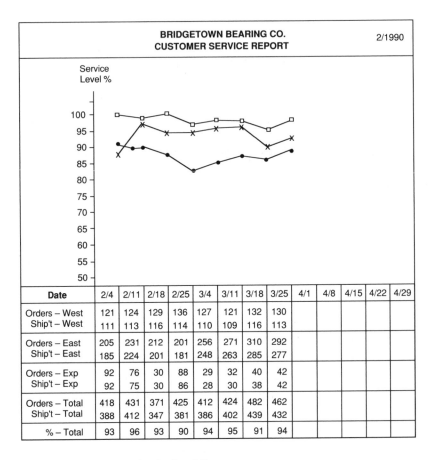

BRIDGETOWN BEARING CO. CUSTOMER SERVICE REPORT													2/1990

Date	2/4	2/11	2/18	2/25	3/4	3/11	3/18	3/25	4/1	4/8	4/15	4/22	4/29
Orders – West	121	124	129	136	127	121	132	130					
Ship't – West	111	113	116	114	110	109	116	113					
Orders – East	205	231	212	201	256	271	310	292					
Ship't – East	185	224	201	181	248	263	285	277					
Orders – Exp	92	76	30	88	29	32	40	42					
Ship't – Exp	92	75	30	86	28	30	38	42					
Orders – Total	418	431	371	425	412	424	482	462					
Ship't – Total	388	412	347	381	386	402	439	432					
% – Total	93	96	93	90	94	95	91	94					

Figure 4-20. Customer Service Level Report

lower number than the first but, in many industries, will be a more useful way of assessing service level. In a measurement using this method, the order mentioned previously as having all lines shipped 90-percent complete will have a service level of zero. The order which has nine lines shipped and one line not shipped will score a 90-percent level of service.

A more exacting method of measuring service level is to record the percentage of orders that have been delivered in full and on time. An order is considered to be shipped only when the full quantity of every line item on the order has been successfully dispatched.

The choice of how to view the calculation of service level percentage will vary according to the type of business and the needs of the customer. If a company sells complex equipment that can be used only if all the constituent parts are available, then the last method (shipped-in-full) will be appropriate. A company selling high volume retail supplies will likely find the first method more satisfactory.

Delivery reliability So far, the discussion has centered around the quantity being dispatched, but the date of delivery is equally important. The question of how to define an on-time delivery varies according to the type of market and the type of products involved. A supplier of birthday cakes who delivers one day late will have many unhappy customers, whereas within another industry this may be less critical.

The usual method for defining on-time delivery is to set a planned dispatch date; a delivery is considered "on time" if it is dispatched prior to the planned delivery date. Most companies having a high volume of deliveries typically will quote a standard lead time, which is used to establish the planned delivery date. In other companies, the planned dispatch date is entered into the system at the time of order entry and is agreed upon with the customer. The service level reports show which orders have been dispatched on time and which were late; many report the average lateness of order lines, and some provide a range of service levels based upon the number of days it took to deliver the product (see Figure 4-21).

Other pieces of delivery information are also valuable when measuring customer service level. The planned dispatch day (calculated when the order is entered) may be quite

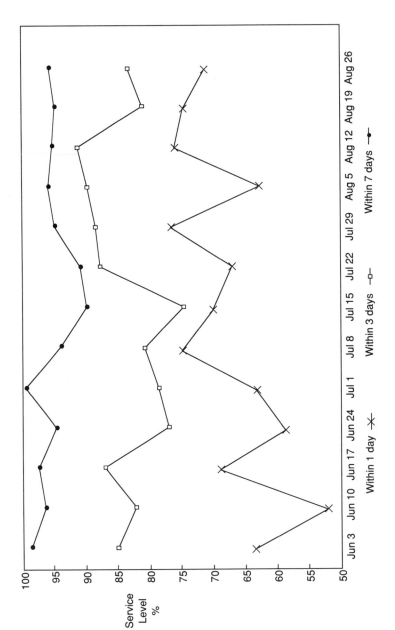

Figure 4-21. Service Level by Dispatch Days

different from the customer's required delivery date. A good order entry and dispatch system will have both dates available so that service level can be measured from the point of view of the customer's stated requirements rather than according to the planned delivery date.

Frequently, during the order entry and dispatch process, particularly for long lead-time products, the planned delivery date has to be changed. There are many reasons for changing dates, some legitimate and some not, but if customer service level is measured in terms of the latest planned delivery date, it may deceptively paint a more pleasing picture than what the customer actually sees. A good order entry and dispatch system will keep track of the original planned delivery date as well the latest planned delivery date. A service level report based upon the original planned delivery date can provide a clearer assessment of the effectiveness of the entire order entry and dispatch process (see Figure 4-22).

Receipt versus dispatch Most customer service level reporting is based upon the date of dispatch to the customer. This approach assumes that the products are delivered immediately to the customer and that there are no delays, breakages, or problems in transit. This assumption is clearly not valid, particularly when the delivery is achieved using common carriers and storage at consolidation warehouses.

From the customer's point of view, the order is not delivered until the goods have been received, and some companies attempt to measure service level at the time the customer takes delivery. The gathering of this information can be difficult and requires additional data entry and processing, but in some industries it is a vital method for measuring the effectiveness of the process from order entry to customer receipt.

The companies that attempt to measure service level in this way have two or three different methods of gathering the

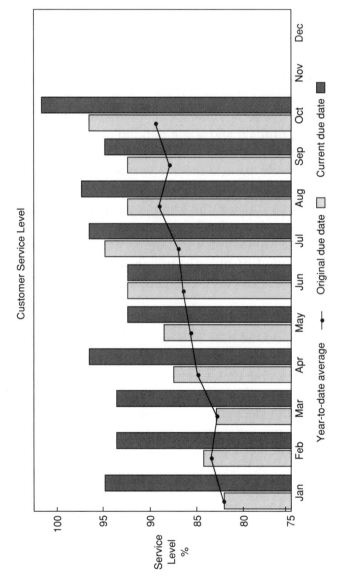

Figure 4-22. Service Level by Original Plan Date

information. One way is to have a reply card attached to every shipping document; when the goods are delivered, the customer signs the card and mails it back to the supplier, who enters the information into performance measurement systems. Another method is to have the carrier mark the delivery date and time on the driver's routing sheet. These sheets are then returned to the supplier and used for analysis.

Unfortunately, the reply method has proven to be of limited value because a large percentage of the cards are not returned and the validity of the information is in doubt. A typical return rate for cards of this sort is around 30 to 40 percent, and there is a tendency for dissatisfied customers not to return the reply cards. The report, therefore, shows a biased picture.

In recent years, the introduction of electronic data interchange (EDI) has opened up the possibility of the customer automatically sending back a confirmation of receipt transaction when the goods are received. This information is received by the supplier's system and entered automatically into the performance measurement data base. While few companies do this yet, as the use of EDI increases, more interest is being shown in this approach.

Number of past-due orders A very simple, pragmatic method of measuring customer service level is to count the number of order lines that are past due at any time. The advantage of this method is its simplicity; it can be easily employed by manually counting the outstanding picklists, shipping documents, or outstanding orders. It can also be produced easily within an order entry and dispatch system by writing a report that counts the number of unshipped orders. Past due orders can be expressed as the number of orders, order lines, or quantity. The report should be available every day and the results plotted on a graph or bar chart. The information can be reported by product group or by customer type (if relevant).

Choosing a method of measuring service level As has been outlined above, there are several different ways of approaching the calculation of customer service level. Each method has merits and there is no "right" way to do it. It is necessary, when deciding which method to use, to select the method that gives the most valid information for your own business. Do not use more than one method of measuring customer service level, because using more than one can create confusion and give people the opportunity to argue and discuss the validity of the methods instead of working for improvement. Pick a method that makes sense in your industry; then go ahead and use it.

Qualitative Service Level Measures

The quantitative methods of measuring customer service level are valuable, but they do not give the complete picture because of assumptions about the way the customer views the service he or she is receiving. A world class manufacturing environment must keep very close to what the customer needs and wants. This information can be gained only by asking the customers directly what they think of the service they are receiving. A customer survey for performance measurement assesses the changes and improvements that are taking place over time. As the company introduces changes into the process aimed at improving customer service, it is important to measure the effect of these changes as they are perceived by the customers.

Customer survey of service level This can be done using simple questionnaires. The key to the effectiveness of this method is that the questionnaires must be short and simple and the survey must be continuous and on-going. A single survey of many customers has some value because it will point out the areas of strength and weakness and will enable the company to adjust its procedures to better meet the needs of the customers. For performance measurement purposes, however, a single survey is not enough.

A method that has been employed successfully by some companies is to have an on-going telephone survey of their customers. The survey is very short — a maximum of six questions — and is aimed at assessing the customer's view of the most important aspects of the suppliers distribution business. In the example (shown in Figures 4-23 and 4-24), the factors included in the survey are lead time, on-time deliveries, lines delivered in full, orders delivered in full, the emergency order process, and the product packing. The example is taken from one particular company and may not be applicable to other companies. Each company must select its own short list of key customer service features.

The purpose of the survey is not only to assess how the customer perceives the level of service he or she is receiving, but also to gain an understanding of which aspects of the distribution process are most significant to the customer. There are two questions associated with each topic and each question has a possible score from 1 to 10 (where 1 is lowest and 10 is highest). The first question asks the customer how important each aspect is to that customer; the second asks how good the supplier is at meeting that need. For example:

1a. How important to you are short lead times (less than seven days) for the delivery of electronic components?
1b. Are you satisfied with the lead times offered by Jones Electronics?

The result of this survey is a list of issues that are important to the customer, with a score out of 10 for each one, and an assessment of how well a company is meeting that need.

CUSTOMER SURVEY ANALYSIS

	LEAD TIME	ON-TIME DELIVERY	FULL LINE ITEM QTY.	FULL ORDER ALL LINES	EMERGENCY ORDERS	PACKING
CUSTOMER 1						
IMPORTANCE	2	7	4	2	1	5
RATING	7	3	5	4	5	6
IMPORTANCE FACTOR	-3	2	-1	-3	-4	0
RATING FACTOR	2	-2	0	-1	0	1
NET FACTOR	5	-4	1	2	4	1
CUSTOMER 2						
IMPORTANCE	3	8	5	3	7	2
RATING	6	4	4	5	4	3
IMPORTANCE FACTOR	-2	3	0	-2	2	-3
RATING FACTOR	1	-1	-1	0	-1	-2
NET FACTOR	3	-4	-1	2	-3	1
CUSTOMER 2						
IMPORTANCE	1	7	4	2	4	6
RATING	6	3	5	5	2	5
IMPORTANCE FACTOR	-4	2	-1	-3	-1	1
RATING FACTOR	1	-2	0	0	-3	0
NET FACTOR	5	-4	1	3	-2	-1
TOTAL						
IMPORTANCE FACTOR	-3	2.33	-0.67	-2.67	-1	-0.67
RATING FACTOR	1.33	-1.67	-0.33	-0.33	-1.33	-0.33
NET FACTOR	4.33	-4	0.33	2.33	-0.33	-0.33

Figure 4-23. Customer Survey Table

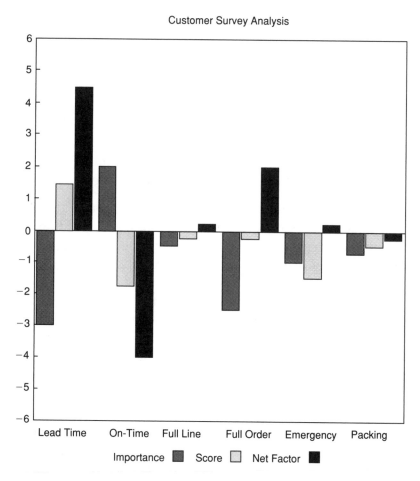

Figure 4-24. Customer Survey Chart

For a continuous telephone survey to be of use, the list of customers to be interviewed must be accurate, the right people within the company must be surveyed, and a reasonable number of customers must be contacted each week or each month. The selection of customers is important if the survey is to be balanced. It is useful for the customers surveyed to have made recent purchases, and it is important not to contact the same customers too frequently.

Analysis of the customer survey When a customer survey is conducted continuously, there must be a simple method of analysis so that the information contained within the survey is readily obtained. These are the steps in the analysis:

1. Subtract 5 from the importance number and from your company's score to obtain the importance factor and the rating factor.
2. Subtract the importance factor from the rating factor to obtain the net factor for each of the survey items.

In Figure 4-23, the first set of data is for Customer 1. Their lead time importance score came to 2 (out of 10), yielding an importance factor of −3. Their assessment of the company's lead times was 7, giving a rating factor of 2. The net factor, therefore, (2 − [−3]) is 5.

This process is repeated for each of the six categories and for each of the customers surveyed. The average importance factor, rating factor, and net factor are then plotted on a bar chart (see Figure 4-24). The bar chart shows at a glance which aspects of your business are well received by the customers and which need improving. When the net factor (the solid block on the chart) is positive, your company is performing above the customer's expectation; when the net factor is negative, then you are performing below expectation. The chart in Figure 4-24 shows that the supplier is offering lead times that are better than customer demand and that the supplier is good at supplying the orders complete and in full. The big negative is that the customers perceive the supplier as being unreliable at delivering the product on time.

These charts have proved very valuable in practice because they not only track how well the customers rate performance, they also track the customers' needs, which may well be changing over time. These charts help match service to customers' stated requirements.

Lost Sales

The ultimate comment on a supplier's performance is for the customer to buy the product from another source. It is sometimes possible to measure the number of prospective sales and/or accounts that have been lost to other vendors. When this information is available, it can be a very pertinent figure.

Some industries, food distributors for example, operate on the basis that if they only partially supply an order, the remaining quantity is lost. They do not backorder and deliver at a later stage. When this is the case, it is easy to identify sales that have been forfeited due to lack of supply. A report showing the difference between booked orders and sales will provide a clear picture of orders that have been lost.

Another method of assessing lost sales is to compare the sales quotations submitted to prospective customers with the orders resulting from them. When an order quotations system is being used, it is common for the sales order to be created by a direct conversion from the previously entered quotation. A report can be produced which lists all the unconverted sales quotes and analyzes the effect of these lost sales.

Summary

The key areas of interest for the measurement of delivery performance are:

- vendor delivery performance
- production schedule adherence
- order and schedule changes
- customer service level
- lost sales analysis

There are several approaches to each of these issues. The methods selected must be directly relevant to the manufacturing strategy and must be simple to gather and use.

CHAPTER FIVE

Measurement of Process Time

A COMPANY implementing a just-in-time approach to manufacturing changes the emphasis from looking at individual products to looking at the production process itself. Performance measures that focus on the process are useful because they reflect this emphasis.

This chapter examines measures of the manufacturing process times and other factors directly related to process times. These measures include production cycle times, lot sizes, the distance a product moves through the plant, machine setup times, and material availability. No company will need to use all of these measures; each example is given to illustrate the kinds of measures that have proven useful to companies taking the road to world class manufacturing. Select the ones that make sense in your plant, or adapt the ideas presented to your own current needs.

Manufacturing Cycle Time

Cycle time is one of the crucial issues of just-in-time manufacturing; a recent article in *Business Week* noted that the "new math of productivity points to time as a manufacturer's most precious resource." The measurement of cycle time is a primary feature of performance measurement for world class manufacturers. A study[1] conducted in the early 1980s, which sought to test by simulation the effect of changing various aspects of the manufacturing process, concluded that the most significant benefits are gained by reducing lot sizes and cycle times.

When production times are analyzed, the typical American manufacturer finds that less than 5 percent of the cycle time is spent actually making the product. During the other 95 percent of the time, the product is waiting, queuing, being inspected, or undergoing another non-value-added activity.

What constitutes a *long* cycle time? In a long cycle time, non-value-added activities significantly outweigh value-added activities. The ideal cycle time would consist entirely of value-added activities; in other words no queues, wait time, or wasted activity. The reduction of waste, elimination of non-value-added activity, and the reduction of cycle times is a continuous quest for world class manufacturers.

Problems Caused by Long Cycle Times

Long cycle times create manifold problems for the manufacturer, including the following:

- *High work-in-process (WIP)*. A long cycle time means that it takes a long time to convert the raw materials, components, and subassemblies into finished products. During that time these materials are on the shop floor being worked on or waiting to be worked on. The longer the cycle time, the longer the partially completed products are on the shop floor and the higher the value of work-in-process inventories. Long cycle times cause high WIP inventories.

- *Make-to-stock.* When the manufacturing cycle time is longer than the lead time offered to customers, the manufacturer must hold stock of finished products. If the manufacturing cycle time is shorter than the customer lead time, then products can be made to order. Long cycle times cause high finished goods inventory.

  When a product is made to stock, the production planning must be based on a sales forecast rather than on actual customer orders. There are always uncertainties built into a forecast; it can never be perfectly accurate. To overcome the inaccuracies of the sales forecast, the manufacturer must hold safety (or buffer) stocks of the finished product. This holding causes high finished goods inventory costs and often leads to products being wasted due to obsolescence, deterioration, or its being beyond shelf life.

- *Changes during the process.* When a product has a long manufacturing lead time, it is subject to many changes during the production process. These changes include engineering changes, order quantity changes, and process changes. Changes of this sort are expensive because much work has to be done to make the change; this extra work includes the identification of products, retrieval of the paperwork, scrap or rework of the components, and the work required to make the change. In addition to these non-value-added activities, there are the intangible costs associated with the confusion and loss of focus created by these kinds of changes.

- *Complex systems.* When products are out on the shop floor for a long time, complex systems are required to keep track of them. These systems are needed so that the work-in-process can be accounted for, so that production order statuses can be maintained, and so that the shop floor can be scheduled and monitored. Complex systems cost a lot of money and are wasteful of both time and effort.

- *Uneven loading of work centers.* When products are made in large batches and with long lead times, the work load placed on the production work centers varies considerably. Many companies attempt to create final assembly schedules that are evenly balanced. An evenly balanced final assembly schedule, however, can still cause wide variations in load on the upstream work centers when lot sizes are large. A world class manufacturing plant will employ small lot sizes and short cycle times to facilitate a synchronized production schedule and a level loading of work cells.

- *Inflexibility.* Customer-driven flexibility is a significant objective of a world class manufacturer — including being able to quickly change product mix, to vary production volumes, and to introduce new products. This kind of flexibility cannot be achieved when cycle times are long. The minimum possible time required to make a change to the shop floor schedule is the production cycle time; if the cycle time is long, these flexible changes cannot be made. Production flexibility requires short cycle times.

How to Shorten Cycle Times

There are two keys to shortening cycle times: (1) reduced lot sizes and (2) synchronized production planning and control.

When products are made in large lot sizes, the cycle times must be long because it is necessary to complete a large quantity at each step of the process. For example, a product requires five minutes in production step 1 and ten minutes in production step 2. When making a lot size of 1,000, the total production time (assuming no queuing, waiting, or setup) is 250 hours — nearly one month of single shift days. If its lot

size is reduced to 100, the production time will be 25 hours —
about three days.

This problem can be alleviated to some extent by overlap-
ping the operations, but in practice there is a clear relationship between lot size and cycle time. Lot sizes are large in
most factories because of the need to take advantage of the
"economies of scale" or economic order quantities.

The argument goes like this: "If it takes me five hours to set
up the machine to make a product, I need to make a large
amount of that product. If I only make a small amount, the
cost of the setup is prohibitive." There is a calculation that can
be used to obtain the optimum economic order quantity
(EOQ) taking account of setup costs and inventory costs (see
Figure 5-1). The way to reduce lot sizes is to reduce setup
times so that small quantities of the products can be manufactured without violating the economic order quantity.
Companies engaged in just-in-time manufacturing expend a
great deal of effort reducing setup times.

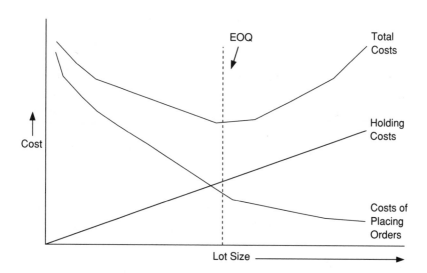

Figure 5-1. Economic Order Quantity

Another key aspect of just-in-time manufacturing is the need to synchronize production. Synchronized manufacturing means organizing the shop floor so that each work cell is manufacturing components, subassemblies, and final assemblies precisely in the right quantities and at the right time. There is an even flow of production through the work cells with each cell scheduled to meet the needs of the final assembly schedule and the customer demands.

A perfectly synchronized production plant has no waiting, queuing, or delays in production. This ideal is, of course, very difficult to achieve, but many companies have made great progress with synchronized manufacturing. The use of kanban cards can help to synchronize production. Lower level products are not made until they are needed; they are "pulled" from earlier work cells frequently and in small quantities — the kanban being the document authorizing production of further products, parts, and subassemblies.

Another way to synchronize manufacturing is to schedule final assembly based upon the rate of flow of the products through the final assembly cells and then to schedule the lower level cells in synchronization with the needs of the final assembly lines. It is still important to control the hour-by-hour execution on the shop floor by the "pull" of parts and subassemblies from preceding cells, but the synchronized planning of production through each cell can be essential to a well synchronized operation.

The development of synchronized production plans identifies any "bottleneck" production cells — cells that are loaded above their capacity. These cells need to be examined both for the resolution of the immediate problem (by moving production to other cells, increasing the capacity by overtime or increased crew size, and so on) and for the longer-term solutions.

Identifying and solving bottleneck problems is a useful tool for the continuous improvement process where the objective is to levelize the flow production. In levelized production, each work cell is making just the right amount of product required to fill the needs of the final assembly schedule. No cell is overloaded and no cell is significantly under-utilized.

Ideally, the final assembly schedule will exactly match the needs of the customers and each work cell will be set up to maintain an even flow of production in support of customer requirements. In order to achieve this ideal, it is necessary to have flexible production cells, cross-trained and flexible people, fast setup times, and small lot sizes.

Measuring Cycle Time

Despite the importance of short cycle times to just-in-time manufacturing, it is not easy to measure cycle times in an economical and meaningful way. There are four primary methods of measuring cycle times:

- detailed recording of cycle times
- analysis of engineering routings
- sampling
- pragmatic

Detailed recording of cycle times Recording the cycle times in detail for each product and each schedule will provide "accurate" measures of the production cycles. Figure 5-2 shows an example of a detailed cycle time report.

Unfortunately, a large amount of effort is required to gather this information. A system similar to traditional work order control is required to keep track of each production batch and to record the start and stop times throughout the process. For some companies, particularly those required to maintain detailed lot number tracking, this amount of data collection is practical. But most companies embarking on a world class manufacturing approach to get rid of a work-order style of

UNITRONIX CORPORATION
DETAILED CYCLE TIME REPORT

PAGE 16
21-JAN-1991

CO BR WORK CNTR	ORDER NO	PRODUCT	STP	START-DATE	STOP-DATE	QUEUE	SET UP	PRODUCTION	MOVE	CYCLE TIME
01 01 FAB7										
	003464	AS10322-A	080	090190	091090	18.0	4.5	62.0	5.0	89.50
	003576	AS9200-AB	060	091090	091390	15.0	3.25	21.5	3.0	42.75
	004365	AS9400-AA	070	091790	092090	24.0	6.75	14.25	12.0	57.00
	005923	AS10322-A	080	092090	092590	32.0	4.25	36.0	12.0	84.25
TOTAL FOR WORK CENTER = FAB7					AVERAGE:	89.00 / 22.25	18.75 / 4.69	133.75 / 33.44	32.0 / 8.0	273.50 / 68.38
01 01 FAB8										
	003341	AS12203-B	060	090190	091290	30.00	4.25	82.5	10.0	126.75
	004569	AS10340-B	030	091490	091890	12.00	6.0	35.75	12.0	65.75
	004652	AS10110-B	040	092190	092890	22.00	3.50	62.0	12.0	99.50
	004722	AS12203-B	060	092890	093090	8.50	3.75	17.5	5.0	34.75
	005476	AS11265-A	090	092890	093090	4.25	3.50	18.25	4.0	30.00
TOTAL FOR WORK CENTER = FAB8					AVERAGE:	75.75 / 15.35	21.00 / 4.20	216.00 / 43.20	43.0 / 8.6	356.75 / 71.35

Figure 5-2. Detailed Cycle Time Report

production control favor a simpler, paperless method of production planning.

This detailed kind of cycle time reporting can be achieved manually using a tracking sheet similar to the one shown in Figure 5-3. Once again the amount of work required to compile and analyze this information makes this procedure a costly and wasteful activity and should be done only if the information is essential and cannot be obtained in another way.

Production Tracking Report						Product Group: CD-6 Week Ending: 02/15/91		
Product	Quantity	FAB. 100	Finishing 200	Assembly 300	Final Assy 400	Pack 500	Total
108-02545	2500	2.5	1.25	3.50	4.75	1.00	13.00
108-05408-1	3500	4.25	1.50	1.75	3.50	0.75	11.75
144-05741	1250	1.25	1.00	1.00	2.50	1.00	6.75
560-12035	5106	2.75	0.75	2.25			
840-70811	325						
644-14369	4000						
380-98415	2600						
Total	19281						

Figure 5-3. Manual Cycle Time Analysis Report

Some companies employ a simple technique of manually tracking cycle times. The schedules, kanbans, or orders are time-stamped when they are released to the floor and then time-stamped again in the final assembly area — often the packing department. The cycle times are then calculated and presented as averages on graphs and charts. This method is very successful for a simple production operation and where the data collection task is not a burden.

Bar codes and automatic information collection Some sources contend that the cost of collecting information can be greatly reduced by the use of automated data collection devices, many of which use bar code readers or other optical scanning devices. This contention is true to some extent; nevertheless, the necessity and usefulness of the data still need to be considered carefully.

The fact that the information can be more easily obtained does not mean that the information is useful and should be reported. The technology is not important — it is the value of the data that must be determined. In 1985, Professors Miller and Vollmann, in an article for the *Harvard Business Review* entitled "The Hidden Factory," showed that every production plant has two factories; the first is making the products and the second is creating transactions in control systems (manual and computerized). Of these two factories, the second is by far the most wasteful and expensive. The best way to reduce hidden costs is to eliminate the transactions, not to find technologically more elegant ways to process them.

Bar coding and other methods of optical scanning can make it easier to gather much of this detailed data and will also improve the accuracy of the information. What is important is what is *done* with the collected data.

Analysis of engineering routing A more practical method of tracking cycle times is to analyze the engineering routings. This method does assume, of course, that engineering routings are accurate and up to date. In many traditional companies, the production routings, drawings, and bills of material are woefully inadequate for this analysis. In a traditional company, the inadequacies of the engineering information are accommodated by the people on the shop floor knowing from their experience the right part numbers and routings. The cost of this approach results in high inventories (to cover poor planning) and low quality owing to the products being made according to the varying experience and knowledge of the operators and supervisors involved.

World class manufacturers, in contrast, frequently are able to use their engineering information for the analysis of cycle times because the detailed work done as a part of the continuous improvement of the process, setup reduction, and production planning requires that this information be accurate. In addition, the simplification of the production process and the use of production cells (rather than work centers) often simplify defining the process and keeping it up to date.

A cycle time analysis report, as shown in Figure 5-4, can either be produced from the production routings for all the company's products or can display the routings and cycle time information for products actually manufactured over the preceding day, week, or month. The report can be sorted and totalled by product and product group or by production cell or line.

As with most of these kinds of performance measures, the trends and the spread of the cycle times are more important than the individual day's results. The trend is important because the gradual reduction of cycle times will show the success of the multitude of small changes that constitute the continuous improvement process.

One change rarely makes all the difference to production cycle times; the setup procedures, lot size reduction, production quality, machine maintenance, shop floor layout, and personnel training all combine to make up the improvements resulting in short cycle times.

Cycle time sampling There are two problems with the use of engineering information to measure cycle times; they are the inaccuracy of the data and the fact that you are not measuring what actually occurred, only what theoretically should have

UNITRONIX CORP
STANDARD CYCLE TIME REPORT

PAGE 11
3-FEB-1991

CO	BR	CUSTOMER	SALES ORDER NO	LINE ITEM	PRODUCT NO	AUTHORIZED QTY	STEP	RUN TIME	SETUP TIME	MOVE TIME	CYCLE TIME
01	01	100	101786PX	002	M1A1	100.00	10	25.00	0.35	0.00	25.35
							20	50.00	0.00	0.00	50.00
							30	15.00	0.00	0.00	15.00
							40	25.00	0.00	0.00	25.00
							50	60.00	0.00	0.00	60.00
							60	25.00	0.00	0.00	25.00
TOTAL FOR SALES ORDER= 101786PX								200.00	0.35	0.00	200.35
01	01	300	143567PX	005	M1A1	150.00	10	37.50	0.35	0.00	37.85
							20	75.00	0.00	0.00	75.00
							30	22.50	0.00	0.00	22.50
							40	37.50	0.00	0.00	37.50
							50	90.00	0.00	0.00	90.00
							60	37.50	0.00	0.00	37.50
TOTAL FOR SALES ORDER = 143567PX								300.00	0.35	0.00	300.35
01	01	500	14367PX	006	M1A2	150.00	10	37.50	0.00	0.00	37.50
							20	37.50	0.00	0.00	37.50
							30	52.50	0.00	0.00	52.50
							40	22.50	0.00	0.00	22.50
							50	15.00	0.00	0.00	15.00
							60	52.50	0.00	0.00	52.50
TOTAL FOR SALES ORDER = 14367PX								217.50	0.00	0.00	217.50

Figure 5-4. Cycle Time Analysis from Routings

occurred. The problem with measuring detailed actual production time is that the cost of collecting this information is often prohibitively high.

A solution to these problems is the use of sampling. Sampling does not require every production run to be measured in detail; just a small sample of each day's production is measured and reported. The purpose is to measure the actual cycle time of a small enough sample that measurement is not a costly burden to production personnel, but yet to have a large enough sample that the information is authoritative.

The choice of how many samples to take and how to decide which particular schedules are to be sampled will vary considerably according to the kind of products and the production processes involved. In addition, the ease of sampling will have a bearing on the amount of sampling that is practical. This approach is similar to sampling techniques used within quality control measurement, which will be discussed later in this book.

Hosts of different methods can be used to take the measurement. Some companies have colored stickers attached to every one-hundredth kanban card. When the production personnel encounter a kanban with a sticker, they write the start and stop times on the sticker. The kanbans with stickers are separated each day and the information is analyzed.

The analysis of the information can be done in different ways. Some companies maintain manual control by calculating the cycle time from the start and stop times and then posting this information on a board or chart at the work cell (see Figure 5-5).

Another approach is to enter the information into a computer spreadsheet and perform some statistical analysis on the data. This analysis will produce averages, summaries by product type, work cell, cell type, and spreads or standard

| CELL | AVERAGE PRODUCTION CYCLE TIME (IN MINUTES) | | | | | | | | | |
	8/5	8/6	8/7	8/8	8/9	8/12	8/13	8/14	8/15	8/16
F101	86	82	82	84	79	80	81	79		
F102	47	42	43	42	45	41	41	40		
F103	66	69	72	66	65	66	67	66		
A001	12	12	12	11	11	12	10	11		
A002	14	12	17	13	12	15	14	13		
B001	8	8	8	8	9	8	8	8		
B002	6	7	6	7	6	6	6	6		
B004	12	9	9	10	8	8	7	7		
D100	18	21	17	16	32*	17	16	14		
D200	5	5	5	5	4	4	4	5		
D300	4	4	4	5	5	4	4	4		
D301	4	3	4	4	3	3	3	3		

Figure 5-5. Production Cycle Time Board

deviations. An example is shown in Figure 5-6. A graph showing cycle times expressed in terms of their spread (upper and lower levels) is given in Figure 5-7.

Cycle time information can be used immediately if operators calculate cycle times and post them onto a chart. These charts (see Figure 5-8) are similar to statistical process control charts and show the standard cycle time and the upper and lower limits of acceptable cycle times. If the cycle time falls outside of these limits, the operator can investigate the rea-

```
                    CYCLE TIME ANALYSIS

CELL:   F23 MOWER ACCESORIES

PRODUCT      WEEK 1  WEEK 2  WEEK 3  WEEK 4

127/441         12-INCH THATCHER
   MON       1.26    1.37    2.65    2.75    AVERAGE  = 2.30
   TUES      2.43    1.17    2.21    3.01    HIGHEST  = 3.66
   WED       2.87    2.87    1.56    2.89    LOWEST   = 1.17
   THURS     1.19    1.82    3.66    1.54    SPREAD   = 2.49
   FRI       3.22    3.49    2.65    1.36  STD. DEV. = 1.84


327/441         18-INCH THATCHER
   MON       4.65    4.44    3.75    4.80    AVERAGE  = 4.11
   TUES      3.55    5.10    4.21    3.01    HIGHEST  = 5.44
   WED       2.87    4.65    3.89    2.98    LOWEST   = 2.87
   THURS     5.44    2.99    5.43    3.66    SPREAD   = 2.57
   FRI       3.50    5.21    3.52    4.52  STD. DEV. = 3.41


682/441         18-INCH READ THATCHER DISPOSER
   MON       3.44    1.18    2.87    3.04    AVERAGE  = 2.41
   TUES      2.11    2.54    2.43    2.79    HIGHEST  = 3.87
   WED       3.87    1.36    2.21    1.78    LOWEST   = 1.11
   THURS     2.89    2.87    1.93    2.66    SPREAD   = 2.76
   FRI       1.11    3.21    1.69    2.25  STD. DEV. = 1.76
```

Figure 5-6. Cycle Time Analysis Sheet

sons for the deviation and resolve (or help to resolve) the problem. This charted information can also be used as a central topic for participation group or quality circle discussion in the quest for continuous improvement.

Other sampling methods may be carried out by production engineers as a part of the wider analysis of the production process in an improvement effort. In these situations the engineers will monitor particular lots of the production through

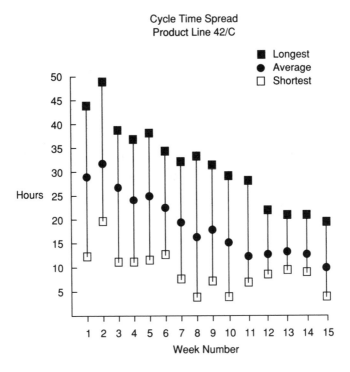

Figure 5-7. Spread of Cycle Times Chart

the entire process. Occasionally, videotaping is used to analyze the strengths and weaknesses of the production process, particularly the setup operations. This analysis provides detailed information about the cycle times of each product through each cell and can be used to track changes in cycle time as the process is improved.

Pragmatic methods of cycle time measurement Many companies employ much less sophisticated methods of cycle time measurement. Frequently, it is not necessary to have anything very complex to report cycle time and a simple idea can be one that everybody in the plant will see as relevant.

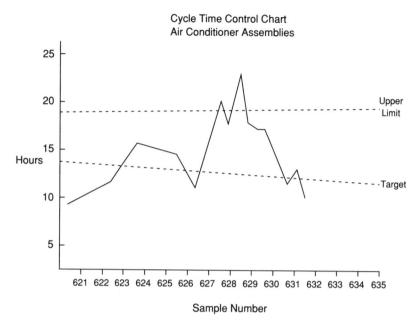

Figure 5-8. Cycle Time Upper Limit Chart

One of these pragmatic methods is to record each day the number of completed product (or product group) lots and to keep track of how many uncompleted lots are in WIP. The number of WIP lots divided by the number of completed lots that day gives the average cycle time for the production of that cell or item. This figure can be reported on a chart or day sheet and can be analyzed more fully to establish trends and spreads over time.

Typically this information is reported for each cell or product group on a daily basis and then summarized and averaged weekly. These reports are distributed to the supervisors, plant managers, and operations manager or vice president. Figure 5-9 shows a production completions report including cycle time calculations.

PRODUCTION SCHEDULE AND COMPLETIONS REPORT
3QTR 1991

FINAL ASSEMBLY CELL - TIMERS

	WK1	WK2	WK3	WK4	WK5	WK6
SCHEDULE	120	130	140	150	150	150
CUM. SCHEDULE	120	250	390	540	690	840
ACTUALS	95	140	125	155		
CUM. ACTUALS	95	235	360	515		
RELEASED	350	145	140	155		
CUM RELEASED	350	495	635	790		
W.I.P.	255	260	275	275		
CYCLE TIME IN WEEKS	2.68	1.85	2.20	1.77		
CUM. ADHERENCE	79.16	94.00	92.31	95.37		

Figure 5-9. Production Completions Analysis Report

Lot sizes When it is difficult to measure cycle time directly, a measure of the lot sizes can be a good indicator of the success of cycle time reduction efforts. Lot sizes can be measured directly from the production planning and control system or they can be surveyed manually. Average lot sizes can be graphed for each level of production, fabrication, subassembly manufacture, and final assembly.

There are many methods used to calculate the "ideal" lot size and many published academic works seek to provide an algorithm that will optimize production lots. A world class manufacturer tends to take a much less academic approach to these issues and just puts into action programs that will systematically reduce lot sizes by reducing setup times, synchronizing the production process, and enhancing product quality.

When lot size reduction is a focus of just-in-time manufacturing implementation, it is helpful to make average lot size a key measure of success. When kanban cards are used to control the flow of production through the plant, measuring lot sizes is easy because the quantities required by each kanban card is the lot size for that product or subassembly. These cards can be analyzed after use and the averages calculated.

Measuring average lot size is an easy concept and can be used as a rallying point for production personnel. Some companies regularly post average lot size each week and set targets for reduction. They then use the report as the focus for all the efforts being made in the plant to reduce setup time and cycle times, to improve quality, and to provide flexibility to customers.

D:P Ratio

The use of a ratio runs counter to the criteria established in Chapter 2 for world class manufacturing performance measures because the requirement for simplicity suggests that ratios should be abandoned in favor of direct and clearly understood measures. The D:P ratio is an exception because it is a measure that makes a clear link between customer requirements and the manufacturing process. World class manufacturers pay a great deal of attention to the customers needs and requirements.

The "D" of the D:P ratio stands for the *delivery lead time;* the "P" stands for the *production lead time.* The production lead time referred to in this ratio is the total or cumulative production lead — which includes the time to manufacture the final assembly, the time to manufacture all components and subassemblies, and the time to procure all parts and raw materials. It is the time taken to purchase the raw materials and to manufacture the product from scratch.

For example, a simple telephone is made up of a plastic case, a keyboard, a printed circuit board with various electronic components, and two microphone/loudspeakers. The telephone manufacturer makes some parts and purchases others; the breakdown is:

Final Assembly	Make	Lead Time = 12 days
Plastic Case	Make	Lead Time = 10 days
Plastic	Buy	Lead Time = 30 days
Coloring Agent	Buy	Lead Time = 45 days
Keyboard	Buy	Lead Time = 45 days
Printed Circuit	Make	Lead Time = 15 days
Circuit Board	Buy	Lead Time = 25 days
Electronic Components	Buy	Lead Time = 50 days
Microphones	Buy	Lead Time = 36 days

The total production lead time for the telephone is 77 days (see Figure 5-10) which is the "critical path" for the purchase of the electronic components, manufacture of the printed circuit, and the final assembly of the product.

Delivery Lead Time

The delivery lead time (D) is the lead time offered to the customers. If the value of D is greater than P, then the product can be made to order. If the value of D is less than P, the product must be made to stock. If a product is made to stock, there must be a significant amount of finished goods inventory held so that the required customer service level can be achieved. If the D:P ratio is small (less than 1), the manufacturer is able to offer more flexibility to the customer; this flexibility includes product mix changes, production volume changes, and custom products. If the D:P ratio is large (greater than 1), the manufacturer must forecast customer needs and can only provide flexibility of mix and volume by holding additional finished products inventory. Custom

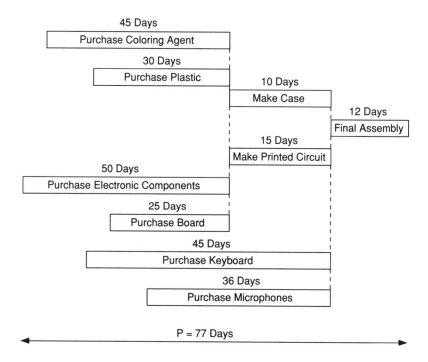

Figure 5-10. Production Lead Time

products cannot be supplied within the delivery lead time because there is not enough time to make them. The delivery lead time is not a single figure. There are at least three variations that the world class manufacturer must consider. The first is the delivery lead time offered to the customer (D1); the second is the lead time the customer would like to have from suppliers (D2); and the third is a delivery lead time that would give the manufacturer a competitive edge over other suppliers of similar products (D3).

All world class manufacturers are concerned with providing a better service to customers. This service improvement covers the whole range of the business including products, quality, price, reliability, service, flexibility, and lead time. The D:P ratio is a good measure of success at improving customer lead times and production flexibility.

Measuring the D:P Ratio

The production lead time can be calculated by reviewing the bill of materials and the lead times associated with each component, subassembly, part, and raw material. From this information the critical path can be discovered and the cumulative lead of the critical path calculated; this comprises the production lead time.

This calculation is laborious when done by hand, but it can be readily calculated from the data contained with the production planning and control system. A good manufacturing resource planning (MRPII) system will have a method of calculating this information because the information is needed when reconciling the lead times used by the material requirements planning (MRP) to the inherent lead times contained within the production routings used to schedule the shop floor.

The delivery lead times need to be studied carefully. The lead time currently offered to customers will be a known number. The customers' preferred lead time (D2) can only be discovered by asking the customers. A good order entry system will retain the customers' required dates for every order and will show the difference between the dates the products were promised and the dates the customers requested delivery. This figure will be an indication of the preferred lead time, but a true figure can only be arrived at by discussion with key customers.

The lead time that gives the company a competitive edge over other suppliers (D3) can be derived by studying the delivery lead times offered by other suppliers and comparing this with the customers' preferred lead time. This method of studying the competition's strength and weaknesses and setting standards for one's own company, based upon the competitor's achievements, is known as *competitive benchmarking.* This concept will be dealt with more thoroughly in Chapter 11.

For the D:P ratio to be a practical measure, the three kinds of D must be reviewed constantly and the latest values of P must be available. The objective of WCM is to continuously reduce the D:P ratio until it is less than 1. This goal is achieved by a host of improvements throughout the entire manufacturing process. The reduction of individual cycle times will help reduce the production lead time, as will better supplier relationships and just-in-time deliveries to the shop floor. The various continuous improvement programs that are under way within the world class manufacturing company will contribute to the reduction of the D:P ratio.

The ratio may be calculated as an average for all products the company manufactures, broken down into averages for different product groups, or reported individually for each product. A ratio like this can be an effective measure only if it is a quick and clear "rule-of-thumb." Ideally, it should be reported as a single number or a short series of numbers (by product group, plant, or line). This way it can be a powerful and motivating measure. The best way to present the D:P ratio is as a graph showing the trends over time (see Figure 5-11).

Setup Times

Setup times within a production plant are another key factor for a world class manufacturer. The reduction of setup times enables lot sizes to be reduced, thus reducing work-in-process inventories. Reduced lot sizes, in turn, will allow cycle times to be reduced; reduction in cycle time will make the company more responsive to its customers, will reduce or eliminate the need for finished product inventories, and will

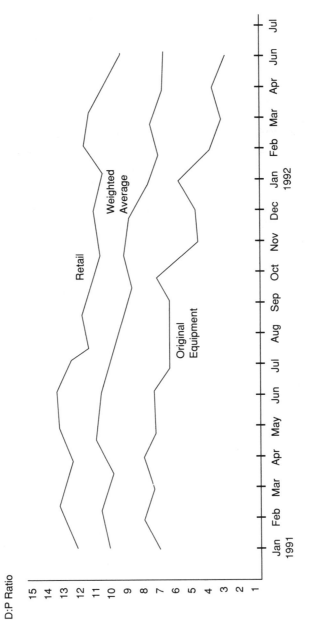

Figure 5-11. D:P Ratio Graph

reduce the D:P ratio. A typical production facility will have hundreds of different setup procedures, and a part of the ongoing continuous improvement process will be the gradual reduction of setup times. When just-in-time manufacturing techniques are first introduced into a production plant, considerable effort is often required to bring setup times down to a reasonable level. Just-in-time production is not practical if lot sizes are large, and lot sizes can be reduced only if the setups are short. In the past there has not been much emphasis on the need for fast setups, but the wide acceptance of JIT methods has brought this issue into the forefront of attention in many plants.

Reduction of setup times is often tackled using a "quality circle" approach. A team of people including operators, supervisors, engineers, and technicians are given the task of reducing setup times within a cell, group of machines, or range of products. There are various techniques that have been devised to assist with fast setups.

Many companies have found that setup times can be reduced significantly (50-75 percent) by merely studying the problem and better organizing the activities. Further significant reductions can be achieved by relatively minor modifications to machines, tools, dies, or the product. Only after these kinds of improvements have been made is there a need for any substantial capital investment. The actual cost of achieving fast setups in most plants is only the time and attention of the operators who work with these machine on a daily basis and of the technicians and engineers whose skill and experience can be brought to bear on these issues.

Measuring Setup Time Reduction

There are two primary methods of measuring the setup times within a production plant. One way is to count the number of setups and divide them into ranges according to the length of time taken to achieve the setup. The second approach is to calculate the average time taken to perform a number of setups within a cell or work center.

The first approach is shown in Figure 5-12. This report analyzes all the setups that have taken place over a date range (day, week, or month) within each work center and divides those setups into six categories:

1. Greater than 2 hours
2. Greater than 1 hour but less than 2 hours
3. Greater than 30 minutes but less than 1 hour
4. Greater than 10 minutes but less than 30 minutes
5. Greater than 1 minute but less than 10 minutes
6. Less than 1 minute

The report lists each work center or cell within a plant and shows the number of setups that occurred within the time period by category. This information is then totalled by plant number.

Such a setup time analysis is significant only when it is viewed over a longer time period (see Figure 5-13). As the effects of continuous improvement begin to be felt, the number of setups in the longer time categories will reduce and the number in the shorter time categories will increase. The company will set objectives to have a certain number (or proportion) of setups in each of the categories.

Average Setup Times

Another useful way of looking at setup times is to calculate the average setup times that occur over a time period within each work center or cell. The purpose here is not only to understand the time taken to set up a machine but also to see the extent to which these setup times vary. The setup time for a particular product on a particular machine should be very

UNITRONIX CORPORATION
CURRENT SCHEDULE
NUMBER OF SETUPS BY TIME CATEGORIES

CO BR	WORK CENTER		>2 HR	>1HR	>30 MIN.	>10 MIN.	>1 MIN.	<1 MIN.
01 01	0420	CASE FABRICATION	0	8	15	2	0	0
	0510	PLATE FABRICATION	7	12	2	0	0	0
	0600	ACID FILL AND CHARGE	0	23	15	8	0	0
	0650	DECORATING	0	0	0	0	63	0
	0700	FINISHING AND PACKING	0	9	18	3	0	0
BRANCH = 01			7	51	50	13	63	0

Figure 5-12. Number of Setups by Time Class

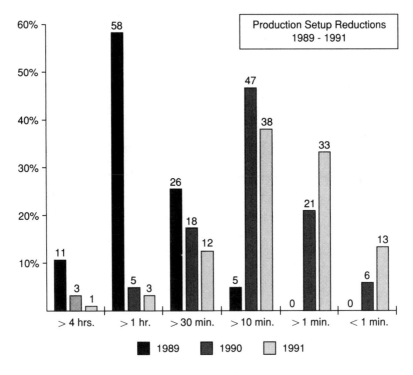

Figure 5-13. Setups by Time Class Graph

consistent. If it is not consistent, then it is necessary to study these setups for reduction; fast setups are those that are meticulously planned and executed. If the setup times vary, then there is room for improvement.

Figure 5-14 shows a detailed average setup time analysis report. The report shows the setups that were performed for each production job within each work center. The report gives the standard setup time, the actual setup time, and the variance between these two. This information is averaged and summarized for each work center and the standard deviation of these setups calculated. The standard deviation is a factor that demonstrates the degree of variability among the setups;

UNITRONIX CORP
AVERAGE SETUP TIMES

PAGE 11
9-FEB-1991

CO	BR	DATE	WORK CELL	OPERATION CODE	PRODUCT	QUANTITY	STD. SETUP	ACTUAL SETUP
01	01	09/10/90	0420	RE1	M1A1	100.00	0.35	0.25
01	01	09/10/90	0420	RE1	M1A2	150.00	0.30	0.25
01	01	09/10/90	0420	RE1	M1A1-12	80.00	0.40	0.50
01	01	09/11/90	0420	RE1	M1A1	120.00	0.35	0.25
01	01	09/11/90	0420	RE1	M1A2	100.00	0.30	0.50
01	01	09/11/90	0420	RE1	M1A1-12	100.00	0.40	0.35
01	01	09/12/90	0420	RE1	M1A1	90.00	0.35	0.35
01	01	09/12/90	0420	RE1	M1A2	170.00	0.30	0.25
01	01	09/12/90	0420	RE1	M1A1-12	100.00	0.40	0.35

TOTAL FOR WORK CENTER = 0420   CASE FABRICATION

						QUANTITY	STD. SETUP	ACTUAL SETUP
						1010.00	3.15	3.05
					AVERAGE		0.35	0.34
					LOWEST		0.30	0.25
					HIGHEST		0.40	0.50
					SPREAD		0.10	0.25
					STD. DEV.		0.12	0.29

Figure 5-14. Average Setup Times Analysis

if the standard deviation is a large number, there is a lot of variability. The plan would be to reduce the standard deviation, ideally to zero.

Figure 5-15 illustrates a more useful report of setup times, as summarized by work center or cell. The report shows the same information but does not show the order number detail. In reality, as a company moves into just-in-time manufacturing, the traditional work order system will be abandoned and setup information will be presented by product or by cell only.

Pragmatic Measures

As with the measurement of cycle times, it is not usually desirable to measure the setup times in the infinite detail required to produce the reports shown in Figures 5-14 and 5-15. More practical and less expensive methods of recording setup times and associated trends are required.

One method frequently used involves measuring a sample number of setups. This method can consist either of measuring a few setups in detail each day and reporting those samples in detail, or measuring every setup one day a month or a quarter.

Another approach is to have the operators and changeover personnel record the time of each setup on charts in the production cell. This way the setups are measured in detail, but measuring them does not require the complexity of recording the information through a computer system.

Many companies change which setups they measure in detail as their setup reduction process continues. When setup time reduction projects are first started, certain key setups are the focus of attention; these are the setups that contribute the most to large lot sizes. As these problems are solved and the attention shifts to other setup processes, the detailed measurement will also change and focus on current priorities.

UNITRONIX CORP
SETUP TIMES SUMMARY

PAGE 2
9-FEB-1991

CO	BR	WORK CELL	OPERATION CODE		AVERAGE	LOWEST	HIGHEST	SPREAD	STD.DEV.
01	01	0420	RE1 BUILD 2-SECTION CASE CASE FABRICATION	STD.	0.35	0.30	0.40	0.10	0.12
				ACTUAL	0.34	0.25	0.50	0.25	0.29
01	01	0510	FL21 24-PANEL PLATE SET PLATE FABRICATION	STD.	0.55	0.30	0.60	0.30	0.22
				ACTUAL	0.49	0.20	0.90	0.70	0.33
01	01	0510	FL29 36-PANEL PLATE SET PLATE FABRICATION	STD.	0.58	0.35	0.75	0.40	0.31
				ACTUAL	0.45	0.12	0.85	0.73	0.47
01	01	0650	DK10 ATTACH SPRAY & DECAL	STD.	0.10	0.10	0.10	0.00	0.00
				ACTUAL	0.15	0.05	0.20	0.15	0.13

Figure 5-15. Setup Times Summary

Whichever methods are used to limit the amount of wasteful activity associated with the production of setup time analysis reports, there is a need to have a periodic audit where setup times are analyzed in detail and the changes in the number of setups by time categories displayed. This aspect is a key measure in establishing the improvements brought about by the setup time reduction program.

Material Availability

Another significant cause of long cycle times is poor planning of raw material and component inventories. Holding up production because of missing parts or materials is anathema to a just-in-time manufacturer, and a key objective of the improvements made to the production planning and control processes is to ensure material availability and reduced inventories.

Measuring material availability can be quite straightforward. If the company is using an MRPII system to plan and control production, then the system will usually detect parts shortages before an order or schedule is launched on the shop floor. Stock balances on each part or product are recorded within the system, and when the schedule is released onto the shop floor, the system can check the available materials and report any shortages. This information can then be shown on a material availability report.

There is more to this story. Because the stock figures held in the system may not be accurate (see Chapter 7 for a more detailed discussion of inventory accuracy), the system may show that sufficient parts are available yet the material, in fact, may not be available in the stockroom or stock point. These stock-outs can be recorded and tracked. If manual systems are used to control inventory, then material availability can be tracked manually, simply by recording how many schedules could be released to the shop floor successfully and how many were delayed due to part shortage.

The method of reporting this information can be the number of schedules or orders, the number of production items, the number of individual parts in shortage, or the quantity of parts short of requirements. Regardless of which criterion is used to measure the material availability — the method will vary from one plant to another — select one that makes sense in your environment and keep track over time. The objective is to maintain 100-percent material availability; nothing less than this is acceptable.

Figure 5-16 shows a typical graph for reporting material availability. Each bar shows the number of schedules or orders released that week and the number delayed owing to material shortages. The graph line shows the percentage of those orders that were released successfully. This graphical combination of quantities and percentages is often helpful for presenting information clearly and concisely.

Distance of Material Movement

Movement of materials within the plant is wasteful activity; it does not add value to the product and causes delays and high inventories. A traditional manufacturing plant divides the factory into machine centers that contain machines of a similar type. Jobs are processed through the factory by moving the semicompleted material from one machine center to another according to the production routing, which defines all the tasks required to complete the product.

This approach has some significant shortcomings. First, it requires that the products be physically moved a great distance during the production process as they are transferred from one machine center to another. Not only does this movement increase labor costs but it also adds to production cycle time, causes additional waiting and queuing, and increases scrap and damage.

The second problem is that a machine center organization usually results in the production personnel specializing in a

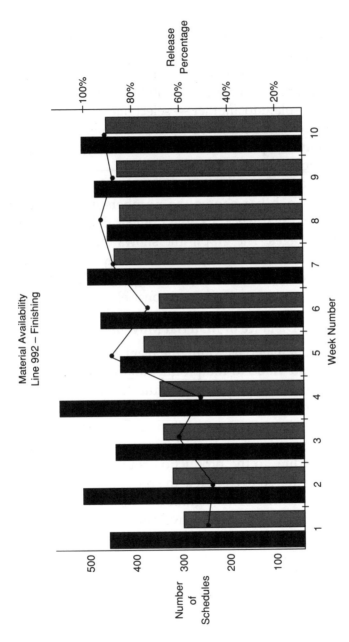

Figure 5-16. Material Availability Graph

particular type of task within the factory, and people rarely move from one specialty to another. An objective of just-in-time manufacturing is to have people cross-trained within the plant so that they can perform many different tasks and so that production capacities can be changed according to market needs. This method is important for providing flexibility to customer requirements. The third shortcoming of this traditional style of organization is that it leads to complex control procedures. It is just not possible to see where a particular job is in the process because the factory has a wide range of jobs, each at a different stage of manufacture. In order to keep track of the overall situation, it is necessary to maintain thorough and careful records of the status of each job — and this is a time-consuming and wasteful task.

A just-in-time approach to shop floor layout (see Figure 5-17) is concerned with minimizing waste; with material movement, people's time and skills, and the use of tooling within the plant. Usually the shop floor is laid out as a series of manufacturing cells where dissimilar machines are grouped together based upon the manufacturing process that is completed within this cell. Instead of a batch of material being moved between three, four, or more separate work centers for different activities, these machines and people are grouped into a cell so that the activities can be completed in series with virtually no movement of materials.

There are several popular styles of production cells including production lines, U-shaped cells, and zig-zag cells. The style of cell chosen will be determined by the kind of process and by the physical constraints of the plant. Whichever styles of cell are employed, the movement of materials will be significantly reduced.

Most companies, when introducing just-in-time production methods, are not able to totally reorganize the production plant in one fell swoop. Cellular manufacturing is introduced

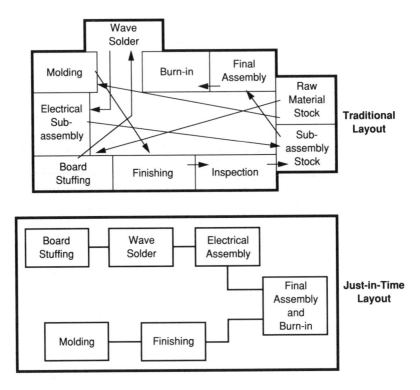

Figure 5-17. Shop Floor Layout — Traditional and JIT

gradually by selecting the particular products or part of the process that can provide the most immediate benefit and by then studying the process until an optimum floor layout is devised. Often the 80/20 rule can be a guide to selecting the right place to start a shop floor layout program; that is, selecting the 20 percent of the process or products that contribute 80 percent of the production costs or cycle time.

Measuring Distance Moved

A report showing the distance moved by products throughout the plant over a time period (a day, a week, or a month) can be a useful way of monitoring the success of shop floor layout reorganizations and of keeping track of the effectiveness of the layout over time as product mix and volumes change. Figure 5-18 is such an example of a distance moved report. The information shows all the production jobs over the selected date range and calculates the distance moved by the production material through the production process.

The report in the example is sorted and totalled by product and product family and shows the plant number (CO/BR), the product number, and the product family code. Each job step required to manufacture that product is then shown for each order or schedule on the shop floor together with the work centers where the jobs are completed. Each work center shows the previous (or from) work center, the distance travelled from that work center, and the time taken to move the product. The distance moved and time taken are then summarized for all orders for that product and for the product family.

Few manufacturing planning and control systems have the distance moved information built into their data base, but it is easy to add this information for the purposes of this report. The report can be produced by reading all the production orders and schedules that have been completed within the date range. The production routings for each of these activities can be accessed and from this the route taken within the plant is available. A new file that specifies the distance between each work center or cell is required within the data base. From this file, the distance moved information can be obtained and totals calculated. The data file of distances may be structured by simply defining either two or more cells or work centers and entering the distance between them, together with other pertinent information such as the mode of transport and standard time taken. Alternatively, the position of each cell and work center can be given a grid reference and

```
                          UNITRONIX CORPORATION - PRAXA SYSTEMS                              PAGE 7
                 REPORT OF DISTANCE MOVED BY PRODUCT & PRODUCT FAMILY                     9-FEB-1991
                               PRODUCT AND PRODUCT FAMILY

CO BR PRODUCT NO PRODUCT   FROM                              TO      DISTANCE  MOVE   ORDER NO  JOB
                 FAMILY    WORK                              WORK    MOVED     TIME             STEP
                           CENTER                            CENTER  IN FEET

01 01  M1A1      EX01
                           0420  COMPONENT INSERTION         0420      0.00    0.00   B101       10
                           0501  COMPONENT TEST              0501     25.00    0.43              20
                           0600  CHASSIS ASSEMBLY            0600     55.50    1.50              30
                           0700  FINAL ASSEMBLY              0700     25.00    0.75              40
                           0500  TEST                        0500     10.00    0.50              50
                                                             0420      0.00    1.20              60
                           0420  COMPONENT INSERTION         0501      0.00    0.00   B110       10
                           0501  COMPONENT TEST              0600     25.00    0.43              20
                           0600  CHASSIS ASSEMBLY            0700     55.50    1.50              30
                           0700  FINAL ASSEMBLY              0500     25.00    0.75              40
                           0500  TEST                        0500     10.00    0.50              50
                                                                       0.00    1.20              60

 PRODUCT NUMBER = M1A1                                                231.00    8.76
```

Figure 5-18. Distance Moved Report

the distance between the cells can be calculated each time based on the distance required to travel from one grid reference to another.

The grid reference idea is a simple one and significantly reduces the amount of work required to set up the table of distances. In practice, however, it is difficult to use because it does not take into account the route required to go from one cell to another — a route that may involve one-way sections, movement up and down stairs, specified gangways, and the like. One company used a combination of the two methods by having grid references with manual override of distance between work centers. When the system produces a report, it looks for an override distance; if that is not on file, it calculates the distance from the grid references. Figure 5-19 shows a summary report of the distance moved analysis which can be used to graph the trends and monitor changes over a longer time period.

```
               UNITRONIX CORPORATION — PRAXA SYSTEMS
               SUMMARY OF DISTANCED MOVED BY PRODUCT     PAGE 14
                  1-FEB-1990 to 28-FEB-1990          9-FEB-1991


   CO  BR   FAMILY   PRODUCT NUMBER              DISTANCE    MOVE
                                                  MOVED      TIME

   01 01    EX01    M1A1       TERMINAL           231.00    8.76
   01 01    EX01    M1A2       TERMINAL           258.00   11.00

   PRODUCT FAMILY = EX01                          489.00   19.76

   01 01    JD12    J1S15      MONITOR            453.21   17.25
   01 01    JD12    J1S21      MONITOR            126.50    5.75
   01 01    JD12    J1S35      MONITOR            554.25   21.50
   01 01    JD12    J1S85      MONITOR            352.00   11.25

   PRODUCT FAMILY = JD12                         1485.96   55.75
```

Figure 5-19. Distance Moved Summary

Manual Methods of Tracking Distance Moved

While distance moved is not an aspect of performance measurement that lends itself to manual tracking, some techniques have been employed in certain companies. One method uses sampling, which was discussed earlier in the chapter for setup time and cycle time measurement. Sampling can be used by selecting a certain number of schedules or orders and by manually tracking their movement through the production plant.

This information can be recorded on graphs or can be entered into a computer for spreadsheet-style analysis. The information required includes the average and spread of distance moved when manufacturing each product or product group over the relevant time period.

A more pragmatic method of measuring distance moved is to select an easy-to-measure factor that represents the distance moved within the plant. The total fork-lift truck mileage can be tracked easily and may be a good gauge of the distances materials are moved within the plant. If the plant employs people specifically to move materials, then the hours worked by the material handling personnel is another good gauge of total material movement.

When kanban cards are used within a plant, they authorize not only the production of component and subassemblies, but they also authorize their movement from one cell to the next. The kanban cards can have the distance moved printed on them (particularly if the kanbans are printed by the planning and control system) and these move cards can be collected, counted, and analyzed.

If kanban cards are not used, the same information can be derived by having an identifying ticket at each work center and stock room. The material-handling personnel take a ticket at each location visited for a pick-up and another ticket when the delivery is complete. The two tickets, stapled together, will show how many material movements have been made. For this approach to be practical, there must be a very limited number of "count points" so that the distances can be quickly and easily reckoned; if the process is too complex, it becomes wasteful instead of useful.

Next Work Center Report

The next work center report, shown in Figure 5-20, is similar to the detailed distance moved report except that it is sorted and summarized by each work center and the next work center's material moved to and from that work center. This report is not an ongoing monitoring report; it is an analysis tool for shop floor layout. This report can be used to analyze each work center and to determine which centers need to be located adjacent to each other.

When a plant makes a wide range of products and the production process is complex, it is often a difficult task to determine the optimum layout. This report can be used to show, for a specified date range, which production schedules passed through the work center and where they went to next. This analysis will show how the work centers should be arranged to minimize material movement or how production cells should be rearranged based upon the current production mix and volumes.

For most companies, altering the shop floor layout is a major task. Some WCM companies with frequently changing production volumes and mixes have taken steps to ensure that cells can be rearranged quickly. This rearrangement can be achieved primarily by choosing machines that can be moved easily, that do not require special installation processes or power sources, and that are flexible and can be adapted readily to changing production needs. The use of a next work center report facilitates this kind of flexible production scenario.

```
                                    PRAXA SYSTEMS
                          ANALYSIS OF NEXT WORK CENTER                      PAGE 9
                             FOR PRODUCTION JOBS                         9-FEB-1991

CO  BR  FROM              TO         DISTANCE   MODE    ORDER NO    JOB
        WORK            WORK         MOVED                          STEP
        CENTER          CENTER       IN FEET

01  01  0420  COMPONENT INSERTION
                         0501          25.00    MANUAL    B101       20
                         0501          25.00    MANUAL    B102       30
                         0501          25.00    MANUAL    B110       20
                         0501          25.00    MANUAL    B113       30

            TO WORK CENTER = 0501                100.00

FROM WORK CENTER = 0420                          100.00

01  01  0501  COMPONENT TEST
                         0600          55.50    CONVEY    B101       30
                         0600          55.50    CONVEY    B102       40
                         0600          55.50    CONVEY    B110       30
                         0600          55.50    CONVEY    B113       40

            TO WORK CENTER = 0600                222.00
```

Figure 5-20. Next Work Center Report

Machine Up Time

The nature of just-in-time manufacturing is that excess inventory of components and subassemblies must be eliminated throughout the production process. The ultimate objective is to eliminate all inventory except that which is needed immediately for the production of finished products. This philosophy assumes a very high degree of reliability in the production process and does not take account of machine breakdowns or stops in the production process due to lack of parts or assemblies.

Just-in-time manufacturing does not seek to utilize production equipment 100 percent of the time; it is better to have a machine idle than to have it making product that is not immediately required. But when a machine or cell *is* required to manufacture product, it must be able to go into action immediately. There are two primary reasons why a machine or cell cannot be used; one is machine failure and the other is missing parts, tools, or supplies.

The implementation of just-in-time manufacturing is often accompanied by the introduction of a thorough preventive maintenance program. Production personnel are trained to perform basic daily and weekly preventive maintenance tasks, and emphasis is placed on the quality of product made by each piece of equipment. This program is augmented by maintenance engineering analyses of the longer-term preventive maintenance requirements of each machine to ensure that the equipment is always in prime condition. Contrary to popular belief, many observers have noted that Japanese companies frequently use old-fashioned production equipment. As a matter of fact, many Japanese manufacturers do *not* use state-of-the-art production technologies, robots, flexible manufacturing cells, lights-out factories, and so forth. Rather, the emphasis is placed on ensuring consistency of production quality by keeping the equipment in peak condition.

The up time of production cells is a major issue for some companies and can be easily measured. Any time a machine or cell goes "down" the amount of time lost is tracked by the operator or supervisor. The total lost time throughout the plant can be tracked and the up time calculated either as a percentage of the total work hours or in real terms.

Figure 5-21 shows a typical up-time graph that can be used to monitor the success of the preventive maintenance program, to measure the efficiency of the production planning process, and also to analyze the reasons for cycle time problems. A chart similar to Figure 5-22 can be used to show the primary reasons for down time. In this example, all failures are assigned to one of four categories: defective parts, missing assemblies, operator error, or machine failure. The changing mix of these problems can be a good indicator of the success of the various continuous improvement programs going on within the plant.

Customer Service Time

A very useful and easy-to-collect measure of the overall efficiency of the production process is to keep track of the customer service time (CST). This measure is primarily useful for make-to-order companies because CST is concerned with the entire process from (1) the customer placing the order through (2) manufacture to (3) the dispatch of the products.

When an order is received from the customer, it is time-stamped, either manually on the order or in the computer system. When the order is shipped, the dispatch time is stamped on the documentation (or in the computer system), and the difference between the two times is the customer service time. The CST is collected for all orders each day and shown on a graph or chart within the plant.

Customer service time is a good measure because it is easy to do, it clearly focuses on the customer, it measures the entire

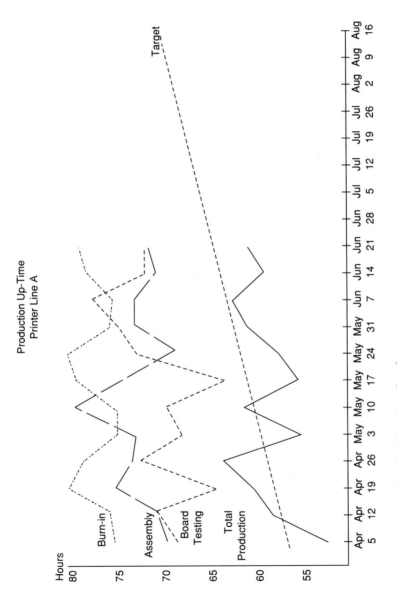

Figure 5-21. Production Up-time Graph

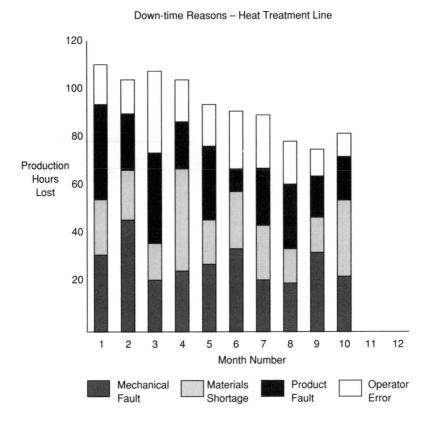

Figure 5-22. Down-time Reasons Chart

process, it is applicable to both manufacturers and distributors, it is readily understandable by all personnel, and it is obviously important to the success of the company. There are controversies concerning how the CST should be gauged; for example, is it the final dispatch of the full order or individual line items, should it take account of delivery time, does it consider quality? These issues need to be resolved and a method selected that is appropriate for the plant involved; then, customer service time can become a key objective to the entire personnel of the company.

Summary

The key areas of interest for a world class manufacturer for the measurement of process times are:

- manufacturing cycle time
- D:P ratios
- setup times
- material availability
- distance of material movement during production
- machine up-time
- customer service time

CHAPTER SIX

Measurement of Production Flexibility

FLEXIBILITY IS becoming a major requirement for world class manufacturers. Production flexibility has been highlighted as a prime objective for the 1990s by some of the largest and best known Japanese manufacturers.[1] Consequently, three aspects of flexibility need to be examined:

1. changes in production mix
2. changes in production volume
3. fast introduction of new products

Changes in Production Mix

As more customers move toward just-in-time manufacturing, they require more frequent deliveries of smaller quantities; and the precise mix of products required each day is not known until the last minute. An example of this situation is the Bloomington Seating Company in Normal, Illinois.[2] It provides its customers (primarily Chrysler Corporation) with a 90-minute lead time for automotive seats that are delivered in a precise mix of model and color and in a sequence specified by the customer. This level of service is provided with less than one-half a day of finished product inventory.

This kind of production mix flexibility is becoming increasingly important to a company attempting to match production to the current customers' needs. Traditionally, the variable nature of customer demand has been accommodated by holding large inventories of finished goods and making to stock. A world class manufacturer strives to eliminate inventory and to provide an excellent level of customer service through flexibility of production. The objective is to make-to-order and to make only what the customers need when they need it; no more and no less.

Changes in Production Volume

Changing production volumes on specific products requires the ability to use the production equipment for many different products, the ability to change production rates through the machines and work cells, and the ability to move production personnel to whatever tasks are currently required. The plant must be able to make as many of any product as the customer requires.

Changing the total output volume of a plant requires excess available capacity. This available capacity can be provided by having additional machines and equipment, additional people (perhaps temporary employees), the use of overtime and additional shifts, variable production rates on the machines, or a combination of all these. For a company to have additional available capacity, it must have a very low cost base within the plant, resulting in a low break-even point. A plant requiring 90-percent utilization to break even will have little volume flexibility because the plant loses money if it is not producing at least 90 percent of its capacity.

A plant with a 30-percent break-even point (the goal for Toyota plants) has plenty of room for flexibility.

New Product Introduction

There are two kinds of new product introduction that need to be considered — (1) the enhancement of existing products and (2) the introduction of an entirely new product. Most companies have difficulty making significant engineering changes to existing products; such changes require a complex process of communication, technical specification, training, and piloting. This process is much more difficult in a traditional manufacturing plant because the long lead times and large lot sizes require the identification and rework of components, subassemblies, and finished goods inventories; and the communications between design engineering and the shop floor is often poor.

Many of the leading Japanese companies have put much effort into this kind of flexibility. Companies like Kawasaki and Honda Motorcycles are able to introduce new models every month with a minimum of disruption. In this way, they are able to continuously react to the demands of the marketplace and reduce production costs. The changes can be piloted between shifts when the extra time is used to try out the new tooling, procedures, and setups. Once the changes have been tested and the people trained, they are introduced into the already flexible production schedule without major problems or delays.

The reduction of product life cycles is a reality that must be faced in a wide range of industries. The fast pace of technology and the demands of the customers for novel and better products require that companies be able to innovate continually and bring these innovations to the marketplace quickly. Further, these will be ever-increasing requirements in future years. Already the automobile companies have realized that they do not have the luxury of seven or eight years to design and introduce a new style of vehicle; this process is being shortened as each model year goes by. The electronics industry is another area where innovative new products are being introduced continuously; a world class manufacturer is able to rapidly turn innovative ideas and technologies into profitable products.

Achieving Flexible Production

Effective flexible production requires a combination of many aspects of world class manufacturing. A company that has short production cycle times is much more flexible than a company with long cycle times. Short cycle times require small lot sizes (ideally of one unit) and fast setup times. These aspects of WCM have been discussed in earlier chapters.

Other factors that affect production flexibility are the amount of cross-training among the production operators and technicians, the degree of commonality of components and subassemblies, the degree of process commonality between products, and the number of manufactured subassemblies. The degree to which commonality of product and process exists within the production plant is a profound measure of production flexibility.

Production commonality is a significant factor in the ease or difficulty of changing the production volumes based upon customer requirements. A high degree of commonality requires less specialization on the part of the work force; therefore, it is easier to introduce cross-training of the operators to perform a wide range of production tasks. Similarly, it is easier to add additional production personnel when increased capacity is required.

The introduction of enhancements and modifications to existing products is very much affected by cycle times and commonality. If the cycle times are short, it is a much less complex task to introduce modifications because it is not necessary to track and modify large volumes of work-in-process products, assemblies, and components. When there is a smooth-running stable production process, it is easier to introduce changes to that process than to a process which is diverse and complex.

The Kofu plant of Yokogawa Electric is an example of how flexibility can be introduced. Yokogawa Electric makes sophisticated production process control equipment like automated flow-rate recorders; the company used to manufacture to stock with a lead time of one month. As a result of introducing world class manufacturing techniques, Yokogawa is able to make products to customer-specified design in batch sizes of one and to offer a delivery lead time as small as 48 hours. The ideas of world class manufacturing have been applied to the entire process of order entry, production, and distribution; the production of a flow-rate recorder starts two hours after the order is received by the sales department. The additional capacity and labor that was made available by the introduction of world class manufacturing techniques enabled Yokogawa to fabricate many components that were previously subcontracted.[3] (These statistics were reported in 1985 and the Yokogawa company has subsequently continued to improve on this level of flexible service to customers.)

The methods used to measure cycle times, lot sizes, and setup times were discussed in Chapter 5. This chapter will examine measurement of commonality, level of variability, and new product introduction.

Number of Different Parts

The logic of this performance measure is simple: the more different part numbers that are required to make your products, the greater the complexity of the production, procurement, and engineering systems required to support production. If the complexity is high — the flexibility will be low.

Another reason to reduce the number of parts required in manufacturing is the need to improve quality. When the part count is reduced, there are fewer parts requiring certification and inspection, and there are fewer suppliers to audit. The task of certification and auditing can appear daunting when there are large numbers of parts; as the part count is reduced, the certification process becomes much more manageable.

Many WCM companies implement component reduction programs with the view to systematically decreasing the number of part numbers used in their products. This goal can be achieved through a greater degree of commonality, by engineering changes such that several parts are replaced by one new part, or by new manufacturing techniques.

An example of a new manufacturing technique is the design of the newer IBM typewriters, which have been engineered for manufacturability. In particular, the machines have been designed so that very few screws, bolts, or fasteners are required in the production process; the majority of parts have been engineered so that they clip or fit together and do not require fastening. This new design has not only simplified the production process but also has reduced significantly the number of parts required in the product.

One General Electric location provided its draftsmen with an incentive to reduce part numbers in their products; the result was the elimination of 1,000 items in two months. This reduction in part numbers led to the elimination of 39,000 shop orders per year and 125,000 fewer pieces being ordered, made, or stocked.[4] As one source recently noted, "Effective manufacturers work from designs that have as few parts as possible, and that can be assembled by methods within manufacturing's capabilities."[5]

Measurement of Part Reduction

Part reduction can be a very simple measure. The simplest method is merely to count the number of part numbers on the part master file of the production planning system. This information can be sorted and totalled by product family or other suitable grouping.

A better picture can be given when the age of the parts is taken into account. Most companies have a large number of obsolete part numbers on their files because these parts were used on products that are no longer manufactured. Ideally, these parts should be removed from the files, but often there are legitimate reasons for retaining them; perhaps spares support is required for an extended period. The part count reports should include current components which can be identified only by including those which have been issued to production in recent months, or by interrogating the bills of material for parts within the effectivity dates of currently manufactured products.

In some production plants the number of different parts is counted by "exploding" the products in the current master schedule. This method ensures that the part count includes only those parts which are currently in production on the shop floor. The advantage of this approach is the concentration on current production; the disadvantage is that the number of parts will vary according to the product mix this week or month which may obscure the engineering changes that are taking place. It is often useful to sort and total these part numbers into different categories so that such parts as hardware items are shown separately from specialist fabrication components, for example.

The objective is to reduce the number of different parts in current production. It is the change over time that is significant, rather than the individual number of a product family.

These figures should be reported on graphs showing how the number of parts is changing.

Percentage of Standard, Common, and Unique Parts

A product made entirely of standard parts will have more flexibility of production than a product made entirely of unique parts. Standard parts are readily available and can be obtained with short lead times and in smaller quantities. The quality of standard parts often can be certified more easily, and the part is likely to be less expensive than a unique part. An extra advantage of standard parts is that if excess inventory does occur on those standard parts, it can be sold on the open market; excess unique parts are usually scrapped at zero value.

A product made entirely of parts that are common to other products manufactured by the same company will have more production flexibility than a product made entirely of unique parts. The company already will be fabricating these parts or will have a certified supplier, and the total usage of the part will be more predictable. If Product B is ordered instead of Product A, and those products have common parts, customer orders can be more easily satisfied than if they each have unique parts. Many world class manufacturers institute a commonality drive. The design and production engineering personnel review the products and increase the degree of commonality and use standard parts wherever possible. Frequently trade-offs have to be made; for example, the standard part may be a higher specification than is necessary and be a more expensive unit to buy. The savings gained (tangible and intangible) by having standard or common parts will often outweigh the additional costs.

Companies that introduce new products frequently will not spend the time reviewing existing products but will put the procedures in place to ensure that new products are designed as far as possible with standard and common components. This approach is usually just one aspect of a wider program aimed at introducing quality and manufacturability at the design stage and at creating closer cooperation between the design, production, and marketing groups within the company.[6]

Definition of Commonality

Defining commonality is not a clear-cut science and varies considerably from one company to another. If a company manufactures 300 different products and a component is used on two of those products, it cannot be considered "common" because it is not used on enough products. Similarly, a component may be used on 170 of those products, but these may be the very slow-moving products accounting for only 5 percent of the company's output; this may not be enough commonality to be considered a common part.

The decisions relating to the definition of commonality need to be analyzed carefully and a reasonable approach used. The approach should be simple; for example:

- A part is considered common if it is used on more than ten products.
- A part is common if it is used on products in more than one product group.
- A part is common if it is used on products totalling more than 15 percent of production output.

Some companies come up with a complex algorithm to define commonality from a combination of four or five different aspects of commonality. This method is a mistake because few people within the company will understand the commonality factor and fewer still will be able to assess the significance of this commonality. The key here (as with other similar performance measurement definitions) is to pick a simple factor that is clearly relevant to your business and start using it. There will always be inadequacies in the approach; maybe 10 percent of the components do not easily fit into the simple model, but you can begin to make progress on the other 90 percent.

Taiichi Ohno, who led the world in just-in-time manufacturing when he introduced the Toyota production system, has a set of rules that he calls his "25 Doctrines." One of these doctrines is "Don't seek perfection — 60 percent is good enough. Move forward."[7] This adage applies to the selection of commonality criteria.

Reporting Commonality

Reporting commonality is a straightforward method where each component on the part master file is reviewed and the degree of commonality assessed and reported. For analysis purposes, the report should show each part number and its commonality factor. Some companies sort this detailed report by the degree of commonality (for example, number of products using this part) and then apply Pareto analysis (the 80/20 rule) to divide the parts into logical groupings.

Parts that are standard need to be identified. Often identification can be done by recognizing the presence of a supplier's part number on the file; if a supplier's part number is given, then the part is a standard part. If this cannot be used, then a simple flag on the part record can be introduced.

For performance measurement purposes the details are not required. A summary report showing the number of standard, common, and unique parts is ideal. This information may be sorted and totalled by commodity type, production plant, product family, or other logical grouping; but the purpose of the report is to track the success of the efforts being made by the engineers to increase the level of commonality within the company's products.

Number of Different Processes

Measure of process commonality is a similar measure to that of component commonality. The fewer processes involved in the production of a product and in the production of the entire plant, the more flexible the plant can be to customer needs.

There are two levels of reports that are of value: (1) a report that shows the total number of different processes available within the plant and (2) a report that shows the commonality of these processes across the products currently available for production or currently on the master schedule.

These two reports are analogous to the number of different parts report and the component commonality report discussed in the previous two sections. The number of different processes report can be obtained manually by examining the production floor, or it can be produced by reading the production control data base. Some systems hold this information on a separate file of standard processes or the information is embedded within the production routings; either way, this information can be readily accessed and reported in a suitable sequence.

The commonality of process report must be produced by examining the production routings of the finished products and subassemblies. The same problem of definition exists in that a suitable, simple definition of commonality must be determined, and the report must show the degree of commonality that exists within the plant. These reports can be tracked over time and the trends analyzed as the engineering personnel are busy expanding the production commonality on the shop floor.

These reports need to be analyzed closely because the introduction of world class manufacturing techniques frequently makes additional production capacity available within the plant. Many companies take this opportunity to bring in-house processes that were formally subcontracted, or to introduce a wider range of products. When either of these occurs, it is likely that the number of processes will increase rather than decrease, and this is, of course, a benefit to the company.

The purpose of these commonality reports is not to give fixed objectives that must be met by the production managers; the purpose is to monitor the progress of the quest for commonality within the plant. The reports must be used intelligently and as a part of the continuous improvement efforts of the company.

Position of Variability

Most companies attempt to provide customers with as wide a range of products as possible, within the company's sphere of activity. Many companies see a wide product range as being a significant marketing tool because the customers are provided with "one-stop shopping" for the kind of products the company makes.

This policy can be expensive, because the wider the range of products being offered, the more difficult it is to accurately forecast customer requirements. This policy also leads to high finished product safety stocks and disruption on the shop floor caused by last-minute schedule changes and expediting. Manufacturers who make-to-order and have short production lead times will have fewer problems than manufacturers who have production lead times longer than the delivery lead time offered to the customer.

Case study: Three circuit breakers differentiated early in the process A simplified example of position of variability is given in Figure 6-1, which shows the bills of material for three electrical circuit breakers. The three circuit breakers (A1, A2, and A3) are the same except that the identification and safety instructions are in three different languages. The bill of material has five levels and the design of the circuit breakers is such that the identification and safety instructions are molded into the case of the switch at the first stage of manufacture. The final assembly lead time is four weeks which is the same lead time offered to the customers and is competitive for the industry. The production lead time for the entire switch is 12 weeks.

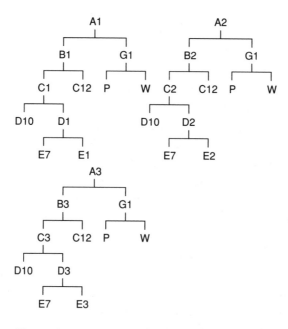

Figure 6-1. Circuit Breaker Bills of Material

Owing to the production lead time being longer than the customer lead time, the company must manufacture subassemblies and components to forecast. In the case of these circuit breakers, the company must forecast subassemblies B1, B2, and B3 separately, and these forecasts drive the production of the unique components C1, C2, C3, D1, D2, D3, E1, E2, and E3.

Demand history indicates that the average demand for this kind of circuit breaker is 50 per week, split into 38 A1s, seven A2s, and five A3s. Variation of the total demand is quite small; the total orders for this kind of circuit breaker has never been more than 55 per week or less than 45 per week; but the variation of mix between A1s, A2s, and A3s is much more marked. The demand for A1 has been as high as 55 and as low as 19; the demand for A2 and A3 has been as high as 20 and as low as zero.

As a result of this analysis, the company has decided to hold subassembly inventories equivalent to the highest possible demand for any of the products, that is, holding 55 B1s, 20 B2s, and 20 B3s. This, in turn, requires holding high inventories of C1, C2, C3, D1, D2, D3, E1, E2, and E3. Thus, the overall policy causes a significant problem of inventory investment because the company has tried to "buy" flexibility by holding large subassembly and component inventories.

But the problem is not solved. When the customers' mix of requirements changes (for example, demand for A2 increases to 25 per week), it will take the company eight weeks to respond to this change, because it takes eight weeks to make B2s from subassemblies C2, D2, and component E2. By the time the increased demand filters through to the manufacture of E2 components, the customers will have experienced significant loss of service and the company's reputation in the marketplace will be damaged.

To worsen the situation further, by the time the company can increase the production of A2s, the customer demand may well have changed and the emphasis moved on to A3s, with the same cycle of shortages, problems, and dissatisfaction.

A long-term solution to this kind of problem is to differentiate the product at the latest possible stage in production, assuming the company cannot significantly improve the production lead times but is able to change the process of production so that the bills of materials look like Figure 6-2. The identification and safety instructions are now printed onto the product as a part of the final assembly. The production of all subassemblies and components is now standard across the three circuit breakers, and the individual products are differentiated in the *final* stage of the production process.

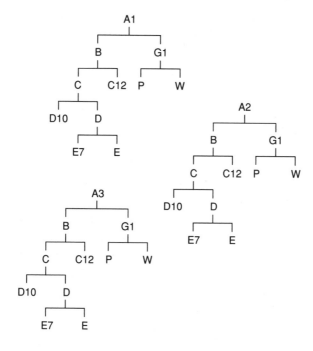

Figure 6-2. Bills of Material with Differentiation at Last Level

The result of this change is an increase in commonality and a significant improvement in flexibility. It does not matter which of the three products the customers order or what the product mix is from week to week; the company can make to order and meet customer needs within the delivery lead time.

Last-minute Differentiation

The example just given is, of course, a simple situation. In reality, the problems facing manufacturers are more convoluted and complex than this, but the principal remains the same. The higher up the production process you can differentiate your products, the more flexible you will be to the needs of the customers.

This method of modular product design has been called "mushroom-shaped" (see Figure 6-3) because a large number of finished products are obtained from a small number of components and assemblies. This approach gives the customers a wide choice, provides flexibility of production mix, and has the added advantage of making it easier and quicker to introduce product enhancements.

Product Enrichment

Another approach to the solution of this problem is to limit the number of finished products available to customers. At first sight, this appears to limit the service offered to the customers, but the opposite can be true if the technique of "product enrichment" is used. The idea is that it is easier and less expensive to manufacture fewer final products; therefore, if you offer a product with more and better features at the same price as an inferior product, then the customer will be more than satisfied and you will have fewer products to make.

An example of this is the techniques used by the Japanese automobile manufacturers when they first penetrated the American and European markets. At that time, most Western auto makers offered a wide range of choice to customers, allowing them to choose from a list of options to meet their needs and their pocketbooks. This policy resulted in the manufacturers having to be able to make thousands of different

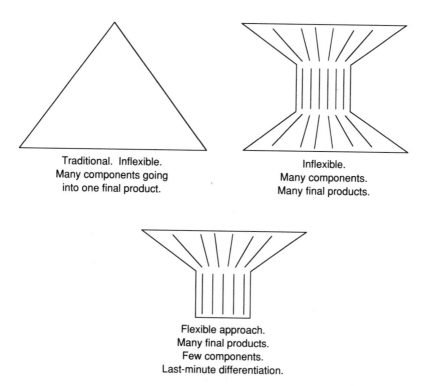

Traditional. Inflexible.
Many components going
into one final product.

Inflexible.
Many components.
Many final products.

Flexible approach.
Many final products.
Few components.
Last-minute differentiation.

Figure 6-3. Product Design Approaches

configurations of the same car, thus causing high cost, unreliable lead times, high inventories, and lower quality.

The Japanese manufacturers offered fewer choices, often just three different versions of a model — standard, deluxe, and luxury. These standard "option packages" resulted in the customer getting more features for less money, and the manufacturer had a much less complex production planning and distribution problem. It is easier and less expensive to fit disk brakes on every car than it is to offer the customer a choice of having disk brakes or conventional brakes.

Measuring Position of Variability

Measuring position of variability is not easy because there can be a large element of judgment involved in determining the position where the variability occurs. The position of variability is determined as the first point in the process at which a unique component is introduced. (The components are designated as unique in the same way as discussed previously in this chapter in the section on the percentage of standard, common, and unique parts.) Position of variability can be measured manually or by producing automated reports.

The simplest method of measuring is to manually review the entire range of finished products and then make a determination where the variability occurs. This position of variability can be expressed in terms of the level on the bill of material or position in the production process. When there are a large number of finished products, it is often possible to perform the analysis by product family rather than by individual product.

When manual analysis is not practical because there are too many products to analyze, there are two methods of producing automated reports. They both rely on reading the entire multilevel bills of material and their related production routings for all the products the company manufactures.

The most straightforward way of presenting this information is to show the position of variability in terms of the level within the bill of material structure where the variability occurs. This information can be shown for each finished product and the average calculated by product family.

A more sophisticated and (in some ways) more precise measure of the position of variability reports variability not at the bill of material level but in terms of the number of days of lead time. For example, if a product takes 12 days to manufacture and the position of variability occurs on day 11, then this can be expressed as a two-day variability.

Reports can be devised that read the exploded bills of material and production routings for all the final products, calculate the lead times of each step within the production process, determine where the first unique component occurs, and then relate the position of variability to the lead time. The report will show each final assembly and the number of days (or hours) for the position of variability.

For performance measurement purposes, the average number of days for the entire product range can be measured. This information is presented graphically to show the change in position of variability as various continuous improvement initiatives are implemented.

The average across the entire product range is the most significant figure, although product family averages can also be important. The factors that affect the position of variability are numerous, and a world class manufacturing company will be looking to decrease the position of variability by a gradual process of continuous improvement as the products and processes are examined and enhanced and as new products are introduced.

Number of Levels in the Bills of Materials

An objective of world class manufacturers is to reduce the number of levels in their bills of materials. Ideally, a product will have just one level, with the product being made from components in a single production process without the need for subassemblies and interim storage of semi-completed product.

The term bill of materials is commonly used in discrete manufacturing, but other industries use terms like recipe, formulation, parts list, and product structure. Whatever term is used, the bill of materials for a product is the list of parts required to make the product and the quantity of each part. The bill of materials often contains a large amount of detailed information about the product and its composition.[8]

The primary purpose of limiting the number of levels in the bill of materials is to reduce inventory and shorten lead times by eliminating subassemblies. Most traditional manufacturers fabricate or purchase components that are held in parts inventory, manufacture subassemblies that are held in WIP inventory, and then make the final assemblies from the subassemblies. A world class manufacturer examines the production process and attempts to simplify and synchronize the process so that subassemblies are no longer necessary.

The ideal is to make to customer order, to make from scratch, and to make the exact quantity required; in this way there is no inventory and there is perfect customer service. In reality, this is rarely the case, even with world class manufacturers, but this is the goal toward which they strive.

The general rule is that the fewer levels within the manufacturing bills of material, the more effective the production process, due to the fact that there will be fewer subassemblies, few transactions, a more flow-style production process, cellular manufacturing with a minimum of movement of materials, and short production cycle times. The measurement of the number of levels within the bills of materials is a good rule of thumb for a world class manufacturer.

Phantom Assemblies

When reducing the number of levels within the bill of materials, it is often useful to retain the multilevel structure of the original bills. There is more clarity to a bill of materials that is structured like a family tree, particularly when the bill is large. A single-level list of parts can be confusing to production and engineering personnel.

To help solve this problem, many companies use "phantom" assemblies — assemblies that exist within the bill of materials to logically group part numbers together. These phantoms are not manufactured as separate subassemblies;

they are used only to provide clarity within the bill of materials structure. When production documents such as pick
lists, pull cards, or kanbans are printed, the phantom assemblies are ignored and just the "real" part numbers shown.
The phantoms are "blown through" to their component
parts. An example of the use of phantom assemblies is given
in Figure 6-4.

DESK LAMP TYPE B62

• **Base Assembly (Phantom)**

• • Base Plate
• • Base Weight
• • Attachment Post (Phantom)

• • • Shaft
• • • Washer
• • • Nut
• • • Collar
• • • Felt Pad

• **Lamp Assembly (Phantom)**

• • Shade
• • Lamp fitting (Phantom)

• • • Insulated Bracket
• • • Bulb Housing
• • • Junction Box
• • • Switch

• • Light Bulb

• **Cantilever Assembly (Phantom)**

• • Cantilever Shaft × 2
• • Cantilever Spring × 4
• • Elbow Joint × 2
• • Base Joint × 2
• • Bolts × 9
• • Washers × 9
• • Nuts × 9

Figure 6-4. Bill of Material with Phantom Assemblies

When components are backflushed as part of the completion transactions within a production planning and inventory control system, phantom assemblies are "blown through" so that transactions are created only for the components themselves.

Engineering Bills of Materials

The requirement for single-level (or flat) bills of materials is for the convenience and efficiency of the manufacturing shop floor. Frequently, the engineering community must view the bills of materials differently from the production personnel. It is useful to have a bill of materials system that allows the manufacturing bills to be different from the engineering bills and yet to keep this information within a single data base.

There are techniques used in some manufacturing control systems that express the same product information in two different ways within the same bill of materials. The bills contain both engineering information and production information. This approach allows bills of materials to be used flexibly without having to duplicate data on different systems with the resultant redundancy and likelihood of error. An example of this kind of dual bills of materials is given in Figure 6-5.

Measurement of the Number of Bill of Materials Levels

The number of bill of materials levels is often an easy figure to measure. A production plant that is laid out in production cells and uses backflushing to report component inventory transactions — the usual case for world class manufacturers — has an assumption of the structure of the bill of material built into the shop floor layout. Typically, a cell relates to a level within the bill and the materials are backflushed as items are completed on each cell.

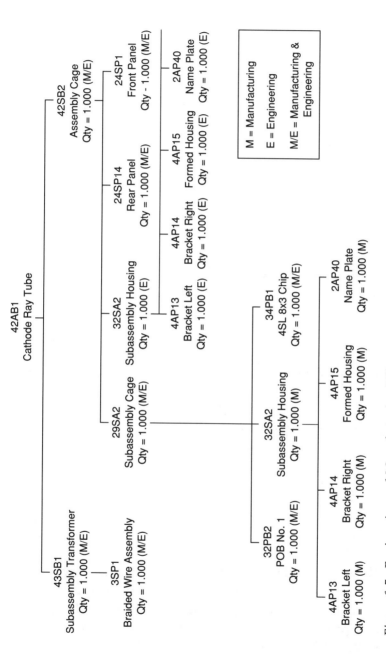

Figure 6-5. Engineering and Manufacturing Bills

For example, if there are three feeder cells supplying a final assembly cell (see Figure 6-6), then the products have a two-level bill of materials (the top level is the final assembly, the lower level is the subassemblies from the feeder cells). A production plant with a single flow line that converts the raw material and components into the finished product in one continuous process typically will have a one-level bill of materials.

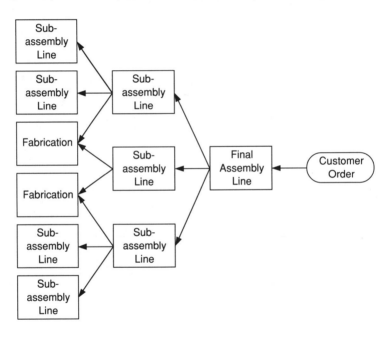

Figure 6-6. Three-level Production Layout

With a focused or specialist plant it is usually easy to determine the number of levels within the bill of materials. When a plant manufactures a wider range of products and has a variety of production process configurations, it is then a more complex task to identify the number of levels within the bills of materials.

Some plants, particularly those which are in the process of introducing just-in-time manufacturing techniques, have production processes that combine elements of both synchronized manufacturing and job shop manufacturing. This so-called "mixed mode" manufacturing can make it difficult to determine the number of levels within the bills of materials. Often during this transition process, this measure is of most significance because it is a good yardstick to measure the aggregate success of the many changes taking place on the shop floor.

The way to measure the number of levels is to have a report that searches the production bills of materials used within the manufacturing control system to determine how many subassemblies have been established within each product. This number of levels is then associated with the products in the master production schedule (either the future master schedule or actual production in the previous week, month, or day). From this, the average number of levels is calculated within the bill of material. Occasionally, it is useful to show this average separately for each product group, but products tend to be grouped by similar production processes and, therefore, have the same number of bill of materials levels.

The ability of a report like this to define accurately and unambiguously the number of levels for a product frequently requires that the bills of materials be structured in a specific way using prescribed standards. It is often necessary to use codes or flags within the bill of materials file or the product master file to identify subassemblies that are built and stocked, as opposed to those that are merely interim items within the process.

The end result of this process is a report (manually or automatically produced) that provides a very practical and pertinent measure of the effectiveness of the changes taking place within the production plant.

New Product Introductions

That companies vie with their competitors to be the first with an innovative new product is a fact of modern industrial life. As the rate of technological advance increases and as competition between domestic and foreign companies heats up, it becomes increasingly important to be able to bring new and improved products to the market quickly. Many world class manufacturing companies have set clear targets for improving the speed and quantity of new product introduction, often incorporating these objectives into the manufacturing strategy.

Many aspects of world class manufacturing lend themselves to the fast and effective introduction of new products or to the enhancement of existing products. The introduction and use of just-in-time manufacturing techniques requires a detailed understanding and analysis of the production process. The examination and perfecting of the production process provides a detailed level of understanding to the engineering and production personnel, enabling them to implement product enhancements quickly and effectively.

The stress placed by world class manufacturers on the education and involvement of all production personnel in the quest for perfection invariably results in a large number of suggestions coming from the work force. These suggestions can frequently result in innovative enhancements to the products or ideas for entirely new products. The introduction of new or improved products is greatly helped when the production personnel are so involved and committed.

A lesson that has been learned from some of the Japanese companies that pioneered just-in-time manufacturing techniques in the 1970s and 1980s is that product enhancement is better managed when there are many small improvements, rather than the traditional Western approach of large major releases or new "model years." The ideas of continuous improvement are just as valid and successful for the introduction of new products and improvements as they are for the elimination of quality and production problems. In order to be able to make a large number of small improvements, it is essential that the production process be under control, that the production personnel can be trained rapidly, that pilot production can be introduced effectively, and that the improvements can be slotted into the production schedules with a minimum of disruption. The reason traditional companies prefer large releases is that they do not have effective control of the production process and are not able to effectively manage a large number of small releases.

The short cycle times enjoyed by world class manufacturers enable them to introduce new products more quickly. If a product takes 12 weeks to manufacture, it will take a minimum of 12 weeks to change over to a new or improved product. If the cycle time is four days, then it takes only four days to introduce the new product.

The lack of inventory (both component and work-in-process) significantly helps with the introduction of new products because there is no need to delay introductions while excess inventories of old components and subassemblies are used up. In addition, the orderly nature of a just-in-time production plant eases the introduction of product enhancements because changes can be introduced in a more orderly manner.

Measuring New Product Introductions

There are two basic ways of measuring new product introductions: (1) measuring the speed of introduction and (2) measuring the number of new products over a time period. The speed of introduction or "time-to-market" is a measure of the company's effectiveness at converting ideas into products. This process can be measured simply by keeping track of when a project was initiated and when it was completed and the new product launched onto the market. The time-to-market is the time taken from initiation to completion.

When a company has a formal suggestion system — as most world class manufacturers do — then the date of the original suggestion is logged and the progress of the suggestion tracked. The time-to-market can be established for all those suggestions related to new products or product enhancements that are accepted and implemented.

There is often a need to categorize the kinds of product changes and measure the time-to-market separately for each category. These categories can simply be *minor, moderate,* and *major* enhancement. The categories can be assigned by the judgment of either an engineer or production manager — or they can be defined strictly in terms of the number of component changes, number of changes to the production process, number of changes to the marketing process, and so forth.

Measurement of the time-to-market for a significant new product does not need to be done on a weekly or monthly basis because there are relatively few introductions of this kind. In the case of an industry like automotive, the time-to-market is measured in years. Remarkable improvements have been achieved by such companies as the Chrysler Corporation, which in recent years has been able to halve its time-to-market for the design and manufacture of an entirely new automobile.

Another method of measuring new product introduction that is useful in some industries is to measure the number of new products (or enhancements) introduced each year. This is a measure of the amount of innovation taking place within the company as well as the company's ability to bring those innovations to the market.

The number of new products can be easily measured by merely keeping track of a new product release and counting how many releases occur within the time frame. Again, it is often useful to categorize these improvements according to their size and complexity. In addition, it is sometimes useful to differentiate the source of the innovation — employee suggestion, customer suggestion, engineering enhancement, and so on.

When the number of enhancements is very large, it can be useful to have a report that reads the bill of materials for finished products and identifies the date of introduction (effectivity date) of new revisions. These reports can then be sorted and counted. The bill of materials revision can have a category associated with it so that the report can show the number of changes by category.

Cross-training

The ability to have production personnel move from one task to another is a key ingredient of production flexibility. As the volume and mix of products ordered by the customers change, a sure sign of a flexible manufacturer is that the production personnel are able to adapt quickly to changes.

A measure of the flexibility of the operations personnel is a good measure of the flexibility of the production plant. In order to measure cross-training and to use it in practice, it is necessary to have good methods of assessing which people can do which jobs. In most companies this implementation requires a formal training and certification process. Each production skill is analyzed, and all people within the plant are certified to do the tasks for which they have the relevant skills and experience. In order to actively pursue cross-training, it is necessary to implement a training and experience program within the plant. The objective here is to maximize the degree of cross-training among the work force both by formal training and by giving people experience within the plant at doing new tasks. Once a person is trained in a new skill, that person must be given the opportunity to exercise that skill on a regular basis. There are two measures that are valuable: (1) the degree of cross-training within the plant and (2) the average number of tasks performed by each individual. The degree of cross-training within the plant can be measured by adding up all the numbers of tasks all people are certified to perform and dividing by the number of people. This figure will give the average amount of cross-training among the production personnel.

The average number of tasks *performed* is a better measure, but it is more difficult to capture the information. To have people certified to perform certain tasks is not of much value if they do not do those tasks on a regular basis. They cannot be considered cross-trained just by having attended a training session; they have to use their training regularly in order to be truly valuable to the plant's flexibility. This situation is like a pilot's license; in order to renew a pilot's license, the pilot has to prove that he or she has flown a certain number of hours over the previous 12 months. Pilots cannot be considered competent unless they are "in practice."

Measure of tasks requires that detailed records are kept of who performed which tasks each day, and the number of different tasks performed by each individual each week can be added up. The average number of different tasks performed by the production personnel is a good measure of how flexible the people really are.

J. Sainsbury, the British supermarket chain, has a planned policy of cross-training. Each branch employee is gradually trained in the various tasks required, including shelf stacking; meat trimming; preparation of produce; packing of cheese, butter, and cold meats; cash register; reordering; customer service tasks; back office tasks; and others. Each branch has a large board showing the branch personnel and their trained tasks; the daily activities within the branch are also shown on the board. People are allocated to daily tasks based upon their skill set and to ensure that their skills in each task are exercised on a regular basis. Colored strips are used to annotate who has worked on which tasks when and to identify which tasks each person is trained to perform.

J. Sainsbury, and many other companies, compensate their employees according to the number of skills they are cross-trained to perform. There are some difficulties with this criterion; it requires that the tasks are clearly identifiable and that each new task is of equal difficulty and importance as another. But these kinds of problems can be overcome and in some instances provide a good way to motivate people to accept cross-training as a natural part of their working life.

Output Compared To Capacity

Any company — in order to be flexible to significant changes in production volume — must have more capacity than demand. In contrast to a traditional manufacturer who is always striving to reach high levels of plant utilization, a world class manufacturer would always want the plant to have spare capacity so that changes in customer demands can be more easily accommodated.

The measurement of capacity can be quite complex because capacity can often be difficult to define without having a predetermined product mix, but most companies define capacity in terms of production hours (if there is a wide range of products made) or output per day (if the products are more homogeneous). A report of capacity against output shows the total number of standard hours of product manufactured during the previous week or month, compared with the total available hours of capacity. The ratio of output and capacity is expressed as a percentage.

In most manufacturing plants the capacity is not fixed, and there can always be some variation based upon overtime or utilization of the production personnel. In the reporting of capacity against output, it is common for capacity to be stated in terms of the average capacity and the maximum capacity, and the output ratio is calculated for both capacities. These ratios are then plotted on graphs.

Summary

The key areas of interest for world class manufacturers for the measurement of production flexibility are:

- the number of different parts in the bills of materials
- the percentage of standard, common, and unique parts within the bills of materials
- the number of different production processes
- the position within the production process where the products are differentiated
- the number of levels in the manufacturing bill of materials
- the number of new products launched each year and the time taken to launch them
- the cross-training of production personnel
- comparison of production output and production capacity

CHAPTER SEVEN

Measurement of
Quality Performance

T O SAY THAT QUALITY is an important aspect of world class manufacturing is a ludicrous understatement. Some experts contend that quality is the *only* important aspect of world class manufacturing — that all the other techniques are merely the application of the ideas of total quality control.

The success of many major Japanese companies truly is rooted in their long-term commitment to the improvement of quality. These companies learned the fundamentals of quality control in the 1950s and 1960s (many of them from Dr. W. Edwards Deming, the American consultant and educator) and applied them with considerable success during the 1970s and 1980s. The techniques taught by Dr. Deming and others provide no "quick fixes" for the improvement of quality because they stress that quality is improved by the long-term application of a philosophy of continuous improvement.

Dr. Deming has asserted repeatedly that only a small number of quality problems (less than 15 percent) are caused by production personnel; the rest are caused by the company's managers. If the problem of quality is to be addressed seriously, it must be tackled across the entire company and be given the highest priority.

Definition of Quality

There are several approaches to the definition of quality. Philip Crosby, in his popular book *Quality Is Free*,[1] asserts that quality is "conformance to requirements." Does the product, part, or service do what it is supposed to do? If it does not, then there is a quality problem. Another pioneer in this field, J.M. Juran, takes a different view.[2] Dr. Juran's definition of quality centers around "fitness for use," does the product perform according to the requirements of the user? Robert W. Grenier takes the view that quality can only be defined in terms of customer satisfaction; "customer satisfaction must be the goal that drives the total quality assurance system."[3]

Within the context of manufacturing, the definition of quality would include the following factors:

- *Form.* All dimensions, appearance, and configuration of manufactured product must meet prescribed requirements.
- *Fit.* The features of the product must be applicable to its use, including proper function, interchangeability, consistent geometry, and so forth.
- *Function.* The product performs as it is designed to and meets customer application.
- *Reliability.* The product item functions according to expectations over a reasonable lifetime. The probability of its functioning for a long time is high.
- *Consistency.* Every product has the same properties, functions, and performance. Customers can expect consistent service from each product.

Improvement of Quality

The improvement of production quality is a long-term commitment to continuous improvement in every aspect of the production process. A world class manufacturing approach demands that quality must be designed into the product and the production process, rather than an attempt to remove poor quality by inspection.

The objective of quality assurance within a world class manufacturing environment is not to just reject defective products, but to systematically investigate the causes of defects so that they can be gradually eliminated. The goal is zero defects; the method is continuous improvement.

Quality Through Design

Estimates are that about 40 percent of quality problems on the shop floor are caused by inadequate design. There is a tendency within traditional manufacturers to divorce design engineering from production engineering. Frequently, design is done in a separate building (sometimes miles away from the factory) and the needs of the production plants are not taken into account during the design phase of the product.

World class manufacturers take the opposite approach by having the design engineers very much involved with the production process. Often there is no distinction made between design and production engineering, and the engineers are physically located adjacent to the shop floor. Design projects are performed by project teams consisting of personnel from each area of the company — engineering, marketing, and production. This method has the effect of breaking down the barriers caused by the strict departmentalization of traditional manufacturers.

Vendor Quality

Another prime cause of quality problems is the quality of raw materials and components from suppliers. A traditional approach to this problem is 100-percent inspection of incoming materials, holding additional inventory to cover for rejects, and castigating the vendors every time a quality problem occurs.

A world class manufacturing approach is to work very closely with vendors to solve problems that cause poor quality, to reduce the number of vendors by single-sourcing all materials, and to certify the suppliers so that items can be delivered directly to the shop floor without the need for incoming inspection. The objective is that there should be zero rejects of components and materials because the supplier's quality is assured.

Many world class manufacturers insist that the suppliers themselves introduce world class production techniques. Instead of inspecting the materials as they are delivered, these companies require the vendor to show evidence of the statistical process control of the manufacture of the product.

The Velcro Company came across this problem when General Motors told them that they would no longer be a certified supplier if they did not improve their quality. The irony was that Velcro had always delivered on time. There had never been a quality problem with the products they delivered to GM because GM products were 100 percent inspected prior to dispatch and any defective material was eliminated. General Motors required Velcro to implement world class manufacturing techniques so that 100-percent inspection was not necessary because reject rates were close to zero.[4]

Production Quality

Quality problems caused on the production floor are addressed by world class manufacturers by changing the roles of the shop floor operators. The responsibility for quality is given to everybody within the plant. Inspection (or quality assurance) is built into every stage of production, with the shop floor operators being given the training and equipment required to assure the quality of their own work. Quality problems are identified quickly, the cause of the problem investigated, and the problem solved there and then on the shop floor.

Workplace organization A series of techniques used by many world class manufacturers helps to gradually eliminate quality problems of the shop floor. There are changes to the shop floor itself so that an orderly, disciplined environment is provided. This kind of environment lends itself to the improvement of quality.

Workplace organization improvements include organizing the workplace, giving every tool, gauge, and instrument a specific place, and removing unneeded materials, supplies, and personal items. The layout of the workplace should locate frequently used items in convenient places, mark tools and gauges with easy identification, and create a disciplined environment where items are returned immediately after use. Visible signals (such as lights, schedules, chalkboards, and color codes) and the posting of colored photographs of the products in each work cell so that operators can see how to make the item correctly are also techniques that add up to an environment of orderliness and control.

The physical layout of the shop floor, often using U-shaped lines and production cells to simplify the shop floor, aids communication and provides good visibility. Establishing an atmosphere where everyone works by the rules, as well as keeping the workplace tidy and effective, creates a working environment conducive to the production of high quality products.

Statistical process control Another technique widely used in the implementation of total quality assurance within production is statistical process control (SPC). The purpose here is to gain control of the process by continuously measuring and analyzing the quality of the product at each stage in the production process. SPC will be discussed more fully later in this chapter.

Preventive Maintenance

Preventive maintenance is important in a world class manufacturing environment because machines and equipment used within the plant *must* always be in good condition. It is not good enough to wait until the machine breaks down before it is repaired. World class manufacturers frequently give the operators on the shop floor the prime responsibility for the preventive maintenance of their own machines; maintenance engineers are available to assist the operators and to perform the more specialist tasks. A planned and systematic preventive maintenance program can improve quality significantly, reduce down time, and extend machine life.

Quality Circles

Quality circles have commanded considerable attention in companies committed to world class manufacturing. The purpose of quality circles (sometimes called participation groups) is to bring together a team of people from diverse departments within the company and have them collectively apply their skills to the resolution of quality problems. A quality circle will meet regularly — at least once per week — and review the latest information about quality in their area of concern. Quality circle members will study the results of such things as statistical process control charts and will implement programs to gradually eliminate the problems causing production defects.

Implementing Quality Improvement and
Measuring Quality Performance

The starting point for implementing quality improvement is performance measurement. It is not possible to understand quality performance without measuring it. But merely measuring quality does not improve it; the measurement must be part of a systematic quality improvement methodology. In one system, Dr. Deming has characterized his methodology as the *Deming Circle* consisting of four steps: Plan, Do, Check, Action.

1. *Plan* the quality improvement changes that are needed, set specific targets for improvement, and determine what has to be done to bring these changes into being.
2. *Do* the tasks you have just planned.
3. *Check* the effect of the changes you have implemented. At this point, effective performance measurement comes into the picture. It is important to be able to monitor clearly how the actions you have taken have affected the process.
4. Finally, put the new methods into *Action* by standardizing the new methods into permanent practice. This step is essential. It is easy to see improvement when the process being examined is in the limelight, but if the improvements are to continue, they must become part of the standard operating procedures.

It is not the purpose of this book to give a detailed explanation of how total quality control or total quality assurance can be implemented; many other books do this. The purpose is to examine performance measurement as it relates to world class manufacturing. The remainder of this chapter will examine the measurement of quality performance. There are five aspects of quality performance that need to be addressed — vendor quality, production quality, data quality, preventive maintenance, and the cost of quality.

Vendor Quality Performance

Vendor performance consists of two primary features: (1) delivery performance and (2) quality performance. The measurement of vendor delivery performance was discussed in Chapter 4 and we now turn our attention to vendor quality.

Traditional manufacturers attempt to ensure the quality of incoming materials and components by performing inspections. Every plant has a team of people called goods inward inspection, purchase quality assurance, or some such title. These people inspect the materials coming in from vendors and make sure they conform to the specification outlined in the purchase order. In contrast, world class manufacturers are looking for vendors to become long-term partners who will provide zero defects and on-time deliveries. For this goal to be achieved, a number of things have to be in place, including single-sourcing, relationships based on mutual trust, sharing of information, and certification.

Most WCM companies have a policy of single-sourcing purchased components and materials. The purpose is to lessen the number of vendors the company has to deal with; because it is not possible to have close cooperative relationships with thousands of vendors, it is necessary to deal with relatively few vendors. In addition, single-sourcing means that the vendors receive larger orders from the company and are therefore more able (and inclined) to meet the stringent needs of just-in-time deliveries and 100-percent quality.

The world class manufacturer will typically share information freely with vendors. This information includes future production plans, engineering information, forecasts, costs, new product plans, and so forth. In return, the vendor is expected to provide the company with additional information about their own production process, quality procedures, costs, and future plans.

Measurement of quality performance is a critical aspect of the relationship between the vendor and the company. The objective is 100-percent quality (zero defects) and a minimum of inspection. A world class manufacturer is typically very concerned about value-added and non-value-added activities; procedures are changed so that more time and attention is given to value-added activities and less time given to non-value-added activities. The inspection of incoming materials is a non-value-added activity and does not improve the product or make it more valuable to the customer. It is done merely to identify shortcomings and mistakes on the part of the vendor.

As these ideas of vendor relationships and quality are introduced within a company striving for world class status, the needs of incoming quality measurement change. Initially, the company will want to continue to perform 100-percent inspection of incoming material, but as the quality program progresses and supplier companies become certified, it is no longer necessary to inspect everything — and sample inspection becomes the normal method. This sample inspection is used to validate the certification of the supplier and to ensure conformance.

As the vendor quality program progresses further, the need for sample testing becomes less important because the company requires the certified vendors to be using statistical process control (or other quality measurement techniques) and to report the results of the SPC with each delivery of materials. The company can then ensure vendor quality by reviewing the SPC charts supplied with the goods. This way quality can be verified without the need for further physical inspection.

Measuring Incoming Quality

The measurement of incoming quality is quite straightforward; the materials and components received from suppliers are inspected according to the specifications given in the purchase order. The number of rejects is counted and reported.

The frequency of inspections is determined by the vendor's certification status. Uncertified vendors will receive a significant amount of inspection, perhaps 100-percent inspection. Fully certified vendors will receive no incoming inspection at all, except for the ongoing monitoring of their certification status.

Most companies institute a certification verification procedure that will require detailed inspection of incoming materials from vendors on a monthly, quarterly, or semiannual basis. If a company is fully certified, the review of certification may be semiannual, in which case every six months the incoming products over one day or one week from that vendor will receive a thorough inspection and the reject rates recorded. A newly certified vendor or a vendor whose products have caused a quality problem in the plant may be inspected thoroughly one day per week. Semi-certified vendors may be inspected monthly.

The frequency and method of inspection for certified, semi-certified, and uncertified vendors will vary from one company to the next and will be different for different kinds of products supplied. The certification review process also includes analysis of delivery reliability (see Chapter 4), flexibility (see Chapter 6), the production process, and the supplier's financial stability and business strategy.

An example of an incoming quality report is shown in Figure 7-1, and a vendor performance summary report is shown in Figure 7-2. The vendor performance report combines both delivery performance and quality performance into a single report. This report, usually summarized over a monthly period, is useful for providing a more thorough analysis of the vendor's performance. Many companies send a copy of this report to the vendors each month and take this as an opportunity to discuss changes, problems, and improvements with their suppliers.

Supplier Quality Lots												
Supplier	1	2	3	4	5	6	7	8	9	10	11	12
Kent Moor												
Killeen Machine	█											
Klock Corp.												
LaPresicion	4	4	█									
Laser												
Laurel Manuf.												
Lea Manuf.												
Lindco												
Lucas, Joseph												
M & L Prods.												
Maclean-Fogg	2	█	█	█	█	█						
Magnetic												
McQuay Norris												
Metalcraft, H. K.												
Microfin Co.												
Milford Rivet												

Figure 7-1. Incoming Quality Chart

Manual Methods of Reporting Incoming Inspection

The simplest manual method of reporting incoming quality is to keep track of the number of deliveries (or lots) rejected at inspection. This recording can be done by using a list of the expected deliveries each day from each supplier and then marking the quantity accepted and the quantity rejected. This information is then collated and graphed to provide a measure of total supplier quality and to show the trends in quality performance of individual suppliers.

UNITRONIX CORP - PRAXA SYSTEMS

VENDOR DELIVERY PERFORMANCE SUMMARY

PAGE 2
30-NOV-1990

CO	BR	VENDOR	AVERAGE VARIANCE	% LATE	% EARLY	% ON-TIME	LINES REC'D	LINES LATE	LINES EARLY	LINES REJECTED	QUALITY PERCENT
01	01	00100 FRANKLIN SUPPLY	0.1200	65.15	31.82	3.03	132	86	42	12	90.9
01	01	00200 GREENLEY & STUBBS	0.0720	3.33	51.67	45.00	120	4	62	6	95.0
01	01	00300 ARKLAND COMPANY	0.0500	60.20	39.80	0.00	98	59	39	0	100.0
01	01	00400 SETTLESON INC.	0.3500	43.23	37.41	19.36	155	67	58	15	90.3
01	01	00750 BEST-TECH	0.1100	21.95	17.07	60.98	82	18	14	1	98.8
01	01	00850 EECI	0.0667	13.00	13.90	73.10	223	28	31	7	96.9
01	01	EAST BANK PLANT	0.2618	32.34	29.14	38.52	810	262	236	41	94.9

Figure 7-2. Vendor Performance Summary Report

A more visual method of tracking vendor quality is the use of a vendor quality chart. This more graphic method shows the rejects against specific suppliers. Figure 7-3 gives an example of a vendor quality chart. When a delivery is made with no defects, the inspector shades the first available square in the supplier's row. If there are any defects, a code is written in the next square. This code can show the percentage rejected, or it can be a code showing the reason for the rejection (or some other simple and meaningful coding system). This chart can be drawn on paper or it can be a large chart fixed to the wall in the receiving department.

Reject information is then summarized and used to analyze changes in supplier quality performance and to discuss quality issues with the supplier. A supplier quality graph is shown in Figure 7-4.

Quality and Certified Vendors

Ideally, their materials and components can be delivered directly to the shop floor from the vendor's plant. Certified vendors are subject to a systematic certification verification process whereby their products are inspected at regular time intervals to ensure that there is no change in quality.

A frequently used method of ensuring the continued quality of certified vendors is to inspect the vendor's quality control information for the delivered batches of material. The vendor is required to ship quality control documentation with each delivery. This documentation (usually SPC charts) enables the customer to review the SPC criteria used by the supplier and to verify that the batches of material or components received meet the SPC criteria.

It is possible to track and report the number of rejects based upon the supplied SPC information. Few companies find this necessary because certified suppliers who are effectively using SPC (and other quality control methods) have very few rejects after shipment.

```
                    VENDOR QUALITY REPORT              PAGE 6
                                                30-SEPT-1990

VENDOR:  2162     ALCOTT ENGINEERING, MARLBORO, MA
BUYER:   JLT      JOHN TERTELLI

ITEM:  196-18-001A     FORMED HOUSING

 DATE          QTY. RECD. QTY. INSP. QTY. GOOD  QUALITY %
9-12-90           120         10        120       100.0
9-15-90           120         10        120       100.0
9-24-90           100        100         87        87.0
9-29-90           120         10        120       100.0

196-18-001A       460        130        447        97.2%

ITEM:  196-18-007B     FORMED HOUSING

 DATE          QTY. RECD. QTY. INSP. QTY. GOOD  QUALITY %
9-02-90          1010         25       1010       100.0
9-04-90          1010         25       1010       100.0
9-06-90          1010         25       1010       100.0
9-08-90          1010         25       1010       100.0
9-10-90          1200       1200          0         0.0
9-12-90          1200       1200        720        60.0
9-14-90          1200       1200        800        66.7
9-16-90          1200       1200       1200       100.0
9-18-90          1200       1200       1200       100.0
9-20-90          1200        200       1200       100.0
9-22-90          1000         50       1000       100.0
9-24-90          1000       1000        420        42.0
9-28-90          1000       1000       1000       100.0

196-18-007B     14240       8350      11580        81.3%

    2162        14700       8400      12027        81.8%
```

Figure 7-3. Vendor Quality Report

Production Quality

World class manufacturers do not try to improve the quality of their products by increasing the number of quality inspections; instead, they attempt to gain control of the production

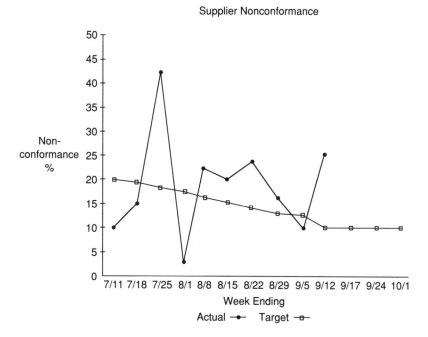

Figure 7-4. Total Supplier Quality Graph

process so that variances can be reduced to the point where every part is made perfect every time. The goal is perfection. Gaining control of the production process requires methods for measuring the variations and identifying how these variables can be reduced or eliminated.

Statistical Process Control

Statistical process control (SPC) is one method widely used for measuring, identifying, and reducing variations in the production process. SPC is a simple and effective tool for continuously monitoring the process and calculating the average (mean) performance.

For instance, a certain performance may be actual length of a metal bar. The product design may require a 42cm bar, and numerous measures yield an average length of 42.07cm. The spread of acceptable lengths can be determined by statistical analysis or design specification — for example, 41.91 to 42.09 cm. Appropriate measurement tools are made available to the production personnel, who are trained how and when to make the required measurements. The measurements are plotted on an X-bar chart (see Figure 7-5) by the operator, who can now use the results to identify, investigate, and correct any excessive deviations or trends as they occur.

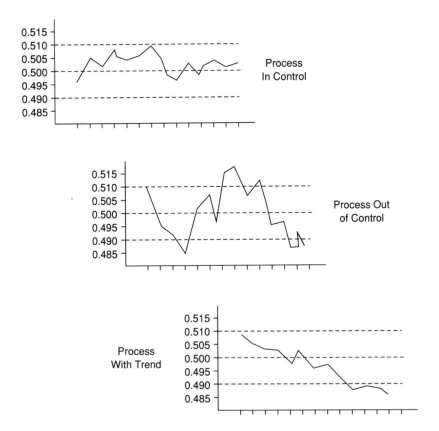

Figure 7-5. Statistical Process Control Charts

SPC and Continuous Improvement

Not only do SPC charts display the accuracy of the process, they also provide a simple method for measuring the success of improvements and changes to the process as they are made. For example, the current variation of the bar length may be +/– 0.04cm. As quality requirements improve, this variation may no longer be acceptable, and steps are taken to reduce the variation to +/– 0.02cm. These improvements may be made by changing the manufacturing procedures, by retooling the machine, by upgrading the materials used, by retraining the operators, or by some other method. The SPC chart will continuously show the effect of these changes.

Statistical process control enables operators to monitor the quality of product during the production process and to detect deviations *as they occur.* The traditional approach to quality inspection is to inspect product *after* the product is made. This after-the-fact procedure frequently allows apparently minor deviations to be overlooked and will result in an excessive quantity of waste and unnecessary labor, as there is nothing to do except scrap or rework the product. Even when the variations are discovered, the product could have already gone to the customer. The final result is an unhappy customer, lost sales, and expensive repairs.

Statistical process control allows quality problems to be identified and corrected continuously throughout the process by the production operators. Rather than depending upon inspection to identify defective completed product, SPC ensures that quality is manufactured into the product.

Determining Sample Sizes and Upper/Lower Limits

The determination of sample sizes and the calculation of the upper and lower limits drawn on the charts is an important part of SPC. Here the statistical element of SPC comes into play. There has been much theoretical work done on the calculation of "correct" sample sizing and setting of upper and lower limits.[5]

This complex and subtle science is definitely the realm of statisticians and specialists. However, it is not necessary in the early stages of the implementation of SPC to get too involved in the finer points of the statistical analysis. SPC is based upon quite simple calculations of means, standard deviations, and acceptable variations. The choice of upper and lower limits can be made from engineering requirements and pragmatic assessments of past performance. Typically, a process consistently producing parts within three standard deviations of the mean is considered in a state of statistical control.

The important issue to remember within world class manufacturing is that the purpose for using SPC is to facilitate improvement. Many companies have implemented SPC for the purpose of monitoring quality but have not used the technique as a guide for continuous improvement. Without continuous improvement, SPC is a fruitless exercise.

Demos Control Charts

A criticism of statistical process control is that its concentration is on the individual operation or process; that there is no way to aggregate the SPC information so that it can be used as a measure of the total production process. A second criticism of SPC is that it is good at handling a single variable (like the width of a hole) but does not lend itself to a production process requiring a large number of quality criteria.

There have been a number of methods devised to overcome these weaknesses. Many of these methods are specific to a particular company or process, but the Demos control chart method is becoming accepted as a widely applicable extension of SPC. The purpose of Demos control charts is to measure typical SPC information and to organize the attributes and variable quality data into an integrated plant-wide SPC chart system.

A good example of the use of Demos charts is in the Wilson Sporting Goods plant in Humboldt, Tennessee.[6] The plant makes golf balls and Wilson managers were primarily concerned about rejects at each stage in the process. The process consists of primary operations including molding, grinding, injection molding, stamping, painting, and packing. The control charts provide detailed SPC information at each stage in the process, and that information is then aggregated up through a hierarchy of control charts for each level of management, culminating in a control chart for the top manager. From this single control chart the plant manager can effectively administer the entire production program. This hierarchy of control information enables each level of managers to actively manage the plant's production quality.

These charts identify when and where the process goes out of control and also identify improvements and other trends in the process. The charts also show where corrective action is needed.

An example of the top manager's control chart is shown in Figure 7-6. The upper part of the chart looks like an SPC X-bar chart and shows the average reject percentage and its upper and lower limits. In the lower part of the chart this information is broken down into the seven production steps. Each of the steps has an average reject rate (shown in the first column) and the actual reject rate is plotted for each day's production. When the reject rate exceeds the upper limit, it is boxed in red; if the reject rate falls below the lower limit, it is circled in green. For example, the plant-wide reject rate exceeded the upper limit on May 18th by reaching 6.5 percent (upper limit is 6.4 percent); this reject rate was caused by a 3.1-percent reject rate in injection molding (which is also boxed in red). From May 20th onward, the plant-wide reject rates are circled in green because they are all below the lower limit of 5.4 percent.

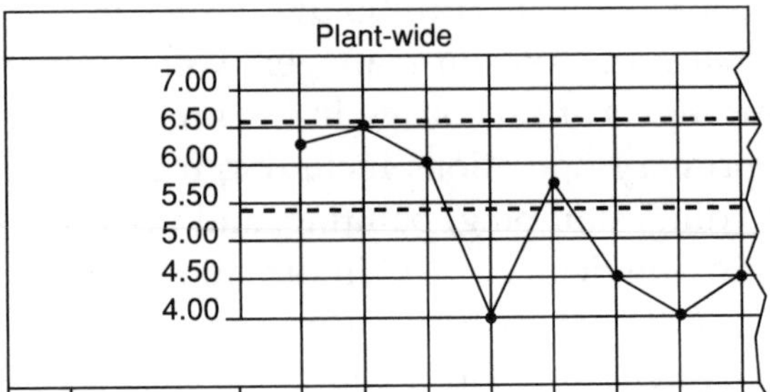

p%	Operations	17	18	19	20	21	22	23	24
.1	Mill/Barwell	.1	.1	.0	.1	.0	.1	.1	.1
.1	Core Mold	.0	.0	.1	.0	.0	.1	.1	.0
.6	Core Grind	1.1	1.0	1.0	.9	2.0	1.6	1.0	1.2
2.6	Inj. Mold	2.6	3.1	3.0	1.5	2.3	1.2	1.5	1.7
.5	Surlyn	.6	.6	.2	.3	.4	.2	.1	.4
1.4	Stamp	1.0	1.3	1.0	.4	.6	.9	.9	.5
5.9	Total	6.3	6.5	5.9	3.9	5.8	4.5	4.0	4.4

Source: Reprinted, with permission of APICS, from Allan F. Scott, "SPC for Continuous Quality Improvement," APICS International Conference Proceedings 1989, p.442.

Figure 7-6. Top Manager's Control Chart

Figure 7-7 shows one of the control charts which provided information for the plant manager's control chart; it shows the reject rates in the injection molding department. The reject rates are broken down to show the rate by shift. It can be seen that shifts 1 and 3 were in control on May 18th, but shift 2 was out of control and was largely responsible for the overall reject rate of 3.1 percent.

Figure 7-8 shows the detailed control chart for the injection molding department on shift 2. The overall reject rate of 3.5 percent on shift 2 on May 18th is made up of rejects from 17

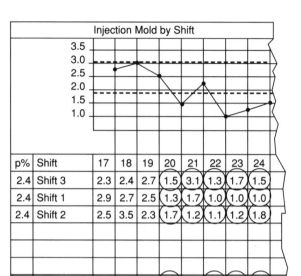

p%	Shift	17	18	19	20	21	22	23	24
2.4	Shift 3	2.3	2.4	2.7	1.5	3.1	1.3	1.7	1.5
2.4	Shift 1	2.9	2.7	2.5	1.3	1.7	1.0	1.0	1.0
2.4	Shift 2	2.5	3.5	2.3	1.7	1.2	1.1	1.2	1.8
2.4		2.6	2.9	2.5	1.5	2.0	1.1	1.3	1.5

Source: Reprinted, with permission of APICS, from Allan F. Scott, "SPC for Continuous Quality Improvement," APICS International Conference Proceedings 1989, p. 442.

Figure 7-7. Injection Molding Control Chart

different presses. The reject rate from each press is monitored, and the red box and green circles show which presses are above limit and which are below limit. This information shows which presses are responsible for the poor reject rate and also shows that corrective action was taken to alleviate the problem.

The end result of this method of statistical process control is that it investigates and monitors not only the quality of specific production points but summarizes this information into management control charts, thus allowing the company managers to effectively control the production process. Wilson Sporting Goods was able, using this method, to gain a 67-percent improvement in production quality over a one-year period.

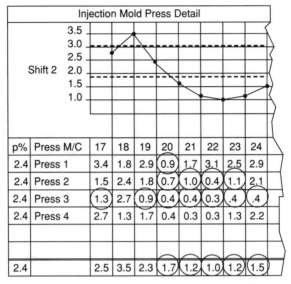

p%	Press M/C	17	18	19	20	21	22	23	24
2.4	Press 1	3.4	1.8	2.9	0.9	1.7	3.1	2.5	2.9
2.4	Press 2	1.5	2.4	1.8	0.7	1.0	0.4	1.1	2.1
2.4	Press 3	1.3	2.7	0.9	0.4	0.4	0.3	.4	.4
2.4	Press 4	2.7	1.3	1.7	0.4	0.3	0.3	1.3	2.2
2.4			2.5	3.5	2.3	1.7	1.2	1.0	1.2	1.5

Source: Reprinted, with permission of APICS, from Allan F. Scott, "SPC for
Continuous Quality Improvement," APICS International Conference
Proceedings 1989, p.442.

Figure 7-8. Injection Molding Detail Chart

Control Charts for Multi-variation Processes

Most quality problems have more than one cause. In some cases it is necessary to identify the individual causes of quality problems and track them separately. Many world class manufacturers use Pareto analysis (the 80/20 rule) to determine which causes are most significant and then record the defects by cause for the process. A Demos control chart is also useful in this kind of situation.

Figure 7-9 shows a typical control chart for a screw machine department.[7] The upper part of the chart shows the total defects and identifies which days are above the upper limit by boxing in red; the days when rejects are below the lower limit are circled in green. The lower part of the chart

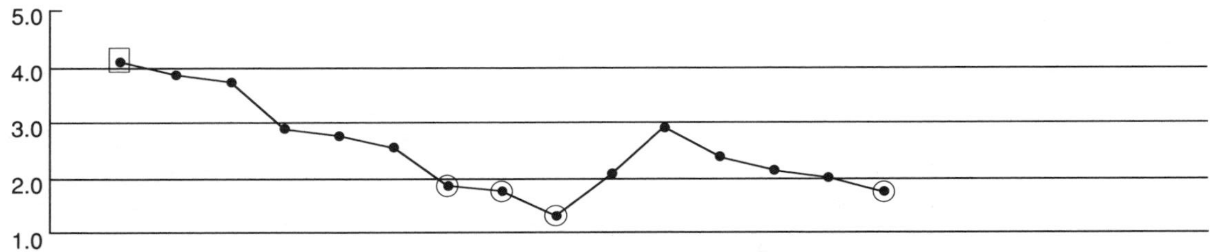

pn	Defect	1	2	3	4	5	6	7	8	9	10	11	12	13	14	15	16	17	18	19	20	21
.4	Width-O/S	510	500	400	350	300	302	250	330	227	420	620	390	400	427	380	230					
.4	O.D.	450	490	300	390	380	500	398	350	200	370	490	390	360	280	260	210					
.30	Width - U/S	200	360	360	480	300	340	200	220	261	330	430	361	287	340	210	250					
.35	M/C Crash	370	460	520	390	385	320	342	215	315	360	400	398	327	330	321	280					
.30	Setup	340	350	340	467	358	327	217	175	201	310	327	356	311	347	260	213					
.28	Bore - O/S	300	298	340	303	420	325	207	201	75	110	1052	1292	295	206	240	200					
.25	Bore - U/S	450	200	300	400	300	283	200	15	41	210	405	200	260	134	94	137					
	Qty. Scrap	2620	2658	2526	2780	2443	2397	1814	1486	1320	2110	3724	2387	2240	2064	1765	1510					
3.0	Scrap%	4.2	3.8	3.7	2.9	2.8	2.5	1.9	1.8	1.6	2.1	4.1	2.9	2.8	2.3	2.1	1.7					

Reprinted with permission

Figure 7-9. Demos Control Chart for Multi-variation Process

shows the defect information broken down into the seven primary causes and an additional "others" cause. The first column shows the mean rate of defects for each cause, and the data are given for the number of defects each day for each of the causes. Red boxes and green circles are again used to show which of the causes is violating limits.

This kind of chart can be used effectively to identify trends in the causes of defects and for gradually eliminating these causes by continuous improvement techniques. In addition, they can be "pyramided" up through each level of management, in a similar way to the example given previously, so that managers at each level of the company can effectively control production quality.

Number of Processes Using SPC

World class manufacturers widely accept statistical process control as one of the cornerstones of world class quality. A good measure of the successful implementation of world class manufacturing techniques is to count how many processes within a plant are using SPC.

The introduction of SPC into a large production plant takes a considerable amount of time. It cannot be forced overnight by management decree; it must be implemented as a part of a total approach to world class manufacturing. The profitable use of SPC requires considerable training and education on the part of managers, supervisors, and operators. It frequently requires the institution of formal methods for problem resolution including such techniques as quality circles and quality review boards.

A simple count can be taken every week of all the processes within the plant that are now using SPC fully, and this count can be graphed over time. It is sometimes useful to juxtapose this measure of SPC use with a graph of total production quality; the trend of SPC use should follow the trend of total production quality.

Quality Improvement Boards

A technique for monitoring employed by some world class manufacturers is the use of quality improvement boards. These large boards, located at each work cell, list the major causes of quality problems within the area, the number of defects for each cause, and a graph or bar chart showing the monthly defect costs.

The purpose of these boards is to provide communication of quality problems, failures, and successes directly within the plant. Reporting the information in this manner has proved to be a valuable tool in the resolution of quality problems for a number of reasons. One reason is that the boards become talking points within the plant, and the production personnel can use the information to discuss the problems and suggest solutions. Another reason is that frequently a certain amount of rivalry is created between production cells to have the best results on the board. This positive competition helps generate an atmosphere where problem resolution becomes the normal approach.

The boards are either kept up to date by the operators in the cell or by a quality specialist and are updated daily, weekly, or monthly according to the needs of the cell and the company. This direct visual presentation of performance measures is typical of a world class approach to manufacturing.

Customer Satisfaction

World class manufacturers have a clear picture that the customer's satisfaction is the ultimate measure of production quality. The measurement of customer satisfaction is not a precise science and varies significantly between companies in different industries. Nevertheless, the customer's view of the products and services is high on the list of concerns for world class manufacturers.

Obtaining realistic information about customer reaction to products is difficult and does not lend itself to objective reporting of facts. Yet, the way customers view your product is the most important sales tool you have. One good measure of customer satisfaction is to count the number of complaints and compliments received. Some companies encourage their customers to respond by doing such things as printing a toll-free telephone number on the product and asking customers to call in comments. Even when this information is not deliberately elicited, many world class manufacturers take careful note of the direct response received from customers. Spontaneous response to a product tends to attract only the negative comments; people will go out of their way to complain and usually do not make the same effort to compliment, but the information is useful nonetheless.

A better way of getting the direct response of customers is to conduct a continuous survey. A survey can be done either by having customers interviewed on a regular basis and collating the information or by providing an inducement for the customers to send in a questionnaire. Some companies offer a free extended warranty, some cash back, or free entry to a competition. These methods are inexpensive and simple to apply, but a thoroughly conducted marketing survey provides sounder information.

Snake Charts

A type of survey that has proved successful with some products is the kind that results in a *snake curve* (see Figure 7-10). The curve lists various attributes of the product or service and provides two columns for response, one labeled "importance" and the other labeled "rating." In the importance column the customer responds to how important they feel that feature is to them; in the ratings column the customers shows what they think of the product.

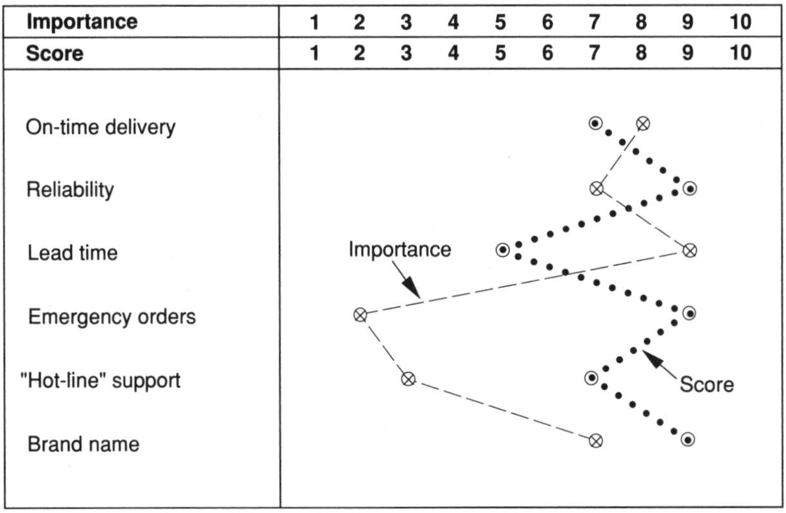

Importance	1	2	3	4	5	6	7	8	9	10
Score	1	2	3	4	5	6	7	8	9	10

Figure 7-10. Customer Service Snake Chart

The resultant graph shows the match between what the customer thinks is important and how the product matches those expectations. This can be powerful information, and it very often provides surprising results. Most marketing departments feel they have a clear understanding of customer needs and preferences, but a survey like this can prove them to be very wrong in their assumptions. A snake curve chart can enable a company to adjust the features, functionality, and service offered to the customers so as to more nearly meet customer needs and desires.

A world class manufacturer is very concerned about producing products that fully meet customer needs and wants.

Irwin Bross pointed out in his book *Design for Decision* that the "purpose of studies in consumer preference is to adjust the product to the public, rather than, as in advertising, to adjust the public to the product."[8]

Percentage of Repeat Sales

If a customer comes back and buys the product a second or third time, then the company must be filling at least some of the customer's requirements. The percentage of sales that are repeat business is a measure of this success. This information can be obtained from the sales analysis files in the order entry and distribution computer system. The report can locate all the orders received during the previous month (or week) and then check to see if these customers have bought from the company before. If appropriate, the report can check to see if each customer has bought that particular product before. The resulting report will show the percentage of orders that is repeat business and the percentage that is new business. An analysis of this information can shed some light on the customer feelings about specific products.

Works First Time

Another more quantitative measure is the "works first time" figure. This measure typically applies to larger, more expensive products that are installed by the company on the customer's premises. Companies that use this method usually have some fancy name for this measure, but it really is a measure of whether the product works correctly when it is first installed and plugged in. This is a basic measure of quality — does the product work? There are hosts of reasons why a product will not work the first time; it may be production errors, damage in transit, incorrect installation, and others. It does not matter to the customer what the reason is. A product that does not work can infuriate someone who has just spent a lot of money on a new piece of equipment.

Time Between Service Calls

Another quantitative measure used by companies that service their own products, the time between service calls, is a measure of the reliability of the equipment and the effectiveness of the post-sales service and maintenance. The longer the time between calls, the more reliable the equipment and (presumably) the more satisfied the customer is with the product.

A variation is a measure of unplanned service calls. Many companies that provide service for their own products conduct systematic preventive maintenance. The purpose of this program is to keep the product in good condition so that it will not break down and require an unplanned service call. A measure of the time between unplanned service calls is a good measure not only of the product but of the preventive maintenance program.

Data Quality

It may seem surprising that the measure of inventory accuracy and bill of material and routing accuracy should come in the chapter dealing with quality. In reality, accuracy of the inventory, bill of materials, and production routing information is quality internal to the company's process and procedures.

Significant inaccuracy in data areas clearly results in less than world class production methods. If the inventory records are not accurate, then the company will have both shortages and excess inventory because the material planning personnel will be purchasing the wrong materials at the wrong time.

If the bills of materials are wrong, then the inventory planning will also be wrong because the components and materials purchased to meet the master production schedule are calculated from the bill of materials information. This situation is exacerbated when backflushing is used to issue material, because the backflushing uses the bill of materials to calculate which components have been used to manufacture a product.

If the production routings are wrong, then the operators on the shop floor are being given wrong instructions about how to make the product — leading them to take action, based upon their knowledge and experience, which inevitably results in longer cycle times and lower quality. In addition, production routings are often used to calculate capacity and load requirements when attempting to balance the production plan within the plant. If the routings are wrong, then the production plan will not be balanced, thus leading to confusion and longer cycle times.

The information contained within the inventory control and production planning systems must be very accurate and complete. The methods of operation introduced by world class manufacturers inevitably lead to greater accuracy. Because the procedures put into place ensure the accuracy and because the procedures are simpler, it is easier under world class manufacturing conditions to keep the information accurate.

Measuring Inventory Accuracy

There are many direct and indirect ways to measure inventory accuracy. The most obvious one is to keep track of variances when a physical inventory or cycle count is performed. Many companies perform a full physical inventory count once each year as a part of the annual audit and inventory valuation process. It is possible to measure the inventory accuracy at this time.

All physical inventories yield an inventory accuracy measurement, but the result is usually given in financial terms and often reports the total dollar accuracy without taking account of the fact that this total figure is made up of positive and negative aggregated amounts. The figures used to measure inventory accuracy for financial purposes are not useful for performance measurement.

A better measure of inventory accuracy from a full physical count is to measure the number of parts that have a variance; a percentage variance greater than 2 percent, for example. Another way is to measure the total percentage error in the stock count without netting the positive errors from the negative errors; in other words, calculate the normalized error. Both these measures provide a good indication of inventory accuracy.

The measure of inventory accuracy at an annual physical inventory is not of much help to a world class manufacturer because once per year is not a frequent enough measure, and most world class manufacturers do not take annual physical inventories. To measure the accuracy of a cycle count is more helpful. If the company has a cycle counting program whereby the component and material stocks are counted on a continuous basis, then a measure of the accuracy (either by number of products inaccurate or a normalized percentage of error) would provide useful information.

An aerospace component manufacturer, recognizing that inventory accuracy was a serious company problem, instituted a thorough program of cycle counting.[9] The prime purpose of the cycle counting was to uncover the problems that caused inventory inaccuracy. The federal government requires 95-percent inventory accuracy for aerospace and defense contractors; this factor is a part of the MMAS standard which lays down the procurement requirements for all government contractors.

As a part of this inventory accuracy program, three kinds of measures were used simultaneously. First, a control group of representative parts was established and the control group parts were counted frequently. This control group acted as a

"Dow-Jones Index" of inventory accuracy. Secondly, the company set up random counts based upon ABC class of the parts. "ABC class" is a way of categorizing the products according to their demand characteristics; the higher volume products with the most impact on sales are coded as "A" parts, the slow-moving products as "C" parts, and the medium-selling products are considered "B" parts. This procedure ensured that the high volume, high cost items were counted more frequently. The third group were parts deemed to be problem parts. These parts represented a range which was identified as having caused a greater than average number of problems in the recent past.

The use of these three views of cycle count accuracy, and the process changes implemented as a result of examining the causes of inaccuracies, enabled this company to improve inventory accuracy from 47 percent to 98.1 percent over a period of just 60 days.

Another method of keeping track of inventory accuracy is to count the number of times a storekeeper or shop floor operator is not able to obtain a product from stock when the system shows the product to be in stock. This very blunt measure shows the information only when a crisis has occurred (that is, an out-of-stock situation) and measures the inaccuracy only when the part is overstated on the system, not when it is understated on the system. But this method does have the distinct advantage that it is easy to measure and does not require any additional, non-value-added activity.

Simplified Counting

There are many aspects of world class manufacturing that simplify the process of stock counting and inventory accuracy. These include the facts that:

- World class manufacturers reduce the number of different parts used in the production of their products; so there are fewer parts to count.

- World class manufacturers hold significantly less inventory; so there is less inventory to count.
- World class manufacturers use standard containers which make it easier to count because the quantities are the same in each container and the products and quantities are easy to identify.
- The inventory of each part is often kept in the same place and is not stored in random locations. This practice makes it easier to find the material.
- The inherent tidiness of a just-in-time production facility with everything labeled and in its place lends itself to accuracy and easy identification of parts.

These factors make stock counting quick and easy to perform. Many companies find it possible to take a total physical inventory as often as once per week without expending a great amount of time and effort. As a result, some world class manufacturers, contrary to what one would expect, can frequently perform full physical counts. From this information, inventory accuracy measures can be obtained.

Purpose of Checking Inventory Accuracy

A world class manufacturing plant holds very little inventory, there are no safety stocks or material brought in ahead of time, and there are no planned scrap quantities. The materials are brought in when they are needed and kept in small lot sizes. When inventory levels are low, it is important that the inventory records be accurate; an inaccurate inventory record could stop production because there is no "fat" in the system.

Whenever errors in inventory records are detected, it is important that these errors be investigated immediately and that the reason for the error be discovered. This step is a part of the continuous improvement process where an error is detected, the reason discovered, and steps taken to eliminate that kind of error. The way to improve inventory accuracy is not to keep checking it. Just like product, data quality must be improved by a detailed understanding of the process used to update the information and by the gradual and systematic elimination of the causes of inaccuracy.

Reporting Inventory Accuracy

A good way of reporting inventory accuracy is to post results on a board adjacent to the stockroom. These data can be in the form of a graph, table, or just the latest figure. This practice can be a good motivator; everyone understands the need for inventory accuracy, and it is a useful figure to report so that the people in the stockroom and on the shop floor can readily see how well they are performing in that area.

Inventory accuracy also can be reported using hard-copy graphs or tables. Figure 7-11 shows a typical inventory accuracy report and, as with most of these reports, it is the trend that is important; as the techniques of world class manufacturing are introduced, the levels of inventory accuracy should increase significantly.

Bill of Materials and Routing Accuracy

Accuracy of the bills of materials is important because inventory planning uses the bills to plan future material requirements, and the backflushing of completed products uses the bills to calculate the amount of components, subassemblies, and materials to issue. The accuracy of the routings is important because these reflect the method of manufacture of the product. The federal government MMAS standard requires 98-percent bill of materials accuracy for aerospace and defense contractors.

These methods often are used as the instructions to the shop floor operators for manufacturing the product. The routings also are used to estimate the load on the plant and

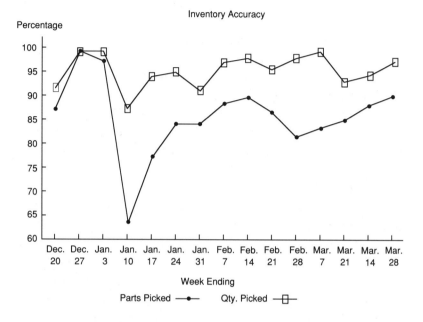

	No. of Parts	Parts Picked	Non-Picks	% Pick	Quan-tity	Quantity Picked	Non-Picks	% Pick
Dec 20	195	170	25	87	638	580	57	91
Dec 27	58	57	1	99	190	188	2	99
Jan 3	67	65	2	97	219	217	2	99
Jan 10	322	206	116	64	1053	916	137	87
Jan 17	265	204	61	77	867	815	52	94
Jan 24	288	242	46	84	942	895	47	95
Jan 31	254	213	41	84	831	756	75	91
Feb 7	299	263	36	88	978	948	29	97
Feb 14	297	264	33	89	971	952	19	98
Feb 21	232	200	32	86	759	728	30	96
Feb 28	221	179	42	81	723	708	14	98
March 7	244	203	41	83	798	790	8	99
March 14	265	225	40	85	867	806	61	93
March 21	254	224	30	88	831	781	50	94
March 28	269	242	27	90	880	853	26	97

Figure 7-11. Inventory Accuracy Report

to assist with the calculation of level loads within each production cell. Both the bills of materials and the routings are used by the costing systems to calculate standard costs.

It is possible to initiate a thorough review of all the bills of materials and routings in order to establish their accuracy. This kind of procedure is often undertaken as a part of the initial implementation of new manufacturing techniques. Companies commonly perform a thorough review of the bills and routings as a part of the implementation of an MRPII system or as a part of the introduction of just-in-time manufacturing methods.

To make this kind of review an ongoing exercise, however, is not practical or effective; it is better to introduce methods whereby any inaccuracies are identified and corrected as a normal part of production operations. Inaccuracies in the bills of materials are identified whenever the people try to make the product and do not have the right parts. In a traditional factory these errors are compensated for by the operators obtaining the correct parts from stock and using their own experience and knowledge to correct the error. Routing errors are handled similarly; the supervisor will manually make corrections to the production routing sheets.

In a world class manufacturing environment, supervisors, operators, and engineers all must see these issues as a part of the company's quest for quality. Whenever bill of routing errors are discovered, they need to be reported and corrected. A mechanism needs to be put in place so that the operators and supervisors can quickly and easily alert the production engineering department of any errors so that the errors can be corrected.

Measuring bill and routing accuracy requires having a method of tracking changes to the bill of materials and identifying the reason for the change. A report showing the number of changes to the bills of materials and routings sorted and summarized by reason code will show the accuracy of the bills and routings. This information can be presented on a graph either as the total number of changes per week or month or by showing the changes as a percentage of the number of bills and routings on file.

Forecast Accuracy

When a company offers a lead time to the customers that is longer than the total manufacturing lead time, then the company must perform some kind of forecasting of requirements. Many companies that make-to-order have to forecast component and material requirements because, in fact, they only do the final assembly process to customer order. The manufacture and purchase of subassemblies and components have to be done from a forecast.

A prime objective of most world class manufacturers is to so reduce the total production time that a forecast is not required, because the company can manufacture (from scratch) within the lead time offered to the customer. In other words, the company's D:P ratio is less than 1 (see Chapter 5). The shorter the production lead time, the better; all world class manufacturers work hard to continuously reduce lead time and cycle times.

If a company still requires a forecast to manufacture components and purchase materials, it is important that the forecast be accurate. Forecasts are made more accurate by giving detailed attention to the calculation, by the people preparing the forecasts having a clear understanding of the variables involved, and by having accurate data from which to calculate the forecasts. The forecasting method used is of less importance than the intelligent understanding of the reasons why the forecasts vary and the extent to which past history is relevant to future demands.

Forecasting requirements become easier and more accurate as the production lead times are reduced. Because to forecast the near future is easier than to forecast the distant future, many of the techniques implemented by world class manufacturers to reduce the production cycle times have the spin-off benefit of improving the accuracy of the forecast.

Measuring Forecast Accuracy

Measuring forecast accuracy requires comparing the forecast with the actual occurrence being forecast. In most cases, this comparison will examine the forecast of customer demand in relation to actual customer demand. There is a difficulty deciding which forecast to compare the actuals with; should the forecast be one week out, two weeks out, ten weeks out, or what? Forecast accuracy should be measured at the total production lead time of the product. If the total production lead time is four weeks, then the forecast accuracy should be measured by comparing the actual demand for this week with the forecast for the same week as calculated four weeks back. The reason for this comparison is that it was four weeks ago that the final decision was made about the quantity of materials to buy and which products to schedule on the shop floor and how to levelize the load on the plant; any changes made inside of lead time require time-consuming and wasteful expediting. A world class manufacturer studies and improves the production process so that expediting is largely eliminated; all expediting is non-value-added activity.

Automated Forecasting Systems

Many forecasting systems use demand history and employ various arithmetic and statistical methods to forecast future demand for the product. Some of these forecasting methods are very complex and require considerable statistical knowledge to understand and use. Other forecasting systems employ more pragmatic methods that can be readily understood. Most forecasting systems allow the user to manually override the forecast that has been calculated by the system; often the master scheduler or marketing personnel have additional information not known to the system, which has an effect upon the forecast. This additional information needs to be included in the final forecast.

For the purpose of measuring forecast accuracy, being able to differentiate between the system-generated forecast and the manually overridden forecast is a valuable factor. The forecast accuracy report should show the accuracy of the forecast actually used in the generation of the master schedule and also show the accuracy of the system-generated forecast. Thus, the person responsible for forecasting can have an assessment of the quality of the manual overrides.

Reporting Forecast Accuracy

The forecast accuracy report should report all products that have been forecast and should show the actual demand, forecast, variance, and percentage variance. This information can then be summarized by product family and the average accuracy of the forecasts within a family calculated. It can be useful to sort and summarize the forecasts by ABC class in addition to product family.

The report should highlight those parts where the forecast is significantly inaccurate, perhaps simply by flagging those items where the actual demand is significantly larger or smaller than the forecasts, for example plus or minus 20 percent. A more complex method of approaching the same situation is to have the report calculate the standard deviation of the historical demands and flag any product where the demand falls outside of 2.5 standard deviations (for example) from the mean.

Either way, this method highlights products having significantly inaccurate forecasts. A good way to measure forecast accuracy is to count the number of products with inaccurate forecasts and plot these on a graph each week to show the trend in forecast accuracy. This method of assessing forecast accuracy can be more lucid than a graph showing the percentage of forecast accuracy over all products.

Preventive Maintenance

Preventive maintenance is significant in many WCM plants. It is a characteristic of many world class manufacturers that they do not necessarily have the latest high-tech machines and equipment. It is a principal of just-in-time manufacturing that capital investment in new plants and machinery is not the first priority when implementing these new techniques. There is a tendency among world class manufacturers to change equipment only when all possibilities of improving productivity with the existing equipment have been explored.

As an example, consider the World Company, a Japanese clothing manufacturer that is a leader in world class manufacturing and has seen astonishing improvements in productivity and profitability as a result of introducing just-in-time manufacturing methods. The company's approach to capital investment is not atypical among world class manufacturers. One of the company's "beliefs is to not spend money on unnecessary capital investment. The seamstresses voluntarily took saws and hammers and fashioned legs and stands out of two-by-fours to raise the machines to a better height. At World's plant, one notices not only that the sewing machines and other equipment look handmade but also that they are laid out in a very efficient manner."[10]

Similarly, many Japanese automotive supply companies have achieved outstanding productivity using old-fashioned machines and equipment. The reason for this achievement is that they take very good care of the equipment and they modify to precisely meet the needs of a world class manufacturing approach. This system invariably requires a thorough preventive maintenance program.

World class manufacturers make sure that machines and equipment are in very good condition because high quality cannot be maintained and enhanced with poorly operating machines. In addition, the machines must be available whenever they are required. When there is no safety stock available within the plant and the components and subassemblies are made only when they are needed, it is vital that every machine is up and working effectively. A preventive maintenance program can go a long way to ensuring this level of effectiveness.

Setting Up a Preventive Maintenance Program

A traditional company employs maintenance personnel whose job is to maintain the machines. These mechanics are responsible for the proper working of the machines and equipment within the plant. In world class manufacturing plants it is common for the prime responsibility for preventive maintenance to lie with the operators. It is more likely that the operators will be able to detect problems with machines when they are using them day in and day out, and the emphasis placed on quality within WCM companies ensures that the operators see a clear need for the machines to be working effectively at all times.

Maintenance personnel are used within WCM plants as trainers and advisors to the operators, and they are called upon to perform the more complex and specialist maintenance and repair tasks. Maintenance personnel are also responsible for establishing the preventive maintenance procedures, defining what maintenance is needed for each machine, determining the frequency of the maintenance, and teaching the operators how to perform these tasks.

Some world class manufacturing companies deliberately run two ten-hour shifts with a two-hour gap between shifts, allowing the operators time to perform preventive maintenance tasks. In addition, this extra time can also be used for training, quality circles, pilot introduction of new products, and other non-direct tasks.

Measurement of Preventive Maintenance

There are several different ways of measuring the success of a preventive maintenance program, and one can be selected according to the needs of the plant. A simple method is to count the number of machines that are on a preventive maintenance program. As WCM techniques are introduced, it takes time to implement a thorough preventive maintenance program. Consequently, measuring each week or month how many machines have been included in the program becomes quite useful information. A variation on this procedure is to also count how many of the machines are having preventive maintenance performed by the operators who have been trained for this additional task.

Other methods include measuring the down time of the machines (see Chapter 5) during each week or month, measuring the total number of unplanned maintenance tasks performed, or measuring the average time between breakdowns. All of these methods give a picture of the success of the preventive maintenance program. As always, the trend is more important than an individual result; as a thorough preventive maintenance program is introduced, there should be significant improvement in the losses due to machine failure.

Cost of Quality

Another way of looking at the measurement of quality is to try to ascertain how much it costs the company to have a high quality product. In a traditional plant, with its inspections, reworks, and scrap, calculating the total cost of creating a high quality product is done by adding together all the tasks associated with ensuring that quality.

Philip Crosby, a leading educator and consultant in the realm of quality control, has listed the following items as the primary elements of quality costs:[11]

- scrap
- inspection labor
- rework
- engineering changes
- warranty
- purchase order changes
- service (except preventive maintenance)
- software correction
- audit
- acceptance equipment costs
- quality control labor
- test labor
- other costs of doing things wrong

This approach is similar to the measurement of non-value-added activities. Any tasks performed only to ensure the quality of the product is non-value-added. As world class manufacturing techniques are introduced, these activities will be eliminated gradually and systematically, and the cost of quality will fall. Mr. Crosby gives a rule-of-thumb that the cost of quality should not exceed 2.5 percent of a company's revenues.

Weekly or monthly calculation of the cost of quality is a good measure of the overall effect of the many quality improvement activities being undertaken by a company that is striving to reach world class status.

Summary

The improvement of quality in every aspect is a major goal of world class manufacturing. There are many aspects to the measurement of quality, and some of the most commonly used measures include the following:

- incoming quality from suppliers
- production quality, including the use of statistical process control charts and direct measures of the customer's satisfaction
- data accuracy within the system including inventory accuracy, bill of materials accuracy, routing accuracy, and forecast accuracy
- effectiveness of preventive maintenance programs
- cost of quality

CHAPTER EIGHT

Financial Performance Measures

T HE USE OF nonfinancial performance measures was
listed in Chapter 2 as one of the criteria for world class manufacturing. There are, however, a number of performance
measures expressed in financial terms, or derived from
financial information, that can be useful and meaningful in
the new manufacturing environment. None of these performance measures are included in traditional cost and management accounting, but most world class manufacturers use
one or more of these measures.

Not all of the reports and measures discussed in this chapter are expressed in financial terms; several are presented in
other metrics. They are included here because, although they
are not expressed in financial terms, they are designed to
measure information directly related to production costs.

There are two primary reasons for using financially based
performance measures; the first is that companies having a
diverse range of products or production facilities need to
have a "common denominator" in which to express performance measures. This reason is particularly applicable when

the performance measures are attempting to show comparisons between two or more plants, and where those plants are dissimilar. The second reason is that financial measures can often give a clear, summarized view of the total effect of the multitude of changes and improvements being implemented simultaneously within a plant or a company.

The Harley-Davidson motorcycle plant in York, Pennsylvania, has very little need of financial reports for performance measurement purposes because the plant makes a single product range — motorcycles. The company does, of course, have many different kinds of motorcycles, but for performance measurement purposes these machines can be considered the same. Productivity reports, for example, can be based on motorcycles completed per person each day, production lead time can be measured as a single figure irrespective of the specific model being produced, and the calculation of product costs is greatly simplified.

In contrast, a company making cars, motorcycles, trucks, and power boats will not be able to consider each product the same for performance measurement purposes because the manufacturing process, the cycle time, the needs of the customers, and the product engineering is significantly different. Under these circumstances, financial reporting methods can be helpful.

Two words of caution:

- The use of financial reporting methods should be approached carefully. Do not use a financial report if a nonfinancial report can be used instead. The reasons are given in Chapter 2; try very hard to find suitable nonfinancial reports.
- As mentioned above, financial reporting can be useful when making comparisons between dissimilar plants or departments. It is important to remember that one criterion within world class manufacturing is that per-

formance measurement should foster improvement rather than merely monitor. There are few instances where comparison between locations or departments is helpful for fostering improvement; interdepartment comparison tends to be based upon the traditional ideas of monitoring who is good and who is bad. In general, world class manufacturers view performance measurement in terms of the changes and improvements over time, rather than pitting one faction against another. The concept is one of cooperation rather than competition, of assisting in the process of continuous improvement.

Waste Rate

Just-in-time manufacturing aims to reduce waste in all its forms from the production process. A key measure of the success of this approach is a performance report measuring the amount of product scrapped or reworked throughout the process. Scrap and rework represent a failure of the process to produce high quality products; these failures need to be identified and examined carefully so that the causes can be eliminated.

Most world class manufacturers use very simple methods of cost accounting (see Chapter 12) and do not collect detailed cost information for production batches or jobs. Costs are recorded in terms of total expenses for the plant or division of the company, and many expenses which are traditionally considered to be direct costs (for instance, labor costs) are treated as indirect costs and are rolled into overheads.

However, most world class manufacturers keep very detailed information relating to the costs of scrap and rework. The objective is, of course, to eliminate any kind of scrap or rework, and it is not unusual for scrap rates to be removed from the bills of materials and production planning information. The company will make no provision for this kind of poor quality.

There are two aspects that make it important to record scrap and rework in detail. One is that a world class manufacturer will want to keep these issues in the spotlight so that they can be eliminated. The weekly scrap and rework rates are often posted on bulletin boards to give them high visibility. Many companies have quality circles whose sole purpose is to investigate the causes of scrap in the process and to devise methods of ensuring that these errors are not repeated.

The second aspect is the practical problem of keeping inventory records accurate. If detailed issues of material to a production job are not recorded and the component issues are posted by backflushing from the bill of materials for the completed item, then the inventory control system will not have any record of material that is scrapped. Similarly, the inventory control system will not have any knowledge of reworked materials because they simply are not included in the production schedules. To overcome this problem, the plant must keep track of all scrap and rework activities so that the quantities on the inventory records are accurate (see Figure 8-1). In addition, a world class manufacturer will use the information to analyze where and when the scrap is being caused and to monitor the progress being made toward the elimination of scrap from the process.

Other Kinds of Waste Reporting

The recording and reporting of scrap and rework is an important measure of material wastage throughout the process, but there are many other forms of waste that can be measured — some of which have been discussed in previous chapters. These include:

- Unnecessary queuing of production on the shop floor (This is measured using cycle time reporting.)

```
            HALLMARK ENGINEERING — ACOUSTIC DEVICES      PAGE 5
                  PRODUCTION SCRAP REPORT              2-JUN-1990

   REASON CODE: PP      PRODUCTION PROCESS ADJUSTMENT ERROR
   CELL: B101       FINAL ASSEMBLY — FAZER BRAND SIGNAL DEVICES

     DATE    SHIFT  PRODUCT                        QTY  VALUE  INS
   1-JUN-90    2    Z32  TYPE 32 SEMI-PRO PHASER  27  276.48  JJD
   1-JUN-90    2    Z31  TYPE 31 SEMI-PRO CHORUS   9   83.88  JJD
   1-JUN-90    2    J22  TYPE 22 JUNIOR FUZZ BX   13   72.11  JJD


   TOTALS FOR REASON CODE: PP    SHIFT: 2        49  432.47


   1-JUN-90    3    J22  TYPE 22 JUNIOR FUZZ BX   11   61.02  DAS
   1-JUN-90    3    L133 SIGNAL SPLICER JUNCTION   7   34.22  DAS

   TOTALS FOR REASON CODE: PP    SHIFT: 3        18   95.24

   TOTALS FOR REASON CODE: PP  DATE: 1-JUN-1990 67  527.71
```

Figure 8-1. Scrap and Reject Report

- Unnecessary movement of materials through the plant (This can be measured using a distance-moved report.)
- Tracking of non-value-added activities (This is discussed later in this chapter.)

Another measure that is particularly important to companies in transition from traditional manufacturing to world class manufacturing is the rate of inspection rejects. A full-fledged world class manufacturer will perform a minimum amount of inspection because the quality assurance responsibilities lie primarily with the operators and supervisors on the shop floor, who are accountable for the quality of their own work. But the introduction of total quality assurance throughout the production plant takes time, and most companies maintain a hybrid system of inspection and in-line quality control for some time; and even after in-line inspection has been fully introduced, sample quality assurance testing is commonly continued. The reject rates from inspection should consistently fall as the techniques of world class manufacturing are introduced. These rejects should be measured and reported.

Inventory Turns and Work-in-process Turns

Inventory reduction is a cornerstone of world class manufacturing and many of the techniques of just-in-time are aimed at bringing inventories down, including raw material, component, work-in-process, and finished goods inventories.

There are several ways to measure inventory levels; world class manufacturers use measures like stock turns or the number of days of stock. Although stock turns is expressed as a nonfinancial measure, it is calculated from the financial measures of inventory valuation and cost of goods sold. Stock turns or days of stock is not a new measure, and has been used by manufacturers and distributors for many years as a key indicator of the efficient use of inventory.

The inventory turns reports can show raw material, WIP, and finished goods separately or as a single summary figure. The reports can be produced daily or weekly and are used as indicators of success with just-in-time techniques, production scheduling, and cycle time reduction.

ABC Analysis

A useful practice is to break manufacturing inventories down into ABC classes, where an "A" part is a component having a high usage value, a "B" part has a medium usage value, and so on. The characteristics and inventory management techniques used to control parts with different patterns of usage are different, and it is informative to show the inventory levels for each of the classes.

The method used to assign the ABC classes varies according to the usage patterns of the components. A company with a diverse range of components and materials needs to subdivide these components using two indicators, one showing usage value and the other showing usage volume. A component with a high usage value and low usage volume (that is, a high cost, slow-moving part) will be treated very differently from a component with a low usage value and high volume part (that is, a very inexpensive part with a lot of demand).

These classes can be assigned by the use of Pareto analysis — the 80/20 rule. The usage value of each component and material is calculated by multiplying the average monthly (or weekly) historical demand by the standard cost of the part. The ABC class is established by assigning A-class to the parts that comprise the top 80 percent of the total usage value (approximately 20 percent of the part numbers); B-class is assigned to the parts making up the next 15 percent of the value, and C-class is assigned to the rest. The specific break points between classes vary from one company to the next, and some companies find it useful to have more than three classes and will assign A, B, C, D, and E codes.

The usage volume class is assigned in a similar manner except the parts are divided according to the average quantity used instead of the usage value. This class is assigned values from 1 to 3, with 1 being the fast-moving parts and 3 being the slow-moving parts.

The combined codes provide a clear picture of the demand pattern of a part. An A1 part is fast-moving, high value; an A3 is slow-moving, high value; C1 is a fast-moving, inexpensive part; and so on. Figure 8-2 shows an example of an inventory turns report which makes use of ABC classes.

```
                    HURON MANUFACTURING
                 HEATING & A/C DIVISION      PAGE  7
                 INVENTORY TURNS ANALYSIS    SEPT 27


       LOCATION    722        BUNTER ROAD ANNEX

                              1      2      3      4

                    A        63.2   57.4   18.9   21.2
                    B        39.4   42.1   12.0    3.3
                    C         4.7    2.2    3.1    1.4
                    X         2.7    0.4    0.9    1.3
```

Figure 8-2. Inventory Turns Report by ABC Class

Turns by Product

Some companies divide the amount of inventory according to the product group for which that inventory is held. All components and subassemblies are assigned a product group related to the final assembly on which they are used, and the inventory turns reports are broken down into inventory levels for each product group.

This method works well when there is little commonality between products, but is less useful when the amount of commonality is high. In fact, it can be quite misleading when a high value component is assigned to one product group and, for example, 40 percent of its usage is against another product group. Circumstances such as these can distort the true picture of inventory levels. However, reports showing stock turns by product group are popular and give a good indication of the success of a just-in-time, inventory reduction approach. Figure 8-3 shows inventory levels reported by product group; the inventory levels are shown in terms of the number of "months of stock" available for the components, subassemblies, and WIP for each product group.

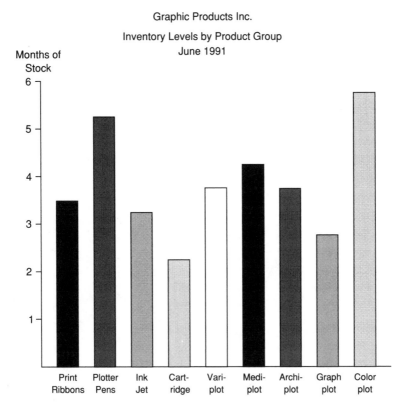

Figure 8-3. Inventory Levels by Product Group

Turns by Plant

Even when the inventory levels are broken down into detailed categories — ABC class or product groups — the aggregate stock turns for the entire production plant is still the touchstone of success within a world class manufacturing environment. Even though there are many aspects of world class and just-in-time manufacturing techniques and these aspects can be applied differently in different situations, a cardinal objective of any world class manufacturer is to reduce the levels of inventory. A report or graph showing the stock turns at a plant level is one of the most important performance measures for managers within a WCM company. Figure 8-4 shows a graph used to display the changes in stock turns for an electronic equipment plant.

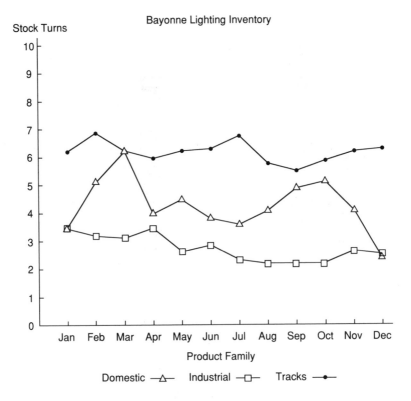

Figure 8-4. Graph of Stock Turns

Calculation of stock turns   There are several methods for determining stock turns, and some of the more common ways are described here.

The definition of stock turns can be the number of times the inventory is totally used within the year. For example, if a company has enough stock to last for three months of production, then the company has four stock turns of inventory. The lower the stock turns number, the better — providing service level and quality are maintained.

For an individual component, stock turns can be calculated by simply dividing the average annual usage by the currently available stock. If the on-hand stock balance is 2,400 and the annual usage is 7,200, then the stock turns is calculated to be 3.00.

When more than one part is involved, it is best to use the *value* of the average usage and the *value* of the on-hand stock balance. The stock turns is the total average usage value of the parts divided by their total stock value.

The total aggregate stock turns for a plant can be simply calculated from the company's standard financial reports. Stock turns equals the total cost of goods sold divided by the total inventory valuation.

Valuation of cost of goods sold Although the cost of goods sold (COGS) is an entirely standard element of traditional performance measurement, the validity of the calculation of COGS is very much open to question. The issues raised in Chapter 3 relating to the shortcomings of traditional cost accounting are very much in evidence with the calculation of cost of goods sold. These shortcomings can be clearly understood when assessing the validity of stock turns calculated this way.

In order to overcome the cost distortions introduced by the inventory valuation procedures, some companies express COGS in terms of direct costs only, for the purpose of stock-turns calculation. An opposite approach to solving this problem is simply to lump the entire plant costs into COGS (for performance measurement purposes) and to use this figure as the basis for calculating the plant-wide stock turns. Although this approach is possible only for the calculation of the total plant stock turns, it does avoid the problems of distorted inventory valuation by making the simple assumption that the entire costs of the operation are (eventually) reflected in the cost of goods sold and that stock turns can be calculated from the total costs of running the plant.

Value-added Analysis

The production process consists of converting raw materials into a useful, saleable item by performing tasks that add value to the product. The only way wealth can be created is by the effective transformation of raw materials into useful objects. This wealth creation process is the root not only of our prosperity and living standards, but also our social and political liberties which (right or wrong) are established and guaranteed by the relative economic strength of a country.

Unfortunately, in the majority of manufacturing plants the amount of time spent adding value to the product (creating wealth) is very small in comparison to the total production lead time. The majority of the time is spent on non-value-added (wealth-consuming) activities like inspection, rework, shop floor queues, moving material, holding inventory, and waiting. All of these activities take time, work, and expend costs; they are wasteful and need to be eliminated.

In a typical manufacturing operation, the total cycle time can be expressed in the following equation:

Cycle = process + move + wait + inspection + setup
(time)   (time)   (time)   (time)   (time)   (time)

The only truly value-added activity within this cycle is the process time; the rest is waste. Because the elimination of waste is a prime objective, a company embarking on a world class manufacturing approach commonly will perform an analysis of what, within the production process, adds value to the product and what is waste. A company that has more than 5 percent of its activities adding value to the product is above the average; most companies find the vast majority of their production activities are wasteful, non-value-added tasks.

A traditional management accounting approach to performance measurement does not differentiate between value-added and non-value-added activities. The efficiency of each operation is measured in terms of variances and standards, but no attempt is made to assess the usefulness of the operation being measured. For a world class manufacturer, that assessment is essential information because the goal of the elimination of waste requires there to be an effective measure of value-added and wasteful operations.

Determining Value-added Activities

Any value-added analysis requires the clear definition of which activities add value and which do not. This differentiation is not always easy, particularly in the early stages of a just-in-time implementation when people become offended and afraid if their jobs are described as non-value-added. However, a company taking seriously the idea of waste elimination must have a clear view of which activities are wasteful and which activities are useful.

Shigeo Shingo has defined "The Seven Wastes" in his classic book *Study of the Toyota Production System.*[1] Any activities that are included in the seven wastes are non-value-added:

1. waste of overproduction
2. waste of waiting
3. waste of transportation
4. waste of processing itself — does this part have to be produced at all?
5. waste of stocks

6. waste of motion
7. waste of making defective products

Each production activity must be studied and a determination made as to whether it adds value to the product. In reality, during the early stages of a world class manufacturing approach, this study can be done in general terms by broadly classifying the production steps; process time will be considered value-added, while material moves, inspection, queuing, and others will be non-value-added. The fact that the process time may contain a degree of non-value-added activities is not important; it is better to have a simple and useful method of differentiation than to attempt pedantic correctness.

Many production planning computer systems define manufacturing activities in terms of process codes that are held on a file or table. All activities within the routings are included in this table. This system greatly simplifies the classification of value-added/non-value-added activities because, instead of each production routing being examined individually, the process code table can be analyzed and each activity flagged as value-added or non-value-added. Reports then can be produced which access this table to determine the value-added status of the activities.

Measuring Non-value-added Activities

Having determined which activities are value-added and which are not, the measurement of value-added activities is simply a matter of measuring how much time is spent on each kind of activity. This measurement can be done by having production operators report their time on each activity and then a report showing how much time was spent on each. In practice, a world class manufacturer will not want operators spending much time and effort on a non-value-added activity like detailed time reporting.

Another way of obtaining this information is to pick up from the routing the standard times taken for each step in the manufacture of a product. This information can be obtained for each product manufactured over a day, a week, or a month; and a report can be produced showing the amount of value-added time compared to the non-value-added. Such a report assumes that the standard times contained within the routings are accurate and valid. In most cases, a world class manufacturer will have studied the production process carefully, and the accuracy of the routings and standards can be relied upon. An example of this kind of value-added analysis is given in Figure 8-5 and a summary report shown in Figure 8-6.

Another way of expressing this information is to report just the number of value-added hours worked over a time period, either in actual hours or in standard hours. These figures can be recorded directly or calculated as the total hours worked less the non-value-added time (queue time, down time, setup time, and so on). A graph showing the number of value-added hours (the truly productive time) is a useful measure of the effectiveness of the production plant. Figure 8-7 shows a graph of the number of value-added hours contributed per person within a diesel engine plant.

As the techniques of just-in-time manufacturing are implemented and the concepts of continuous improvement take root within a company, the value-added content of the production process will increase. The actual size of the value-added content for a company during one week or month is not relevant in itself; what is important is the change over time. A graph showing the change in value-added content over time is a true measure of the production plant's increased efficiency and demonstrates the company's ability to create wealth effectively.

BRANDLEY & PARRY INC.

DETAILED VALUE-ADDED ANALYSIS

CELL: FAB 62 PRE-WELD FORMING

WEEK COMPLETE	PRODUCT NUMBER	QTY	MOVE TIME	WAIT TIME	INSP. TIME	SETUP TIME	NON-VALUE-ADDED	PROCESS TIME	VALUE-ADDED %
11-MAR-1991	12-1A	1000	2.50	6.00	1.00	0.33	9.83	1.67	14.52
11-MAR-1991	12-1B	1200	2.50	4.00	0.67	0.33	7.50	2.00	21.05
11-MAR-1991	12-2A	1000	2.50	6.00	1.00	0.33	9.83	0.82	7.70
11-MAR-1991	13-1F	650	3.00	3.00	0.75	1.25	8.00	1.08	11.89
11-MAR-1991	AB16	45	5.00	3.00	0.33	1.25	9.58	0.75	7.26
11-MAR-1991	AB17	45	4.00	3.00	0.33	1.25	8.58	0.75	8.04
11-MAR-1991	BB16	90	5.00	4.00	1.33	1.75	12.08	1.50	11.05
11-MAR-1991	BB17	90	4.00	3.00	1.33	1.75	10.08	1.50	12.95
11-MAR-1991	DEF1	150	2.75	8.00	1.75	2.00	14.50	2.50	14.71
11-MAR-1991			31.25	40.00	8.49	10.24	89.98	12.57	12.26

Figure 8-5. Value-added Analysis Report

BRANDLEY & PARRY INC.

SUMMARY VALUE-ADDED ANALYSIS

FABRICATION DEPARTMENT — GLENEAGLE PLANT

WEEK COMPLETE	PRODUCT CELL	MOVE TIME	WAIT TIME	INSP. TIME	SETUP TIME	NON-VALUE-ADDED	PROCESS TIME	VALUE-ADDED %
11-MAR-1991	FAB-62	31.25	40.00	8.49	10.24	89.98	12.57	12.26
11-MAR-1991	FAB-65	26.33	33.75	10.25	9.10	79.43	10.10	11.28
11-MAR-1991	FAB-70	40.00	51.20	9.67	12.51	113.38	11.33	9.09
11-MAR-1991	FAB-75	40.00	52.00	10.00	5.69	107.69	15.75	12.76
11-MAR-1991	FAB-80	33.67	43.00	8.50	11.33	96.50	14.20	12.83
11-MAR-1991	FAB-90	38.25	49.50	9.27	17.06	114.08	13.33	10.46
11-MAR-1991	FAB-91	37.25	49.00	12.45	14.79	113.49	13.22	10.43
11-MAR-1991	TOTAL	246.75	318.45	68.63	80.72	714.55	90.50	11.24

Figure 8-6. Value-added Analysis Summary

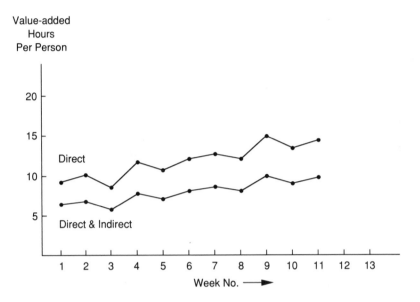

Figure 8-7. Value-added Hours per Person

Value-added Analysis and Cycle Time

There is a close relationship between cycle time analysis and the reporting of value-added activities. The shortest production cycle time is one that contains no non-value-added activities. Many world class manufacturers combine the cycle time analysis (described in Chapter 5) with value-added reporting.

A method of reporting this kind of analysis which is used by some companies is to report the velocity of units through a production cell.[2] A high velocity represents a short cycle time and a high content of value-added activities. This measure is a simple and clear method of presenting value-added analysis without the use of confusing terms such as "value-added."

Value-added Analysis in a Non-manufacturing Environment

A company's efficiency extends beyond the walls of the production shop. The concept of determining which activities are value-added and which are wasteful can be applied equally to such tasks as customer order entry, warehousing, dispatch, invoicing, accounting, and others because the "product" received by the customer is not just the physical product manufactured in the plant, but is the entire service provided by company. This service includes the processing of orders, the dispatch of the goods, and the aftermarket services the company provides. For example, on-site installation of the product for the customer is value-added, whereas a service call to repair or reinstall a faulty product is non-value-added.

For the concept of value-added analysis to be applied in a broader view, the company must determine clearly what the product or service is that is being provided to the customer. Any activity that contributes directly to the supply of that product or service is deemed to be value-added, everything else is non-value-added.

An attempt to apply this kind of approach to research and development activities, marketing, and a company's general administration is difficult and unproductive. For example, is a technical library a value-added activity? But value-added analysis can be a useful tool within the primary flow of the company's sales, order processing, manufacturing, and distribution activities. The analysis is also a useful starting point for bringing the ideas of world class manufacturing into the non-manufacturing departments of the company.

Direct Labor Productivity

In WCM, direct labor productivity (DLP) measurement is different from the traditional DLP measures because it is not concerned with showing the productivity of an individual employee or department. The measurement shows the *amount* of finished products completed each day (week or month) divided by the number of people (or production hours) used to make those items.

When a plant makes a small range of similar products (like Harley-Davidson motorcycles) it is possible to report this information in terms of quantity of products per person, but a company with a more diverse product range will express output in terms of the *value* of the completions in comparison to the number of direct production personnel (see Figure 8-8).

Valuing Production Completions

Measures of production completions raise some difficult issues of how to value the completed production quantities. If production is valued at selling price, there is an assumption that the selling price does not vary; in reality, selling prices vary considerably and in many industries the selling prices at present are falling. If the selling price falls, then the measure of direct labor productivity will also fall, incorrectly showing a reduction in productivity. Even when prices are stable, the selling price is not a fixed figure. The price may change due to negotiation with the customers or, if the products are exported, the selling price may be different in each country. Similarly, if the output is valued in terms of the production cost, there will not be an incentive to reduce costs because reduced costs will lower the productivity measure.

There are ways to overcome this dilemma. The first method is to find a nonfinancial measure; this kind of problem makes financial performance measures irrelevant and misleading.

Another method is to have a standard selling price that does not vary. The standard selling price is sometimes called the "value to the company" or "market value" and is maintained throughout the lifetime of the product. This technique enables the direct labor productivity report to be consistent and to identify trends and changes in productivity.

Unfortunately, the use of fixed values can also present problems because standard prices can quickly become out-of-date and the calculations become divorced from reality. Also,

DIRECT LABOR PRODUCTIVITY ANALYSIS

	STOCKED CABLE PRODUCTS			SPECIAL CABLE PRODUCTS			TOTAL CABLE PRODUCTS MANUFACTURE			
WEEK NO	COMPLETIONS	DIRECTS	DLP	COMPLETIONS	DIRECTS	DLP	COMPLETIONS	DIRECTS	IN-DIRECTS	DLP
1	1782	7	255	2432	8	304	4214	15	12	156
2	1821	7	260	2533	8	317	4354	15	12	161
3	1824	7	261	2765	8	346	4589	15	12	170
4	1795	7	256	2877	8	360	4672	15	12	173
5	1799	7	257	3243	9	360	5042	16	13	174
6	1807	7	258	3768	9	419	5575	16	13	192
7	1832	7	262	4177	9	464	6009	16	13	207
8	1829	7	261	3788	9	421	5617	16	15	181
9	1952	8	244	3822	9	425	5774	17	15	180
10	1936	8	242	3691	9	410	5627	17	15	176
11	1955	8	244	3769	9	419	5724	17	15	179
12										
13										
14										
15										

Figure 8-8. Direct Labor Productivity Report

there is often disagreement about who sets the standard price and what criteria govern the selection. When a new product is introduced, the calculation of the standard selling price can make the difference between the DLP report showing an increase or a decrease in productivity.

To settle for a reasonable compromise is possible. The important factor is to develop a performance measure that is helpful and leads toward increased productivity. The report is not intended to be a precise measure of the use and application of funds; it is intended to be a clear overview of plant productivity.

Production Completions Reports

Reporting the value of production completions is useful in itself, without the calculation of direct labor productivity. Many companies report production completions on a daily basis or by shift. This measure is important to company managers because it shows them at a glance how productive the plant has been day by day.

The problem of how to calculate the value of the completions remains a difficult one with this report, but suitable methods can be devised. The completion valuations can be calculated using standard costs for each product, and these standards can be revised periodically in the usual way.

Unlike the direct labor productivity report, this measure does not attempt to compare changes over a long time period; it shows the completions for a particular shift, day, or week. A revaluation does not invalidate the usefulness of the information. It is possible to recalculate previous information using the new standard costs so that there is some continuity on the graphs of completion values when the revised standards are introduced. An example of a production completions evaluation report is given in Figure 8-9.

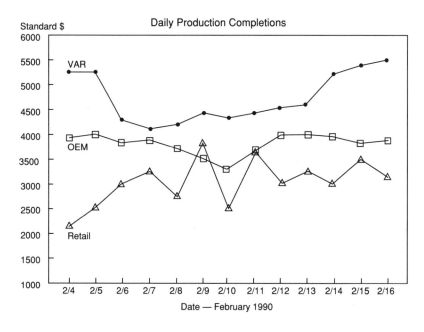

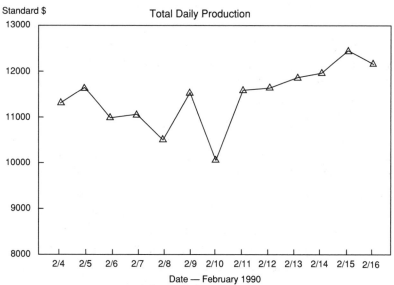

Figure 8-9. Production Completions Evaluation Report

Cost Productivity

There are a number of methods, expressed in financial terms, which are intended to calculate changes in production effectiveness. The purpose of these measures is to monitor the changing characteristics of plant costs over time, particularly during a period in which some world class manufacturing techniques are being introduced into the production process. Three of these methods will be discussed in detail:

- cost productivity per unit
- cost of value-added value per unit
- cost/output ratio

Cost Productivity per Unit

Measurement of cost productivity per unit calculates the cost of producing one unit of a product and is determined by dividing the total production costs by the number of units manufactured. Calculation can be done over a weekly or monthly time period, or it can be expressed cumulatively month-to-date and year-to-date. Whichever version of the measure is chosen, the calculation takes account of the total costs accrued by the production plant over the selected time period and divides by the total number of units produced during that same time period.

This particular measure gives a clear indication of the net effect of all the cost-saving improvements that have been introduced as a result of implementing a world class manufacturing approach. Frequently, the introduction of world class manufacturing techniques will increase costs in the short term. Education costs are high during implementation, as are the costs associated with replanning the shop floor layout, retooling, and enhancements to improve setup times. There are also intangible costs associated with learning curves, mistakes due to new ideas, and time essential for the benefits to become apparent.

The benefits of shorter lead times and lower inventories will manifest themselves only after previous excess inventories have been allowed to dwindle; this process often takes some time. A measure of cost productivity tracks the changing pattern of production costs as changes are made on the shop floor. The change in these costs over time is very important to measure; the information is best presented using graphs or bar charts.

Cost of Adding Value per Unit

Measurement of the cost of adding value per unit is similar to the cost productivity per unit measure except that it is concerned only with the costs of adding value to the product, not with the total product cost.

$$\text{Cost of adding value} = $$
$$\text{total overhead costs} + \text{total labor costs}$$

$$\text{Cost of adding value per unit} = $$
$$\text{cost of adding value} \div \text{number of units}$$

The cost of adding value per unit is a measure of the productivity of the production process. By removing the material and outside process costs from the calculation, this measure focuses on the plant's productivity. This change in focus is particularly apparent when material costs are high in comparison to the labor and overhead costs required to manufacture the product. The effect of any significant change in productivity would not be very apparent because the material costs dominate the productivity measurement.

For example, if product has material costs of $100 and labor/overhead costs of $10, then the cost per unit is $110. If the value-added productivity is doubled, the new cost will be $100 + $5 making a total of $105. A 100-percent improvement in productivity results in a less than 5-percent reduction in total cost productivity. Material costs are not directly affected (in the short term) by improvements in the production process, and the value-added costs per unit are a good measure of the improvement of *production* process effectiveness.

Productivity measures in a vertically integrated company
Measurement of the cost of adding value per unit is particularly helpful in a vertically integrated production environment where there is often additional complexity related to material costs. This complexity stems from the determination of the transfer cost of materials manufactured in one plant and used in another of the company's facilities. The calculation of transfer costs always assumes a certain internal "profit" accrued at the prior plant, and this factor can distort the cost figures of the downstream plants. When materials are moved across international borders during the total manufacturing process, the transfer costs are frequently determined by considerations of the tax and duty implications rather than any consideration of "true" material costs. Under these circumstances, it is valuable to remove the element of material costs from the calculation of plant productivity. The use of the measurement of adding value per unit achieves this objective.

Cost/Output Ratio

The cost/output productivity ratio recognizes the problem discussed earlier, that a calculation based upon cost per unit assumes that every unit can be considered the same for performance measurement purposes. When a plant produces a range of significantly different products, the idea of an average cost per unit can be misleading and confusing. In this situation, it is better to calculate a ratio of the total production costs to the total value of the finished products:

Cost/output ratio = total costs/output value

The total costs can be the total production costs (including material costs) or just the costs of adding value (total costs less materials). Either way, the result is a ratio that measures the changes in production effectiveness.

This measure, like all measures relying on price or standard costs, suffers from the arbitrary assessment of output value. This issue was also discussed earlier and revolves around the difficulty of determining the value of a finished product. If it is the price of the product, what happens to the measure when the price changes? If it is a standard cost, how was the standard established and what assumptions are built into the standard? Also, what happens when the standards need to be changed?

One way of overcoming this problem is to determine which costs can be attributed to which product groups and then to calculate separate productivity measures for each group. This approach, unless the product groups are clearly differentiated, brings into play the whole problem of the allocation of overhead costs to products and will likely cause more problems than it solves.

The purpose of productivity measures is that they should be able to be plotted over an extended time frame. They are not relevant except when seen in the perspective of the changing pattern of production costs and effectiveness over time.

However, a suitable baseline for output values of the products, when it can be determined, can be an effective measure of changing productivity in a plant manufacturing disparate products.

Overhead Efficiency

Measurement of overhead efficiency is a simple measure used to keep track of overhead costs and to relate the size of overheads to the other operational improvements taking place within the plant as world class manufacturing techniques are introduced.

The idea of this measure is that as production cycle times diminish, the production overheads should also diminish. It is vitally important throughout the implementation of world class manufacturing methods to ensure the systematic reduction of overhead costs. One of the subsidiary benefits of a WCM approach is that as production operations are simplified, the associated overheads costs can be seen more clearly. Within traditional manufacturing, all kinds of overheads are commonly "buried" in the general running costs of the production plant; the simplicity of world class manufacturing methods make these costs easier to identify and analyze.

Measuring Overhead Efficiency

Overhead efficiency is measured by dividing the indirect manufacturing costs by the production cycle time. This calculation ensures that as the production cycle times are reduced by the introduction of just-in-time techniques, indirect costs are either similarly reduced or have to be justified by management.

The fundamental assumption built into this measure is that indirect costs should fall in line with the reduction in cycle times. This assumption is not necessarily sound, and some companies will have to plan appropriate targets for overhead efficiency. Nevertheless, the measure provides a simple, elegant method of showing the magnitude of the company's production overheads in relationship to the improvements on the shop floor.

As this measure is put into practical use, it is important to understand the content of the figures used to derive the index. The *precise* content of indirect manufacturing costs and product cycle times used in the calculation need to be understood. Some companies can use the total indirect costs of the entire company or plant and can use the average actual cycle time achieved on the shop floor. For this simple approach to be practical, the company will need to have a single or narrow range of products so that the average cycle time is valid and so that all the overheads can be attributed to a single product line.

Companies with a wider product range will find it beneficial to produce a different measure of overhead efficiency for different product groups, production lines, or plants. This approach, of course, raises all the issues of how to allocate overhead costs to specific products and how to avoid bringing distortion into the manufacturing accounting process (see Chapter 3). The use of activity-based costing techniques (see Chapter 12) whereby overhead costs are allocated in a more relevant manner than with traditional costing techniques is helpful. But using an overhead efficiency measure without implementing a full activity-based accounting system is possible, providing the limitations of the overhead allocation methods are clearly understood.

Even when overhead efficiencies are measured for individual products, production lines, and plants, it is still useful to provide the net measure across the whole company. A good rule of thumb is for senior managers to keep track of how overhead cost reduction efforts are progressing in relationship to improvements on the shop floor.

Other Methods of Measuring Overhead Efficiency

Relating overhead costs to cycle time reductions make good sense in most manufacturing companies striving for world class status, but there are other methods of measuring overhead efficiency. The key to the choice of method for measuring overhead efficiency is to determine which aspects of the production process are the primary drivers of overhead costs and which factors of the process significantly affect the production overhead costs.

In some companies, daily production rate may be a more appropriate factor, and overhead efficiency can be measured as a ratio of overhead costs to production rate. Daily production rate is, of course, just another method of expressing production cycle time, but in some industries it is a more familiar measure.

The measurement of average overhead costs per unit produced is used by some companies to keep track of the changing patterns of overhead costs. This simple measure can be used to initiate overhead efficiency improvements, but it does not have the direct relationship to other changes on the shop floor which is so useful with an overhead efficiency ratio based on cycle time.

Companies that have a diverse product range and where production mix and volumes change rapidly often find that expressing overhead efficiency in terms of total production costs is more meaningful. This approach assumes that production costs are coming down as a result of the introduction of world class manufacturing techniques and that overhead costs will also be falling. The ratio of direct costs to indirect costs can be a powerful measure of production efficiency but, as with other financial measures, can be an obscure measure to the company's non-accounting personnel.

Checkbook Accounting

In a quest to include shop floor supervisors and operators into the company's cost management efforts, some world class manufacturers have devised techniques that make individual production cells, lines, product groups, or plants responsible for their own revenues and costs.

This idea is not new. The technique of making departments or product groups cost centers or profit centers within a larger organization has been in use by thousands of companies for a long time. General Motors and IBM have made this approach into a company philosophy by setting up within the companies autonomous divisions that then compete with each other for market share and profitability. The idea is to break a large organization into units small enough for the managers to exercise an entrepreneurial approach to running their divisions while the benefits of free market competition can still be achieved within a large corporation.

The Amoeba System

An elaborate form of the same concept has been developed and used very successfully by the Kyocera Corporation, a Japanese company that primarily manufactures ceramic materials, industrial ceramics, and semiconductor parts for the electronics industry. Kyocera devised the Amoeba System which, based on the idea that small groups can achieve more than large groups, organizes the company into many small autonomous units. Consisting of three to 50 members each, the amoebas are controlled by supervisory divisions. The company has approximately 400 amoebas and 50 divisions.

Each amoeba is given authority and responsibility over its own work and is able to set prices, profit levels, and performance goals. Many amoebas provide product or services to other amoebas, and there is considerable competition between amoebas to obtain orders from within the company. This internal competition is, in fact, often sharper within Kyocera than with outside companies; successful amoebas prosper and unsuccessful ones die.

These methods have developed within the corporation a keen awareness of the need to provide better quality and lower cost goods and continuous attention to cost control and reduction, and the system enables each group of people to be entrepreneurs within their own amoeba. In addition, the amoeba system provides the people with management skills that are invaluable as the company grows and prospers.[3]

Checkbook Accounting in World Class Manufacturers

This small-is-better, focused responsibility approach has been applied by some world class manufacturers in a much simpler way.[4] Checkbook accounting allows factory managers and superintendents to monitor departmental spending. Actual spending is tracked using a checking account that is assigned to every supervisor, and a deposit is made to that account when scheduled units are produced. Materials, labor costs, and other expenses are credited from the account as they occur.

The checkbook accounting system produces statements that are similar to a domestic checking account and also provides the supervisor with other reports that analyze the costs and revenues. Figure 8-10 shows a report used within a checkbook accounting system. The methods used to calculate revenue and costs must be clearly defined and understood. Revenue debited to the account by completed assemblies can be calculated as the standard cost of the product or as standard hours multiplied by the standard rate per hour. Labor costs can be the actual payroll for the department or the reported hours worked multiplied by the standard hours, and the material costs can be credited at standard cost.

The precise methods of applying costs and revenues to the checkbook accounts will vary from one company to another, but checkbook accounting provides a simple and realistic method of bringing financial accountability and responsibility to the shop floor, workshop, office, and warehouse.

The ideas of checkbook accounting can be extended. Budgets can be set up and actual costs and revenues tracked against budgets; the budgets and actuals can be consolidated up through each profit center so that the checkbook accounting can be integrated with the company's management accounts, and so forth. But the most useful aspect of checkbook accounting is that it is simple and straightforward for the supervisors to use. If it is extended significantly into a complete management accounting system, there is a danger that this simplicity will be lost.

DEPARTMENTAL SPENDING WEEK ENDING ___ - ___

DEPT CHARGED	PURCHASE ORDER	BLANKET RELEASE	TOOL CRIB CHARGES	ELEC. PLUMBING CRIB CHARGES	OIL CRIB CHARGES	TOTAL DEPT. CHARGES	PROD HOURS	STD. COST/HR	STANDARD DOLLARS	BALANCE
MANAGER: SMITH										
111			$673.60	$26.46	$38.40	$738.46	812.32	$2.42	$1969.88	$1231.42
112	$4553.60	$22.00	$1213.30	$42.54		$5831.44	401.10	$2.08	$834.29	($4997.16)
113		$68.00	$1514.58	$35.09	$459.80	$2077.47	552.46	$2.03	$1124.26	($953.21)
114				$1.65		$1.65		$0.55	$0.00	($1.65)
115		$9.47	$14.67	$33.27	$16.16	$73.58	242.20	$0.79	$191.34	$117.76
TOTAL	$4553.60	$99.47	$3416.16	$139.01	$514.36	$8722.60	2008.09	$7.88	$4119.77	($4602.84)
MANAGER: JONES										
211		$242.00	$1244.07	$15.24		$1501.32	131.40	$16.49	$2166.52	$665.20
212			$20.25			$20.25	55.52	$5.52	$308.02	$287.77
213		$172.40	$243.15	$26.50		$442.05	126.90	$12.70	$1611.12	$1169.07
214	$232.74		$712.58	$16.26		$961.58	190.80	$14.70	$2804.00	$1842.41
215	$802.50	$956.27	$1474.51	$42.50	$384.00	$3659.79	204.00	$24.62	$5023.30	$1363.51
TOTAL	$1035.24	$1370.67	$3694.57	$100.50	$384.00	$6584.99	708.90	$74.02	$11912.95	$5327.96
GRAND TOTAL	$5588.84	$1470.15	$7110.73	$239.51	$898.36	$15307.60	2716.99	$81.91	$16032.72	$725.12

Figure 8-10. Checkbook Accounting Report

System Complexity

The more complexity that exists within the systems of a production plant, the less efficient and effective the plant will be. System complexity is not restricted to the computer procedures; the term "system" refers to the entire administrative process used to run and monitor the plant. This overall system includes the processing of orders, invoices, purchase orders, engineering drawings, production worksheets, shop floor routings, rejection slips, expedite documents, inspection certificates, production and inventory control reports, and financial analyses, as well as letters, memos, and reports.

If you visit the average plant and ask the people working there to explain the procedures used to initiate, control, and monitor the production process, likely you will receive several different explanations. Usually, the processes are not clearly understood by the people who use them every day, not because the people are stupid or ignorant, but because the systems are so sufficiently complex (and often so nonsensical) that the people are not able to understand the process.

If the people using the systems find them so complex that they cannot understand them, it is hardly surprising that things frequently go wrong. If the people do not understand the purpose of the procedures, they are unlikely to be able to cope with changes, problems, and unforeseen circumstances. The world class manufacturing approach to these kinds of problems is to simplify the systems. Everyone working in the plant must understand the procedures used within the plant; therefore, those procedures must be simplified.

Measuring System Complexity

Mr. Carlos del Rio of SmithKline Beecham Pharmaceuticals developed a penetrating and simple measure of system complexity. Mr. del Rio's production plant in Puerto Rico was investigating methods of simplifying its systems and performed a detailed study of the usage of reports produced within the plant. This study resulted in a significant reduction in the volume of paperwork used and, as a by-product, yielded a useful method of measuring complexity.

The analysis showed a clear correlation between the amount of paper used in the plant and the complexity of the systems. When the systems were simplified, the amount of paper used was reduced proportionally. The method used by SmithKline to measure system complexity is the amount of paper used by the plant. This amount should be measured in terms of the weight of the paper (in tons or kilos), but in reality it is easier to measure the amount of money spent on paper because this figure can be readily derived from the accounts payable history. Figure 8-11 shows an example of the system complexity analysis.

SYSTEM COMPLEXITY ANALYSIS

BASE YEAR 1986

	EXPENDITURE IN $K	INFLATION FACTOR	ADJUSTED EXPENDITURE	COMPLEXITY
1986	792	0.00	792	1.00
1987	846	3.24	818.59	1.03
1988	799	5.12	758.09	0.96
1989	791	8.42	724.40	0.92
1990	813	12.21	713.73	0.90

Figure 8-11. System Complexity Analysis

This measure has now been adopted as a standard measure for use by SKB plants throughout the world. The measure has been refined by adding an adjustment factor to compensate for price inflation and another for changes in production volumes.

Transactions per lot Another useful measure of system complexity is the average number of transactions created per production lot. A system is complex if it requires a large amount of information to be processed throughout the production cycle. The processing of transactions (both manual and computer transactions) is costly and often wasteful activity. The total number of transactions that occur throughout the plant over a one-week or one-month period can be measured, and this figure can be divided by the number of production lots completed in order to calculate the average transactions per lot.

Pages per lot A similar but more pragmatic measure of complexity and transactions is to measure the number of pages printed. These pages are printed either by copy machines or by computer printers that typically have counters or odometers on them, making it quick and easy to keep track of how many copies have been produced.

The pages-per-lot figures can be calculated simply by dividing the number of pages by the number of completed production lots over a time period. The advantage of this method is that the information is readily available and does not require any extensive analysis.

As always, it is the resultant change in the measures of system complexity over time that is of significance. The individual measure is not meaningful — the trend over time is the meaningful information.

Summary

Financially based performance measures should be avoided by world class manufacturers because nonfinancial measures are clearer, more relevant, and easier to use. There are some circumstances when financial measures can be beneficial and these usually apply when a company has a diverse range of products or operations and requires a common denominator for reporting purposes.

Financially based performance measures that are used by world class manufacturers include:

- waste rate
- inventory turns
- value-added analysis
- cost productivity measures
- overhead efficiencies
- checkbook accounting methods
- system complexity

CHAPTER NINE

Measuring Social Issues

ALL THE PERFORMANCE measures discussed so far have been directly related to the efficiency and effectiveness of manufacturing and distribution operations. But there is much more to life than making, buying, and selling. This chapter will discuss some of the social issues related to manufacturing and suggest some methods of measuring these aspects of modern industrial production.

In the early part of this century the "Scientific Management" movement attempted to define in very mechanistic terms the role of people in the industrial landscape. Frederick Taylor proposed that efficient production could be achieved by using people to do repetitive tasks in a predefined manner; that there was only one efficient way of doing a job and the people must be trained to work with machine-like adherence to pattern. Although the concepts of the scientific management movement have been shown to contain an inadequate understanding of human needs and aspirations, the legacy of this approach to the management of people is still very much with us.

Similarly, the business leaders of the industrial revolution in Europe and the United States paid scant regard for the safety of their employees, their neighbors, and the world around them. Until recently, William Blake's description of production plants as "dark Satanic mills" has been appropriate. Not until the last 30 years have manufacturing companies become aware of their responsibilities toward their employees, the surrounding community, and the environment.

Sadly, these changes have largely come about through government regulation and public pressure; the advent of the Occupational Safety and Health Administration in the United States, the Department of Trade and Industry in England, and similar organizations in other countries has required companies to provide adequate safety in the workplace. The rise of the "green" movement throughout the 1970s and 1980s — together with a few appalling incidents like the Love Canal in Niagara Falls, New York, the Bhopal disaster in India, and the pollution of oceans and beaches by nuclear installations like Sellafield in Cumbria, England — has made it a requirement for manufacturing companies to consider the environmental effect of their business. In recent years, many companies large and small have developed policies or credos that not only relate to their business objectives but also take account of the company's responsibilities to its employees, neighbors, and the community. These aspects of industrial life need to be reflected in the company's performance measurement system.

Morale and Teamwork

The truth is that it is the people who make a company successful. A firm can have a wonderful product, excellent financial structure, and superior marketing plans; but only the effective recruitment and management of the people working for the firm brings success. The suggestion has been made that (if such were possible) the skills and talents of a company's work force should be shown on the balance sheet because these are the most significant assets.

World class manufacturers realize that employees need to be led and managed very differently if the company is to succeed on the world market. The traditional approach to labor is largely based on the ideas of Frederick Taylor and the scientific management movement. The adversarial relationships that exist in most companies between management and production personnel must be changed; cooperation and common goals are the fertile ground in which world class success can grow and flourish.

As discussed in Chapter 1, the approach to people within a world class manufacturing plant differs greatly from that of a traditional company. More authority and responsibility is given to the shop floor operators and supervisors. The shop floor personnel are frequently responsible for the quality of their own work, for scheduling the production cells, and for customer service levels.

Thus, education has a high priority for world class manufacturers so that production personnel can have the tools and techniques they need to continuously improve their performance. Operators are cross-trained so that the plant can provide more flexibility of both product mix and production volumes.

World class manufacturers do not see production personnel merely as pairs of hands; the operators and supervisors are given opportunity to use their intellectual skills to solve problems and implement continuous improvements to the production process. Techniques like quality circles, cross-functional design groups, and an effective suggestion process are used to enable the work force to participate fully in the development of a world class manufacturing environment.

The overall objective is to build a team — a world class team. Such a team is committed to making the company successful; it is not satisfied with minor achievements, but is working toward the radical improvements required to bring a traditional company into world class status. These changes are difficult to introduce within a production plant and often require many years before an atmosphere of trust and mutual respect can be built up. Methods of performance measurement that can assess the achievement of these lofty objectives are required. They need to be objective, understandable, and relevant.

Measuring Morale and Teamwork

To measure intangible issues like morale is always difficult and yet the way people feel about their work, their managers, and their colleagues is most vital to the performance of a company. A number of programs have been developed to attempt to measure the feelings and attitudes of working people within their organizations. This chapter will later discuss how these can be used in practice.

There are, however, other more objective indicators that can provide a gauge of morale and feelings. These indicators include some of the traditional measures of staff turnover, absenteeism, and days lost. These are negative measures rather than positive but do give an indication of the situation.

The introduction of world class manufacturing techniques should, in the medium term, result in a significant lowering of staff turnover because the people in the company will become involved more closely with their work and have greater commitment to what they are doing. In addition, the movement of responsibility and authority from middle managers to the shop floor will result in the people's jobs becoming more interesting, challenging, and satisfying.

However, in the early stages of the implementation of world class manufacturing techniques a significant number of people often do leave the company because they are either unhappy with the changes taking place or they are suspicious of management motives. Many people working within manufacturing industry do not want to embrace significant changes to their work, they do not want to have greater responsibilities and authority, and many have become "case hardened" to traditional management styles and are distrustful of the company's motives.

These attitudes are very understandable and they are part of the challenge facing a company attempting to bring about the radical changes required to implement a world class manufacturing approach. The people issues are by far the most complex and difficult aspect of world class manufacturing. For the managers and the work force to create cooperative working relationships and to develop mutually advantageous goals take a long time and a lot of commitment on both sides.

Sometimes these issues are simplified by the urgency of the situation. Many companies move into world class manufacturing as a desperate measure to prevent the loss of their markets to other companies. When the issue is this stark, creating a common purpose among the people within the company is often easier. This situation has been the case, to some extent, within the U.S. automobile industry where companies like Chrysler and unions like the United Auto Workers have seen the nearly fatal situations that occurred in the early 1980s and necessitated agreements requiring great commitment and concession on both sides. This cooperation on a common purpose has enabled these companies to pull themselves back from the brink of disaster.

In the long run, the introduction of world class manufacturing will reduce staff turnover, reduce absenteeism, and reduce the loss of productive days due to industrial disputes. Measures of these factors are helpful rules-of-thumb to indicate the morale and cooperation across the company. Care must be taken, however, in the way those measures are administered. A prime objective within a WCM company is to create an atmosphere of trust and mutual respect among the company's personnel; this goal can be jeopardized if the people feel that their activities are being unnecessarily checked. Some tact is required in the way the information is gathered for these measures.

Involvement of the People

World class manufacturers put great stress on the teamwork and involvement of their people in broader areas than their immediate job responsibilities. The ideal employee within a world class manufacturing environment is:

- willing to take on responsibility for the quality of his or her work without additional inspectors being required
- working cooperatively with other employees in programs like quality circles where teams of people from various functional areas work together to resolve ongoing problems within the production process and apply the ideas of continuous improvement
- cross-trained in many different functions within the production plant so that he or she can be flexible when the product mix and volumes required by the customers change

There are simple, objective measures that can be used to gauge the level of involvement throughout the company. These include:

- quality circle participation
- number of suggestions per employee
- number of suggestions put into practice
- amount of training/education time per employee
- number of skills per person

Quality Circle Participation

For quality circles (participation groups) and other similar programs to be effective, the people must *want* to participate; the best quality circle programs are voluntary. It is easy to assign people to attend quality circle meetings, but only those who have "caught the vision" of world class manufacturing will be effective.

When quality circles were first introduced into Western companies, many of the programs failed and the concept fell into disrepute. There were several reasons for these failures, and one reason is that the people were "press-ganged" into taking part. The nature of participation and cooperation needed to make these approaches successful is much higher than just attending the meetings and doing a few tasks; it requires a real commitment on the part of each participant.

Companies serious about promoting this participation among their work force must persuade people to take an active part by educating them in the principles of world class manufacturing, by showing the purpose and usefulness of these quality programs, and by providing the training required for each person to be a valuable member of the team. Once this kind of training is completed, the employee should then be able to choose if he or she wants to participate.

Some companies make it positively difficult for people to take part in these groups by making the groups meet outside of working hours. As a result, fewer people will attend the meetings, but the ones that do will have a higher degree of commitment and involvement.

Under a voluntary approach, a simple measure of the amount of participation is to count the number of people within the company who are actively involved in these quality circles or participation groups. As the concepts of world class manufacturing take root within the company, and as the people see the improvements and the benefits, then the percentage of the work force actively involved in quality circles will increase. Care must be taken to ensure that the gathering of this information is not used to coerce people to attend and that there is no suggestion that attending the quality circles will look good on an employee's pay review. To be effective, voluntary participation must be genuinely voluntary.

Suggestions for Improvement

A key note of some of the best Japanese companies is the active involvement of all personnel in the continuous improvement process. The workers within the plants are never satisfied with their quality, productivity, and effectiveness; they are continuously striving toward higher levels of achievement. In addition, there is a high degree of participation in the suggestion program.

Most Western companies have some sort of suggestion program where each facility has a mail box or similar system for employees to relay ideas to managers. Good ideas that are put into practice can earn the employee a financial reward or other benefits. In reality, in most companies, this suggestion process is not widely successful and little is truly achieved by it.

The degree of commitment and participation evident within world class manufacturing companies is such that the employees seem to be bursting with suggestions for improvements. Few of the suggestions are major changes — most are small improvements — but when a large number of these small enhancements are added together, they become major steps on the road of continuous improvement.

An example of this kind of participation was cited in Chapter 2 where Nissan employees at one plant made over 28,000 suggestions when asked to contribute ideas for reducing production costs. This figure, which represented more than three suggestions per person, is a striking example of the degree of participation that is possible.

Participation of this magnitude differentiates a world class manufacturer. The Nissan work force did not just suddenly make up 28,000 suggestions; there was an ongoing atmosphere of participation and continuous improvement so that when a special need arose the people were able immediately to focus their ideas on resolving that need.

The way to measure the success of this kind of program is to count the number of suggestions received each month and to calculate the number of suggestions per person. Sometimes, reporting the number of suggestions per person by department, plant, or product group is helpful. Keeping track of this program over a long period so that trends can be seen is also important. The involvement and cooperation of the work force is something that builds up gradually (and with ups and downs) during the implementation of world class manufacturing techniques, and this aspect needs to be continuously tracked.

One of the most important aspects of a suggestion program is to treat the suggestions seriously! If people are to participate, they must see that their suggestions are being reviewed and considered and are valued by the people who are able to put the ideas into action. They must also be able to see that some of the suggestions are acted upon and implemented. Not all suggestions will be useful, some will be downright silly; but they must be taken seriously and acted upon. When people see that their ideas are being put into practice and the benefits are being felt, they are encouraged to come up with more ideas and suggestions.

As a general rule, it is better not to reward individuals for suggestions. A reward system leads to people being secretive about ideas and to rivalry emerging as to who had the idea first, and so on. One of the purposes of participation and suggestions is that the people working in the production plants should discuss ideas among themselves and together come up with practical and important improvements. The incentive of individual rewards limits this free flow of ideas. If rewards are to be used at all, they should be rewards that benefit the whole group. One company that makes wide use of a suggestion program also has a favorite children's charity that the employees are involved with in fund-raising and other activities. When major suggestions are implemented and improvements seen, the company donates a substantial sum to the charity fund.

If the number of suggestions per employee is measured, the number of suggestions that are put into practice must also be measured. In some ways, this process measures management commitment to the suggestion program, but the employees also see in clear terms the effect of their suggestions.

Some companies attempt to quantify the value of the implemented suggestions and to report the amount of money saved (or earned) by the program. There are differences of opinion about the usefulness of this approach because quantifying the improvement accrued by a specific suggestion is very difficult; very often, several changes working together produce the desired result, and calculating how much benefit has come from one or more suggestions is not possible. Quantification by this mode tends to be misleading.

Amount of Education and Training per Employee

"If you think education is expensive; try ignorance!" This piece of homespun philosophy has great bearing on modern manufacturing industry. Traditional manufacturers put very little effort into the education and training of their people. World class manufacturers put a great deal of time, attention, and money into education programs. Quite simply, a world class manufacturer requires everyone within the company to be actively involved in the process of continuous improvement, wants their shop floor personnel to be cross-trained to provide flexibility, and expects employees to take more responsibility for their own quality, schedules, and customer service. If these additional things are required of the people, then they must be trained to achieve them.

When world class manufacturing techniques are being introduced into a manufacturing plant, the people working in the plant must be educated not only in the techniques themselves, but in the entire philosophy of world class manufacturing. This program cannot be completed in a few short sessions, as this kind of fundamental education requires a systematic and extensive education program.

A world class manufacturer is concerned about quality. Quality applies to every aspect of the company's process from receipt of customer orders through manufacturing to dispatch of the product and post-sales service. For quality to be consistently and systematically improved, the people have to be highly skilled in all aspects of their work; this level can be achieved only by consistent and systematic education.

A criticism of traditional manufacturers is that they do not care about the people working for them. They are concerned primarily about turning the people's labor into profit as cheaply and quickly as they can. This is not, of course, true of all companies; many companies are compassionate and caring toward their employees, but the general attitude within traditional companies is that profits take precedence over people. This attitude gave rise to the labor movements in the early part of this century and is the source of the majority of the labor disputes that have blighted so many industries in post-war Western countries.

World class manufacturers frequently attempt to change these basic attitudes. This effort has given rise to such practices as providing guaranteed lifetime employment for selected employees and other similar schemes that are common among the best Japanese companies. One way of showing long-term commitment to the employees is to provide long-term, systematic education and training for each employee.

The objective of fundamental education programs is to earn the active commitment of each employee to the radical changes associated with world class manufacturing. It is not good enough just to reorganize and tell the people what to do. A world class manufacturer is interested in harnessing the employees' minds and hearts as well as their hands. This goal requires a concerted commitment to education, training, and personal development.

The average amount of education and training provided to each employee is a valuable measure and can be done by keeping track of the amount of money spent on education and dividing by the number of employees. A financial measure like this, however, is not a true measure and does not take account of the varying costs of different classes and programs. If a senior executive attends a three-week management symposium in Switzerland, the cost would be included in the total education costs but would distort the performance measure.

A better way is to keep track of the number of days of training each person attends and calculate the average number of days per employee. This figure can be calculated for each department or plant within the company. This measure works well if all the education is given in terms of off-the-job classes, but many of the skills required within a world class manufacturing environment can be better learned in short on-site classes, on-the-job instruction, and video or self-study training.

This difficulty can be overcome by having a method of certifying the attainment of each education and training step and then measuring how many "class hours" each employee has completed. From this, the average amount of education and training made available to each employee can be monitored. These measures are more pertinent if the education and training programs are voluntary. If someone has signed up for a class without its being required, that person is likely to gain more from the class.

Cross-training and flexibility Chapter 6 dealt with the measurement of cross-training and production flexibility. Two measures are discussed, the degree of cross-training and the average number of tasks performed by each individual.

Leadership and Working Environment Measures

There have been many attempts in recent years to establish a more objective view of the way that people feel about their work, their managers, and their colleagues. The way people feel about their work is so very important to the success of an organization, and yet to measure these feelings in *objective* terms that can be used to evaluate the social climate of the company and initiate improvement is anything but easy.

To a large extent, the way people feel about their work is determined by the way the company is run. Also, measures of the social climate within a production plant are measures of the leadership abilities of the managers within the plant. Most companies have a detailed method of evaluating employees; each person's work is reviewed by a manager or supervisor annually (or more often); but few companies have any way of evaluating the leadership skills of the managers.

Some would claim that the majority of problems in Western manufacturing companies are caused by inadequate leadership. Dr. W. Edwards Deming puts great stress on leadership. "The required transformation of the Western style of management requires that managers must be leaders. Focus on outcome must be abolished, leadership put in its place."[1]

Leadership — certainly an important aspect in the success of any enterprise from organizing a Little League to winning a war — is a very elusive quality to measure. A production plant is unlikely to be successful with world class manufacturing (or anything else) if managers are not able to provide vision, organization, and motivation to their people. But not only is measuring quality of leadership difficult, it is also difficult to present the information in a useful way as a tool for improved leadership performance.

Work Environment Scale

A number of evaluation tools developed to try to solve this problem are being used by a number of larger corporations including IBM, Xerox, and SmithKline Beecham. One of these tools is the work environment scale, which was developed by Dr. Rudolf H. Moos of Stanford University.[2]

The purpose of this scale is to ask employees a series of questions, about 150 in all, designed to gauge the way the people feel about their working relationships, their own personal growth within the company, and the working atmosphere. There are three kinds of forms: the Real Form where people report what really happens in their company, the Ideal Form where they express their concept of the ideal working environment, and the Expectations Form, which looks into the expectations people have of their work and their company.

The idea of the program is to measure the real feelings the people have about their work, their colleagues, and their company and to contrast these feelings with the conception of an ideal working environment and the current expectations. A clear difference between the Real and the Expectations measures signals areas of concern that need to be analyzed and improved.

The forms examine ten major aspects of the working environment:

1. *Involvement:* the extent to which employees are concerned about and committed to their jobs

2. *Peer Cohesion:* the extent to which employees are friendly and supportive of one another

3. *Supervisor Support:* the extent to which management is supportive of employees and encourages employees to be supportive of one another

4. *Autonomy:* the extent to which employees are encouraged to be self-sufficient and to make their own decisions

5. *Task Orientation:* the degree of emphasis on good planning, efficiency, and getting the job done

6. *Work Pressure:* the degree to which the press of work and time urgency dominate the job milieu

7. *Clarity:* the extent to which employees know what to expect in their daily routines and how explicitly rules and policies are communicated

8. *Control:* the extent to which management uses rules and pressures to keep employees under control

9. *Innovation:* the degree of emphasis on variety, change, and new approaches

10. *Physical Comfort:* the extent to which the physical surroundings contribute to a pleasant work environment

Using the work environment scale Attitude measurement questionnaires need to be used carefully; they can be misleading if the surveys are not administered correctly. The leaders who coordinate the use of the survey need to be trained in the use and purpose of the program so that they can explain to the employees how to correctly fill out the forms.

The purpose of the questionnaires needs to be fully explained to the employees taking the survey, and it must be made clear that the survey is being done to help the company assess its management methods. Understandably, people being asked to fill out forms of this kind for the first time will be suspicious of how the results will be used. They need to be assured that there are no "right" answers and that the results will not reflect back on the individuals taking the test.

The survey is typically used twice per year. In practice, usually about 18 months (or three uses) pass before the employees feel confident that the survey is a helpful tool and not an intrusion.

The results of the survey should not be published widely. The manager of each department needs to see the summarized results for his or her department, and the senior managers need to see the summaries across the plant or division. The results of the work environment scale must be used to improve the working environment and *not* as a method of judging a manager.

The results are analyzed by calculating the average results for each of the ten categories for each of the three forms. These results are displayed on graphs for each department and discrepancies investigated. A discrepancy occurs when the Real result varies significantly from the Expectations and the Ideal results. Although the results are analyzed by calculating averages, the actual numbers that make up the averages are also reviewed to determine the spread of results. These spreads give an indication of the unanimity among the work force.

When serious discrepancies are determined between the Real environment and the employees' Expectations, the department manager is responsible for changing that aspect of the work environment. This task is not always easy to accomplish because some aspects are not directly under manager control and some of the categories do not lend themselves to specific courses of action.

One company using this kind of social climate measure found a discrepancy in the area of control (the extent to which management uses rules and pressures to keep employees under control) for the shop floor supervisors. Investigation revealed that the supervisors had very little real responsibility because all their actions required that forms be filled out and signatures be obtained from higher managers. This rule applied even to the issue of materials to the shop floor. Changes were made in the authorization requirements, giving the supervisors much more responsibility and authority in their work. The discrepancy was rectified by the time the next survey was completed.

In some of the other categories, to determine specific changes that can be made in order to improve the employees' perception of their working environment is more difficult, but this survey provides a useful tool for managers at least to understand the issues from their employees' point of view.

Environment and Safety

All manufacturing companies are required by law to monitor the impact of their operations on the environment. In most countries the law requires detailed and specific reporting of factors such as the emission of regulated substances and others. This information is no doubt useful to the government but for performance measurement purposes is often complex and confusing to the companies and the engineers and scientists who have to do the reporting.

What is needed is a clear and comprehensive assessment of the company's success in adhering to environmental standards. An index is needed that enables the plant manager to keep his or her finger on the pulse of the work being done within the plant to ensure environmental safety.

Environmental compliance can be measured as the number of deviations to standard divided by the number of measurements made. A deviation is a reading that contravenes either the government standard or the company's own standards. The number of measures is the quantity of observations taken in the time frame. The environmental compliance factor typically will be reported weekly or monthly (depending upon the number of measurements taken) and graphs used to display the data and analyze trends.

When deviations from standard do occur, the reasons for the problem must be found and steps taken to rectify the situation in the future. This type of problem can be treated in the same way as any other quality control problem. Techniques like statistical process control, Pareto analysis, and fishbone charts are very useful in the quest for continuous improvement in the area of environmental safety.

Safety in the Plant

In most countries, companies are required by law to keep detailed information about safety problems within their plants, and many companies have safety procedures that exceed the minimum requirements of the law. The needs of world class manufacturers are no different than those of traditional manufacturers in this area, and similar measures are widely used:

- days lost through accidents
- number of days since last accident
- number of accidents or near-accidents reported

Many companies post this information on large notices inside the factory, sometimes showing the figures for each department, so that there is constant emphasis on safety issues. Most companies conduct ongoing training and education in safety procedures and strictly apply the safety procedures throughout the plant.

Johnson Controls Battery Division, which has plants using hazardous materials such as lead and acids, posts the safety record of the plant on a large board outside the plant building near the main entrance. Everyone, employees and visitors alike, is constantly aware of the company's stress on safety.

Johnson Controls also monitors environmental safety within the plant by providing all employees with free medical checks on such vital issues as lead level in the blood.

Some companies go further than just reporting accidents and loss of days due to safety problems and conduct safety audits on a regular basis. The purpose of these safety audits is not only to record actual safety problems when they occur, but also to identify potentially hazardous situations within the plant and take steps to eliminate these problems *before* an accident or injury occurs.

A safety index, which can be derived from these data, provides the plant manager with a simple view of the plant's safety environment. The safety index may be calculated as:

Safety index =
number of audit failures ÷ number of audit observations

This index is then presented as a graph and the trend over time is analyzed. As with environmental measures, safety issues lend themselves to the continuous quality improvement techniques used by world class manufacturers. These techniques can be applied to the issues measured by the safety index, and goals can be set for the total elimination of accidents and injuries within the plant.

The safety index can be extended also to include actual occurrences of accidents or injuries. The safety index is calculated by adding together the audit failures and the days lost through accidents, and then dividing by the number of audit observations plus the total worker days worked over the observation period. This composite index provides a single figure assessment of the plant's safety record.

Summary

The majority of performance measures dealt with in this book provide information relating to the productivity and effectiveness of production plants implementing world class manufacturing techniques. The reality of business life is that there are many other issues, also critical to the success of an enterprise, that are not as easily measured. These measures deal with issues such as:

- morale of the work force
- teamwork within the company
- the extent to which the employees are involved in the company's quest toward world class manufacturing
- leadership abilities of the managers
- the education and training level of the work force
- the company's commitment to safety and environmental issues

There are methods of measuring these kinds of issues. It is vital that they be taken into account by a company moving into world class manufacturing status.

CHAPTER TEN

Establishing Performance Targets

AFTER DETERMINING which performance measures are valid and useful to the company, the question of performance targets needs to be addressed. Companies have always set performance targets and used measurement systems to track the achievement of these targets. What is different about the use of performance targets for world class manufacturing is the degree of improvement expected as a result of implementing world class manufacturing techniques.

Traditional manufacturing companies frequently implement new methods with a view to reducing, for example, inventory levels. The kind of reductions expected are typically in the range of 5 percent to 20 percent. When implementing world class manufacturing techniques, the goal for inventory reduction will be in the range of 75 percent to 80 percent in the short term and significantly more as the company's methods mature. The changes are radical, and the people implementing the new methods do not have any experience to draw on that will help them with setting new targets.

There are some techniques to assist with these decisions, and later in this chapter we will look at competitive benchmarking, price targeting, the "half-life" concept, and some of the common sense approaches to the establishment of performance targets. But the first necessity is to address the issue of whether a company should set targets at all. This controversial issue has strong views expressed on both sides. One camp states that setting targets is contrary to the concept of world class manufacturing and continuous improvement, the other asserts that human beings need goals if they are to achieve anything.

Should Targets Be Set?

Dr. W. Edwards Deming, the American consultant and teacher who was so instrumental in helping Japanese companies become world class manufacturers, believes very strongly that setting performance targets is fundamentally wrong.[1] His contention is that business problems are the result of the system being faulty, not the people. If you give the people targets when they have not the ability to change the system, you are merely adding frustration and fear to the situation. Radical and feisty as ever, Dr. Deming suggests that 85 percent of a company's problems are caused by poor leadership and only 15 percent can be attributed to the work force. Furthermore, a large amount of that 15 percent can be put down to poor training from leaders.

Accordingly, some of the dangers of target setting are:

- It engenders fear. No one can work well when they are not secure. Setting targets creates insecurity and worry, situations that are contrary to the ideas of world class manufacturing. If people are working with fear of their jobs, their bosses, or their colleagues, they will perform in a way to alleviate the fear and will not be the most productive and highest quality team members.

- It establishes mediocrity. For targets to be motivating and not frustrating, they must be attainable. When a large number of people are involved and attainable targets are set, then, by definition, the targets will be attainable by the average person. This practice gives everyone an average target to aim for and establishes an atmosphere of mediocrity.

- It can make people self-satisfied. The problem with a target is that if people attain the target they can, quite reasonably, assume that they have met their manager's requirements, and they will be satisfied with their work. This situation is the opposite of the ideas of continuous improvement. In Dr. Deming's words, "A quota is a fortress against improvement of quality and productivity. I have yet to see a quota that includes any trace of a system by which to help anyone do a better job. A quota is incompatible with never-ending improvement."[2]

- It gives the wrong signal. Performance targets are too often aimed at improvement of inappropriate measures and encourage people to do the wrong things. For example, an official of the postal service was continually annoyed at the mistakes being made by the people sorting the mail. The method of payment for sorting staff was based on the achievement of the quota of 15,000 pieces per day — which did nothing to encourage accuracy.

- It negates pride in workmanship. Establishing targets for people, particularly when those targets are inappropriate, removes from people the ability to use their own creativity and intelligence and removes the opportunity for them to take pride in their work. When people take personal pride in their work, they are able to contribute fully to the achievements of world class manufacturing.

The other side of this debate is equally adamant in contending that it is impossible to expect the best from people without showing them clearly what you expect. Techniques like management by objectives and one-minute management have built into them a large element of self-determination and personal targeting, which solve the issues cited as criticism of the use of performance targets.

Philip B. Crosby, in his book *Quality Is Free*, lays down specific goal-setting as one of his 14 steps to quality:

> *Action: During meetings with employees, each supervisor will request that they establish the goals they would like to strive for. Usually there will be 30-, 60-, and 90-day goals. All should be specific and capable of being measured. Accomplishment: This phase helps people learn to think in terms of meeting goals and accomplishing specific tasks as a team.*[3]

Joseph M. Juran, an internationally respected expert on manufacturing quality, has developed an approach called companywide quality management, which has goal-setting as an integral aspect of success:

- Establish policies and goals for quality.
- Establish plans for meeting these quality goals.
- Provide the resources needed to carry out the plans.
- Establish control to evaluate progress against goals and to take appropriate action.
- Provide motivation to stimulate the personnel to meet the quality goals.[4]

For goal-setting to be valuable, the people responsible for the achievement of those goals must participate in the establishment of the goals. The goals must be specific, measurable, and in line with the manufacturing strategy. Goals should be set only when the people have the resources to achieve and a road map to reach them.

Competitive Benchmarking

Competitive benchmarking is a method pioneered by a number of corporations, including Xerox. The Xerox Corporation was in significant danger of being put out of business by its Japanese competitors in the early 1980s. The Xerox executives realized their situation just in time and implemented some radical (and sometimes painful) new methods that have enabled the business to grow and prosper throughout the late 1980s. One key aspect of these changes was the competitive benchmarking technique.[5]

The idea of competitive benchmarking is to study major competitors and discover what their strengths and weaknesses are. The competitive companies must be studied in detail: design, manufacturing, marketing, customer support, distribution, and so forth. How much of this competitive information is readily available is surprising. There is no need to resort to subterfuge to obtain this information, as the important data are often available in published form in financial statements, industry analysis documents, and trade journals. Japanese companies are particularly open with the kind of information required to perform competitive benchmarking.

This analysis yields a mass of data that is used to determine the key aspects of a company's business. After the key aspects have been established, goals are set for each of those aspects. Generally, the goals are to achieve a level of proficiency in each aspect that is at least as good as the best of the competitors. The competitors will each have strength and weaknesses; goals will be set to emulate the strengths of each of the primary competitors. The achievement of these goals will make a company the best of the best in every aspect of the business.

Benchmarking information can be gained from companies that are not competitors. The distribution division of Xerox obtained detailed operational information from L. L. Bean, the huge mail order distributor in Maine, which had instituted some very effective high volume warehousing operations. Xerox managers also spent time at General Electric Corporation studying its support and distribution operations.

When a company first engages in a competitive benchmarking analysis, the results are often alarming and depressing. It is amazing how good the competitors are. When Xerox completed the first competitive analysis study, it found, for example, that several Japanese competitors could sell office copiers for a lower cost than Xerox could make an equivalent product. To overcome this difference was not a matter of minor improvements; this situation demanded radical change with survival at stake.[6]

The ultimate goals cannot be achieved quickly. The achievement of goals represents, by definition, world class status in manufacturing, marketing, distribution, service, and design. Goals need to be set that are achievable this month, this quarter, this year; but the ultimate goals must be kept clearly in mind. Achieving only this year's goal is not good enough when the competitive benchmark is still much better than this goal.

Competitive benchmarking, to be valuable, must define clear goals for each manager in terms that make sense within his or her area of responsibility. The goals cannot only be large goals for the corporation as a whole; they must be broken down to the specific goals of each department. The benchmarks must be revised continuously (at least once per year) so that performance goals change as the competition changes. This procedure provides a built-in continuous improvement target that is established objectively in clear terms of market success or failure.

The benefit of competitive benchmarking is that goal-setting is done objectively from data obtained outside of the company and does not, therefore, have preconceived ideas or company traditions built into it. These traditions need to be swept away as part of the quest for world class status. In addition, the competitive benchmarks are obtained from studying what is going on in the marketplace, for the marketplace is the ultimate judge of a company's success; it is valuable — even essential — to set goals that are based upon the needs of the market.

Xerox credits competitive benchmarking as one of the major factors in the company's renaissance in the mid-1980s. The first companywide benchmarking was completed in 1980. By 1983, product quality had improved by 70 percent, inventory was reduced to 1.4 months (8.5 stock turns), overheads were reduced from $500 million to $300 million, and manufacturing personnel were reduced from 18,000 to 12,000 while production volumes remained constant. At the end of 1983, the competitive benchmarks were all recalibrated. Quality improvement goals were set to 93-percent improvement, inventory levels to 0.9 months, overheads to be reduced by a further $100 million, and manpower down to 9,000, which is half of the 1980 levels. These radical goals were conceived by the focus of attention brought to bear by competitive benchmarking and were achieved by the motivation and clarity of purpose provided by benchmarking goals.

Xerox credits the technique of competitive benchmarking with making significant cultural changes within the corporation. The attention to competitive capabilities forced Xerox personnel to recognize that they did not have all the answers. A corporation that has been so markedly successful for so long can develop very arrogant attitudes and an extravagant approach to business. Competitive benchmarking helped change those attitudes, eliminate the "not-invented-here" syndrome, and provided the corporation with the vigor and determination required to succeed in the very different market environment of the 1980s.

Price Targeting

Traditional management accountants spend a great deal of time determining production costs. One reason for doing so is that the cost of a product is used to determine the price the company must charge customers. In reality, the price of products in most sectors of industry is largely market-driven. With the exception of government contracts and monopoly organizations, product prices are determined by what the market will bear; this fact is reality in twentieth-century manufacturing industry.

In light of this, techniques have been developed that are designed to enable manufacturers to establish target prices and target costs in line with market needs. Some major Japanese companies pioneered a formal approach to the establishment of price and cost targets in the form of *value engineering*.[7] Value engineering is an integral part of the design process within all divisions of the Toyota group of companies and is used in the earliest stages of new product development.

As with many world class manufacturing methods, value engineering techniques are no different from the steps any company goes through in the development of a new product marketing plan. What makes the difference is the systematic approach used by value engineering and the degree of importance placed on it throughout the design process.

The first step in this process is to establish the needs of the market. This step is done in great detail, and much attention is given to understanding what the customers need before a new product is initiated. This study is one aspect of a broader view of quality; the broadest definition of quality is to consistently make products that fully satisfy the needs of the customer. The starting point of this particular quality quest is to understand in great detail what the customer really needs and to design a product to meet that need.

Furthermore, the needs of the customer must be matched with what the customer is prepared to pay to have those needs met. An understanding of what the customer is prepared to pay is what moves emphasis of product feature from a customer "want" to a customer "need." From this analysis a target price is established, which is a detailed assessment of the market needs and of the price the market will bear.

Senior managers and financial personnel then determine how much contribution — the required profit — is needed by the company from the sale of each unit of the product. The target cost is calculated by subtracting the required profit from the target price. This target cost (or allowable cost) is the basis upon which the design departments perform their analysis of production costs and value engineering.

At this time, the design engineers are also establishing the design concepts of the new product and are calculating the estimated production cost (known as the potential cost). There is usually a gap between the potential cost and the allowable cost; this gap must be bridged through the design phase of the product. The potential cost is not an appropriate cost objective because it does not provide the company with the required profit contribution; the allowable cost becomes the target that must be economical and motivational.

The quest of value engineering is to use the expertise and ingenuity of the people within the company to develop innovative ideas to bring the new product's cost into line with the allowable cost. The cost management department has the task of breaking theoretical costs down into their constituent parts

— separating material costs, labor costs, tooling, depreciation, various kinds of overheads, direct sales costs, administrative costs, and so forth. Costs are also assigned for each major subassembly of the product and to each department within the company. The target costs for each subassembly are assigned to the responsible design departments and, by focusing on both costs and customer needs, the cost reduction process can begin in detail.

The design process goes through many iterations; the techniques of value engineering are applied to every component and production step so that the final production cost is gradually reduced to allowed cost. The suppliers of components and raw materials are also closely involved in the value engineering process, particularly for products having a high material cost (automobiles have a material cost of 60 percent to 70 percent of the total cost). Suppliers also bring their value engineering expertise to bear on the problem and are frequently a major driving force behind the cost reduction effort.

In addition to providing a focus on cost and customer needs, this process also requires that the product and its manufacturing process be very closely examined and refined in the design phase of the project. This aspect has the vital spin-off effect that the pilot production phase is thus a much smoother and more predictable activity than in a conventional approach to design. The problems are not resolved in production — they are examined and resolved in the design stage. This method goes a long way to providing a short cycle time from conception to delivery because there is not a long, drawn-out stage of last-minute fixing of production problems. Northern Telecom saw this procedure as an essential aspect of its quest for world class manufacturing; it "wanted to achieve a mature first cost instead of relying on the usual procedure of continual cost reductions during the product's manufacture."[8]

The final step in this process is to develop the potential costs of the final design and to review this design in line with the original plan that spawned it. Here the final decisions are made relating to cost, price, and market needs. Many months may have elapsed (for a complex product) from the time the original market-driven price was established. During that time, a large amount of analysis and design has introduced new features and ideas into the product and has taken decisions that relate costs to customer needs, and work has been done with suppliers and process engineers. These activities culminate in a product for which the market needs are known, the production costs are estimated in detail, and which become part of the company's strategic plan.

The ideas of value engineering are not new; companies have been employing cost estimating and cost reduction techniques for many years. What is different about the value engineering approach is that it is incorporated closely into the design and development phase of the project. It integrates the needs of the marketplace with the company's cost and profit needs and initiates innovation in design, production process, and manufacturing techniques as the whole development team (consisting of people with diverse responsibilities) brings its talents together in the quest for a highly cost-effective product.

"Half Life" of Continuous Improvement

The "half-life" concept of goal-setting was devised by Mr. Arthur M. Schneiderman, vice president of Quality and Productivity Improvement for Analog Devices Inc. in Woburn, Massachusetts. Mr. Schneiderman studied the improvements attained by a large number of companies that were actively pursuing continuous improvement programs.[9] He found, almost accidentally, that the rates of improvement exhibited similar patterns even though the problems being addressed were very different. He discovered that if one plotted the improvements on logarithmic graph paper, the graphs approximated straight lines (see Figure 10-1).

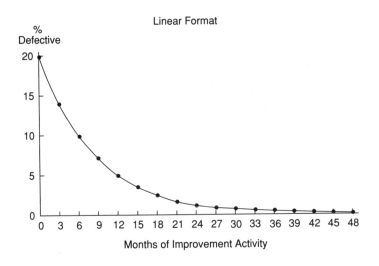

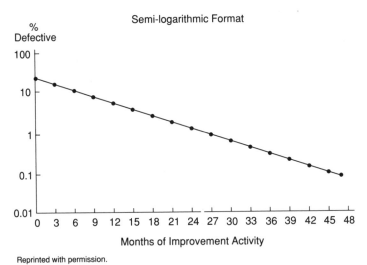

Figure 10-1. Defect Time History

The significance of this analysis is that the rate of improvement (assuming a commitment to continuous improvement) is consistent and can be expressed in terms of the time taken to halve the problem. For example, if a 10-percent reject rate can be improved to 5 percent in nine months, then it can be halved again to 2.5 percent in another nine months. If it takes four months to halve the number of errors in order entry documents, another four months will bring them to one-fourth of the original number, and so forth. This process is called the *half-life* concept because it is a similar technique to the measurement of decay in radioactive compounds, where the half life is the amount of time required for the radioactivity to decay to half its value.

The consistency of this phenomenon, albeit empirical, means that it can be used to predict future levels of defects, setup times, cycle times, and so on. To assist with this use, Mr. Schneiderman has provided a list of 64 different activities (shown in Figure 10-2) together with their half lives and correlation factors. The correlation factor is an indicator of how well the numbers fit the theory; a 1.000 shows a close correlation and a 0.000 signifies no correlation at all.

For occurrences not included in the list of 64, there is a "rule of thumb." In a situation for which a single department has total control of the problem (unifunctional), the half life is typically three months. A situation requiring the cooperation of more than one department (cross-functional) is likely to exhibit a half life of nine months. An activity requiring the cooperation of an outside company will display a half life of 18 months. This estimate is rough and there is considerable variation within the three categories of problems, but the estimate can be used initially for goal-setting until such time as a company is able to develop half-life information.

This method enables managers, supervisors, and operators to establish targets and goals for continuous improvement

The measurement of improvement half life can be done with almost any regression or curve fitting package using the exponential model. A usually adequate alternative is the following graphical method.

- On semi-logarithmic graph paper, plot the defect level (y-axis, log scale) against time (x-axis, linear scale).
- Draw by eyeball the best fit straight line through the data.
- Draw a line parallel to this that intersects the y-axis at an even number, say 10%.
- At a point on the y-axis that is half of the y-intercept value of the best straight line (e.g., 5%), draw a horizontal line.
- Drop a vertical line from the intersection of the horizontal line and the parallel line you drew earlier.
- The time interval between the x-axis origin and your last line's intersection with the x-axis approximates the actual half life.

(This approximation can be improved by dropping by more than one halving of the defect level and dividing by the number of halvings used.)

Description	Half Life (months)	Improvement Cycles	R^2
Operations sheet errors	0.6	4.2	0.834
Days late in delivery	0.8	7.6	0.774
Rejects caused by bends and dents	1.3	1.7	0.590
Process sheet errors	1.4	2.1	0.535
PCB photo imaging resist flake	1.9	3.3	0.748
Errors in purchase orders	2.3	1.5	0.531
Aluminum smears from IC test pads	2.4	5.1	0.717
Yield loss, die coat inspection	2.4	2.3	0.733
Scrap costs, die coat inspection	2.4	2.0	0.754
Defective stockings	2.7	2.2	0.843
Yield loss, PCB photo imaging	2.9	2.3	0.843
Typing errors in bank telegram department	2.9	2.0	0.754
Late orders to customers	3.0	2.7	0.838
Defects in PCB edge polishing	3.3	1.9	0.188
Insertion defect rate	3.3	3.4	0.738
Failure rate, dip soldering process	3.7	8.6	0.980
Down time of facilities	4.5	1.3	0.562
COPQ, goggles manufacturer	4.7	1.9	0.942
Scrap and repair costs	5.0	1.6	0.918
Scrap and repair costs	5.0	0.8	0.746
In-process defect rate	5.3	1.1	0.550
Late spare parts to customers	5.3	1.1	0.471
Defects caused by pits, piston rings	5.5	3.5	0.968
Defects in vacuum molding	5.6	4.6	0.882
Vendor defect level, capacitors	5.7	6.3	0.812

Description	Half Life (months)	Improvement Cycles	R2
Customer returns caused by administrative error	6.3	3.8	0.941
WIP	6.3	1.1	0.979
Accounting miscodes	6.4	2.5	0.709
Manufacturing scrap	7.0	3.9	0.530
Vendor defect level, transformers	7.2	5.0	0.842
Vendor defect level, IC linears	7.4	4.9	0.906
WIP	7.5	2.1	0.759
Failure rate, line assembly	7.5	3.2	0.886
Manufacturing cycle time	7.6	2.7	0.741
Defects per unit	7.6	4.6	0.948
Rework rate	8.0	1.4	0.801
Off-spec rejects	8.8	5.1	0.513
Setup time	9.5	0.6	0.690
Vendor defect level, transistors	9.6	3.7	0.997
Defect levels, customers' incoming QC	10.1	7.1	0.989
Defects	10.4	5.2	0.965
Software documentation errors	10.5	1.2	0.173
Error rate, perpetual inventory	12.1	3.0	0.862
Customer returns because of product	12.4	2.9	0.974
Missing product features	12.5	2.9	0.947
Equipment down time	13.1	2.1	0.940
Scrap costs	13.8	1.7	0.805
Absenteeism caused by accidents	14.8	4.0	0.956
Defects at turn on	14.9	1.3	0.624
Manufacturing cycle time	16.9	2.5	0.937
Defects on arrival	16.9	2.0	0.848
Nonconformances	16.9	0.7	0.666
Vendor defect level microprocessors	18.5	1.9	0.838
Post release redesign	19.0	2.5	0.842
Field failure rate	20.3	1.3	0.857
Accident rate	21.5	2.8	0.907
Defective lots received from vendors	21.6	1.7	0.976
Failure rate, PCB automatic test	23.7	0.5	0.182
First year warranty costs	27.8	2.6	0.950
Computer program execution errors	29.9	0.4	0.364
Late deliveries to customers (+0, −2 weeks)	30.4	0.8	0.994
Warranty failure rates	36.2	2.5	0.769
Failure costs (internal + claims)	37.9	1.9	0.909
Product development cycle time	55.3	1.1	0.733
Average	10.9	2.8	0.770

Reprinted with permission.

Figure 10-2. Observed Improvement Half Lives

programs, and these goals have a degree of objectivity. The goals are realistic only if they are accompanied by a practical commitment to continuous improvement and if the people responsible for the improvement are given the appropriate resources to do the job. These resources can include manpower, equipment, small amounts of capital, training, and expert assistance with both statistical process control and small group problem-solving.

Common Sense Goal-setting

Competitive benchmarking has been invaluable to the Xerox Corporation in its quest for competitiveness in the 1980s. Price targeting and value engineering are an integral part of the quality approach embraced by Toyota and other major Japanese manufacturers in their strategy to penetrate Western markets. The half-life concept is a novel and innovative approach to establishing realistic targets for quality improvement projects.

But these sophisticated techniques are not necessary in order to establish realistic and motivating goals for departments within a company striving for world class status. There is a need at this stage to introduce some pragmatic observations. Simplicity and common sense have a great deal to offer in this area.

The application of world class manufacturing techniques and just-in-time manufacturing can be thought of as the introduction of simplicity into a factory. Most production plants have complex processes and complex administrative systems associated with them. Many of the techniques of world class manufacturing aim at the elimination of these complexities. For example, if production lead times are reduced from 12 weeks to three days, then the need for complex work-in-process accounting is eliminated, the need for control of in-process engineering changes is eliminated, and the need for sophisticated shop floor control techniques is eliminated because there is so much less to control. To achieve simplicity is frequently difficult, and to continuously refine and simplify their production processes is an on-going quest for world class manufacturers.

In light of this, to establish performance targets without the use of sophisticated goal-setting techniques is clearly possible. The application of common sense, coupled with a detailed analysis and understanding of the problems to be solved, gives managers, supervisors, and operators the ability to set goals for themselves.

Goal-setting, however, must be done in accordance with world class manufacturing objectives. The goals frequently will be radically optimistic in comparison to goals set by traditional manufacturers. In traditional plants, an inventory reduction program would typically be associated with a planned improvement in inventory effectiveness on the order of 10 to 20 percent. A world class manufacturer will be looking for reductions of 60 to 70 percent and even then will apply continuous improvement techniques to further eliminate inventory.

Similarly, a traditional manufacturer will set quality goals in terms of rejects-per-thousand parts produced. A world class manufacturer will set an objective of zero rejects, with planned progressive reduction expressed in rejects-per-million. These radical improvements are the hallmark of a successful world class manufacturer, and these approaches need to be incorporated into the production objectives and targets.

There is no need to employ the more sophisticated target-setting techniques; common sense and informed judgment can be equally effective. However, the targets must be radical and in line with a world class manufacturing philosophy. Once the world class manufacturing approach has begun to be applied within the company, the managers and supervisors are able to build up experience. This practical experience can be applied to their previous common sense, and the goals will be yet more realistic.

Interdepartmental Performance Measures

Several major corporations have implemented methods that attempt to translate corporate objectives into specific performance measures for each department within the organization. The idea is to establish a common framework for measuring the performance of each department irrespective of whether the department is directly operational or a support department within the company. The objective is to have the performance measurement systems of support departments like personnel, technical library, and building maintenance integrated with the company's overall performance objectives.

The Xerox Corporation has used this approach with its competitive benchmarking technique; five benchmarks can be established for all departments of the corporation. Benchmarking is not restricted to the major operational goals because these major goals can be broken down into individual components, and each department and each manager can have specific benchmarks.

Competitive benchmarking has permeated the corporation. Every manager at Xerox knows the benchmarks he or she has to achieve because the president of the corporation has made competitive benchmarking one of the foundations of the "New Xerox." The company's "little red booklet" explains the ideas of competitive benchmarking to every employee. The theory is that if everyone in the company has insight into — and a healthy respect for — the competitive challenges of the marketplace, then he or she will be motivated to aim high and achieve.

Northern Telecom has established an innovative method of departmental performance measurement based exclusively on time. All measures are expressed in time, and specific goals can be set for each department. Northern Telecom went through a major readjustment in the early 1980s when competitors began to assault NT's dominance in the massively successful (and profitable) digital-switching technology. After several years of sustained growth, NT saw itself losing market share and volume.

This realization brought about significant changes in operations and outlook. Just-in-time manufacturing techniques were employed in major production plants; new emphasis was brought to bear on customer satisfaction, inventory reduction, and cutting production overheads. At this time, in the words of Roy Merrills, the president of Northern Telecom, "it was suddenly really clear that what was needed to satisfy customer needs was the ability to do things *faster* than ever before. We needed to reorientate Northern Telecom to a whole new operating strategy in which the number one priority was time."[10]

This reorientation resulted in an ingenious approach to performance measurement where every department is measured in terms of the time taken to perform operations, bring new product to market, procure materials, and so forth. This approach does not mean that such vital issues as quality are not measured; they are cleverly incorporated into the time-based approach of the company. This approach has provided Northern Telecom with a companywide focus on what is important and with a clear method of dissemination throughout the company's departments.

Wang Laboratories has developed another method of integrated performance measurement called SMART (Strategic Measurement and Reporting Technique), which establishes a clearly defined method for translating corporate objectives through the primary business operating units to each of the company's departments.[11]

Wang's SMART Way

Figure 10-3 is a diagram outlining the Wang approach. The corporate vision (at the top of the pyramid) is translated into specific market measures and financial measures for each division of the company. These objectives are broken down into division-wide measures of customer service, flexibility, and productivity, where the combination of customer service and flexibility is congruent with the previously defined market measures, and the combination of flexibility and productivity are also congruent with the financial measures.

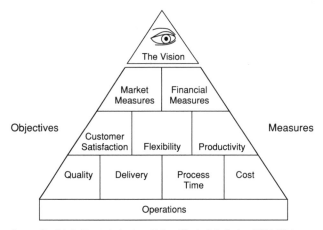

Source: Reprinted with permission from *National Productivity Review*, V8N1, Winter 1988/89. Copyright 1988 by Executive Enterprises, Inc., 22 W. 21st St., New York, NY 10010-6904. All rights reserved.

Figure 10-3. The Performance Pyramid

These broad-brush objectives need to be translated into specific measurable indexes for each department. These specific measures are quantified for each department under four headings:

- quality
- delivery

- process (or throughput) time
- cost

Quality. The definition of quality in the context of Wang's performance measures is broad. Besides considering conformance to specification, it also includes translating the "voice of the customer" into appropriate company requirements at each stage of the life cycle of a product or service from concept to delivery. (Quality measures will differ substantially from one department to another. For a production department, it is dealing with reliability and conformance; for a design department, issues such as innovation and aesthetics will be included.)

Delivery. Good delivery results when performance equals expectations. Delivery, for most departments, includes the twin objectives of quantity and timeliness. The purpose of SMART is to provide measures that align performance with expectations. For example, the customer and supplier may agree on a percentage to be delivered to schedule and a percentage to be delivered on demand; these agreements need to be included in the design of the appropriate measures.

Process time. Process or throughput time refers to the actual time taken for the department concerned to deliver its product or service. The thinking behind this aspect is similar to that of Northern Telecom — that the increase in speed of delivery (of designs, of products, of services, of information) is a primary key to company performance.

Cost. Every department is measured in terms of the costs of delivering the product or service. In the SMART approach, cost is viewed in terms of the excess money (or effort) spent in order to achieve the required quality, delivery, or process time. At the operating unit level, the primary objective is to improve productivity by reducing overall costs; at the department level, the cost objective is often expressed in terms of the elimination of waste.

Using the SMART Way

The intention of SMART is to develop a consistent method of measuring the performance of each department. The method must be appropriate to the department's function within the company and congruent with the corporation's overall objectives.

Departments with direct customer interaction employ performance measures that stimulate the kind of quality and service a world class manufacturer is striving to provide its customers. These measures center around quality, delivery, timeliness, flexibility, and responsiveness. The cost aspects are defined in terms of the elimination of waste (inventory, rework, material movements, and so on) in the process of delivery to the customers.

Other departments in the company that do not have direct customer interaction still use the same four measurement criteria, but the emphasis and importance of each element differs from one department to another and changes over time. Each department determines who is its "customer" and who is its "supplier." For example, the department responsible for the tool crib supplies its products and services to the shop floor departments; its "customer" is the shop floor. Its "supplier" is the machine shop that makes, repairs, and sharpens the tools. The fact that both the supplier and customer of this department are internal to the company makes no difference to the way the SMART concept is applied.

Figure 10-4 shows the SMART system as it applies to a printed circuit board operation. The customer is the final assembly department; the supplier is the materials department. The definition and methods of measurement were established in a joint arrangement between the board department, the final assembly department, and the materials department. The departments jointly define realistic, workable, and mutually acceptable performance indicators for each of the four categories. These measures are in line with the business unit's overall manufacturing strategy and are designed to provide helpful and timely information toward the quality, delivery, cycle time, and cost goals of the department.

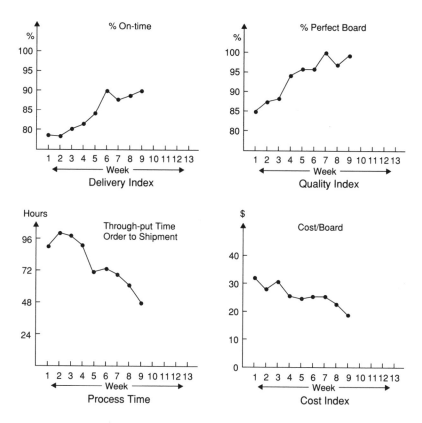

Figure 10-4. SMART System: Printed Circuit Board Manufacturing

Each department has an operational control report that presents the performance of the department in the four primary areas (quality, delivery, process time, and cost) in a consistent format. The control report shows four graphs, one for each of the four areas, containing an index of the department's performance in that area of measurement. The purpose of these control reports is to provide a simple method of presentation so that the information can be presented easily to people in the department and disseminated throughout the corporation.

This process can be repeated in each department; the customers and suppliers are defined and, through negotiation, mutually beneficial performance measures and goals are established. At the time performance goals are established, it is also important to put into place a plan to achieve those goals. This process, done through the interdepartmental teams that determine the new performance measurement methods, provides a valuable forum for the exchange of ideas and the establishment of continuous improvement methods.

The determination of the performance measures is an ongoing process. When a new approach to performance measurement is instituted, the teams will probably not get it right the first time. After the measures have been in use for some time and experience has been gained from their use, they are reviewed and updated. As the business situation changes, the performance measures are changed in method or emphasis, or both. In practice at Wang, the departments have tended to define more performance measures than are necessary or useful. When the measures are reviewed, the number of reports is often reduced and the emphasis changed to make the reporting based more upon exceptions (for example, waste measures rather than total cost) so that the departments can focus more on the process of continuous improvement.

Summary

Although there is some controversy over the desirability of establishing performance targets for world class manufacturers, most companies find it useful to establish clearly defined targets for the performance of each department within the company.

There are a number of sophisticated techniques that can be employed to determine the correct goals for each department, including the following:

- *Competitive benchmarking,* where a detailed analysis is made of the competitors' operations, and an attempt is made to emulate the best aspects of each competitive company.
- *Price targeting,* the application of cost control techniques in detail throughout the initiation and design phases of a new product. This program results in a detailed breakdown of cost and quality targets for each department of the company.
- *The half-life concept,* an analysis of the rate of improvement that can be expected for different kinds of continuous improvement tasks. This system provides a more objective method of setting goals for quality improvement programs.
- *Common sense and a world class manufacturing mind-set,* the application of which provides realistic and motivating targets for companies involved in the introduction of world class manufacturing techniques and continuous improvement.

CHAPTER ELEVEN

Producing the New Performance Measures

THIS CHAPTER WILL examine some practical aspects of the implementation of a new performance measurement system. In reality, the introduction of a new set of performance measures is usually just one step in the introduction of new manufacturing techniques. Implementing world class manufacturing techniques is not a project — it is a total change of approach; and the new techniques are introduced gradually over a period of time. New performance measures can be introduced at the same time.

Some companies have taken the approach that the introduction of new measurement methods is a starting point for the introduction of world class manufacturing techniques; that the measures will highlight the areas requiring change. Other companies have introduced new production methods and then followed up with new performance measurements after the event. The introduction of new performance measures actually should go hand in hand with the introduction of new manufacturing techniques. For example, if you are introducing a world class approach to quality, that is the time to introduce new methods of measuring quality within your company.

Abandonment of Previous Performance Measures

When implementing a new performance measurement approach for world class manufacturing, abandon the old system. This mandate may sound obvious, but it is far from obvious to people who have been using an old system for some time and find it helpful and important.

There are two areas that need to be addressed: (1) the abandonment of financial performance measures and (2) the abandonment of previous nonfinancial measures.

Abandoning Financial Measures

The majority of Western manufacturing companies rely exclusively on accounting reports for performance measurement. That does not mean that they do not have nonfinancial measures, but the financial measures carry far more weight and get more circulation than the nonfinancial measures. The nonfinancial measures tend to be used only in the specific departments that derive them and are not circulated widely. By contrast, the financial reports are widely circulated and accepted as being valid information for the control of the company.

Harvard professor Robert S. Kaplan, co-author of *Relevance Lost: The Rise and Fall of Management Accounting*, draws attention to the inadequacies of current management accounting methods when he says:

> *Many companies use operational measures but they also run their monthly profit-and-loss and budget statements. They have two different systems. The issue is which system gets pushed up from the plant level to the divisional level and*

then to the corporate level. Unfortunately, it tends to be the financial system. My position is that every time you send a financial report from an operating unit to some level of management, you should also include a set of operating performance measures showing physical rather than financial information. These show much better how well the company has been performing and are much more action-orientated than are the usual monthly financial reports.[1]

Changing a company's ethos so that nonfinancial, world class methods of performance measurement become standard practice is not an easy undertaking. The change requires a thorough understanding of the company's needs, a clear assessment of competitive pressures, and leadership at a senior level. It requires the same kind of radical thinking and action that is needed to implement just-in-time manufacturing, total quality control, and other world class manufacturing techniques. These new approaches do not happen by accident or in isolated incidences; they come from decisive and progressive leadership.

Abandoning financial measures does not mean that the company employs no financial reporting. The balance sheets, profit-and-loss statements, budget reporting, and so forth are still required for external reporting and cost control purposes. What is different is that the nonfinancial reports become the authoritative measures of performance for control, improvement, and decision making at the operational level within the corporation.

Abandoning Nonfinancial Reports

The introduction of new performance measures requires that the old measures be abandoned. If the new measures are produced in addition to the old measures, they will not have their intended usefulness and impact. They either will be largely ignored because people are familiar with the previous methods, or both sets of measures will be used and the company will not gain the coherence and focus the new measures offer.

This situation is no different from the introduction of any new approach within a company. The previous system must be eliminated before the new system can be effective. This action is particularly important in the case of performance measurement, because the choice of performance measures and the targets established in their use are designed to influence the behavior of the employees and to coordinate their activities within the manufacturing strategy.

For example, a company previously measured customer delivery service level in terms of the percentage of units shipped within three days of the promised delivery date; and the new method measures delivery service level as the number of orders fully filled on the promised delivery date. The company has a new manufacturing strategy designed to improve on-time, complete deliveries to the customers. Because the old method will yield a much higher service level percentage than the new method, if the old method continues to be reported, the distribution personnel will be receiving "mixed signals" concerning the importance the company places on on-time delivery and may well be content with the more forgiving figures provided by the old system.

It is important to discontinue the old methods of performance measurement when the new techniques are introduced. It is also essential to educate operators, supervisors, and managers in the use of the new methods and in the reasons why they have been introduced.

Establishing the Need for New Performance Measures

Tom Vollmann and his colleagues at Boston University have devised a method for analyzing the performance measurement requirements of a production plant.[2] This performance measurement diagnostic tool has been used at a number of companies and can be tailored to fit the needs of different organizations.

The diagnostic tool consists of a series of questionnaires designed to assess views concerning what is important to measure and the degree to which current reports relate to these issues. The results of these questionnaires are analyzed to establish (1) any congruence between the measurements and the important issues facing the company and (2) where these two aspects diverge.

This approach provides a method of assessing performance measurement needs in a more objective manner. In addition, it is valuable for bringing to light the amount of common understanding of strategies and objectives that exists among plant personnel. Asking people in a company to report the important features of the manufacturing methods can be very revealing. If the answers to these questions are much the same across the people included in the survey, then the company has a widely understood manufacturing strategy. If there is a wide divergence of opinion about what is important, then the company needs to focus attention on establishing and disseminating its manufacturing strategy and approach to world class manufacturing.

The analysis used as a part of the Boston University Performance Measurement Diagnostic Tool provides information about the degree of common thought that exists between the people in the company and shows the extent to which managers, supervisors, and operators are all "on the same wavelength." The analysis then goes on to show graphically the amount of congruence that exists between the current performance measurement system and the people's assessment of what is important to measure. A typical result in shown in Figure 11-1.

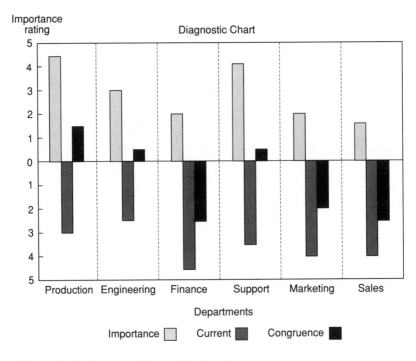

Figure 11-1. Example Diagnostic Chart

When data gathered from the questionnaire are analyzed properly, it is possible to see the areas of divergence — where current performance measures do not deal with the important aspects of the company's operations. These areas need to be addressed first. Performance measures must reflect the manufacturing strategy of the company, and a divergence means that the measures are focusing on the wrong issues and that the company's strategy is not being effectively guided and monitored. The diagnostic tool is a clever idea that has been used effectively in a number of companies. It provides a systematic method for assessing the effectiveness of a performance measurement system in assisting with the achievement of a coherent manufacturing strategy.

Charts, Boards, and Signals

As discussed in Chapter 2, performance measures should be simple and easy to use and should provide fast feedback so that action can be taken quickly to correct problems and build on strengths. Frequently, the best way to achieve this goal is to report the results directly on the shop floor, warehouse, dispatch bay, sales office, or workshop. The use of display charts or boards is useful for such purposes and is common with world class manufacturers.

Performance measurements are recorded by the people doing the work and are shown on a chart in their place of work. The information is clearly displayed so that all the members of that work team can see the results and so that members of other work teams, supervisors, and managers can also keep track of the situation. This approach ensures good communications, creates commitment and team spirit, and motivates people to succeed.

When performance measures are concerned with detecting specific circumstances like a quality failure or a cell overload, then signals can be useful methods of communicating the results. A signal typically will be a light, a buzzer, or a sign used to draw attention to a particular circumstance. Many world class manufacturers use signals to report quality problems in the line. A green light means everything is running well, an orange or yellow light means there is a need for assistance at a work cell, and a red light means that the line has stopped because of a quality problem. A red light will often have an audible warning associated with it; when a red light goes on, everyone knows. A red light causes a flurry of activity as supervisors, engineers, operators, and maintenance people converge on the area to get the problem resolved.

Limitations of Charts, Boards, and Signals

These direct methods of displaying the results of performance measurement are valuable in the plant or office where the work is done, but the dissemination of results to other areas of the company and externally to other interested parties has to be done on paper. The use of charts is again an important aspect of the presentation of the results, particularly when there is a need to discover and analyze trends within the results — trends that can be seen more clearly when the information is shown as a graph or histogram.

Some companies (like Wang Laboratories discussed in Chapter 10) use a standard form of graphical display of performance measurement. The Wang method relies on each department being measured under four criteria: quality, delivery, process time, and cost. These four pieces of information are presented on one piece of paper for each department in the form of four graphs. Each department may have a different method of measuring the four criteria, but the method of presenting the results is consistent.

Graphs and charts should be used to present performance measurement information whenever possible because people are able to understand them better than lists of numbers. However, many aspects of performance cannot be presented in this way, and producing reports that present the information in numerical form becomes necessary. These reports have to be well designed, easy to produce, easy to change, comprehensive, and relevant. In most companies this information is made available through the use of computer systems, and standard computer systems will probably not have the reports available in the right manner. A tool is required that can extract the information from the computer system and present it in the desired way.

Report Writers

The production of performance measurement reports by the management information systems (MIS) department often causes problems. The flexibility and accessibility of the data required by the managers and supervisors in world class manufacturing companies frequently do not fit into the methods of working within the MIS department, because MIS is structured around the needs of longer-term development projects. In most companies, the MIS department does not have a large number of people dedicated to meeting the changing reporting needs of the users, and this situation creates tension between the departments. The users find the MIS department to be unhelpful and obstructive, and the MIS department considers the users to be unreasonably demanding and forever changing their minds. A solution to this problem is the use of a report writer.

A report writer is a software tool designed to allow the managers, supervisors, and specialists within the company's various departments to write their own reports and inquiries and to access information from the computer systems without the need for specialist programming. These tools are called fourth generation languages (4GL) because they can be readily understood and used by people within the company after a minimum of training.

The term "fourth generation" has been coined to designate entirely new methods of computer programming. The "first generation" programs consisted of instructions being built into the early computers and the use of wires and relays to make logical connections within the machine. The "second generation" programming languages were sets of instructions punched onto cards or paper tape that told the computer what to do by giving it a series of complex and specialized codes; these programs could be written only by highly trained technicians. The "third generation" languages like COBOL, FORTRAN, BASIC, and C are widely used for system development on modern computers and employ programming instructions that use (for the most part) real English words and can be more readily understood. Tools called compilers can read these programs and convert them into the detailed and complex codes required by the computer itself. As far as the programmer is concerned, however, the program is written in the third generation language. Third generation programs required trained programmers to develop the systems.

A fourth generation language is designed to be so simple to use and easy to understand that trained specialist programmers are not required. These languages can be used readily by managers, supervisors, and engineers with just a few days of training. They enable the user to extract selected data from the computer system and present it in a useful format that includes printing the data, totalling and summarizing, performing additional calculations and analyses, and dividing the information into relevant sections.

Criteria for a Report Writer

The first criterion for a good report writer is that it must be easy to use. This consideration is highly subjective, but may include the following abilities:

- English-style instructions with no specialist technical codes and syntax.
- Prompted entry allows the program itself to lead the user through the steps required to develop the reports and to ask all the appropriate questions.
- On-line error checking alerts the user immediately if he or she has made a mistake.

- On-line HELP messages that explain how to use the system may appear on the screen to give additional help, instruction, and information.
- A screen design shows what the report looks like as it is developed. The user does not necessarily have to design the report on paper before starting the development; the design can be done interactively using the terminal.
- The ability exists to copy reports, to modify them, and to make changes to existing reports quickly and easily.
- The program automatically creates column headings, page layout, page breaks, subtotalling, and totalling.
- A quick and simple level of use available for the production of ad-hoc, simple reports allows the report writer to do most of the work for the user. More complex levels that provide a large amount of flexibility should be available.
- It includes a well-written, well-presented, and easy-to-read manual.

Another criterion is that the user must have easy access to the data available within the computer system. The data in the system are held on files that are frequently defined in complex and cryptic terms; the fourth generation report writer must have a method of making this information available in ways that can be readily understood. This availability feature will include the use of data dictionary overlays containing descriptive information about the available data, the creation of "views" which logically link several files (or sets of data) together so that the user does not have to learn how the files within the system are structured and keyed, and such helpful additions as predefined headings, field sizes, print positions, and predefined calculations so that the user does not have to define algorithms within the program.

Adequate security must be built into the system so that certain data can be restricted for some users. There is always sensitive data held on these systems, and this information cannot be accessible to all the users. For example, much of the payroll data needs to be secured.

The report writer must be powerful and have the following capabilities:

- It must be able to access multiple files within the system — it is not uncommon for a performance measurement report to employ up to eight or ten files simultaneously.
- It must be able to accommodate several lines to be printed for each piece of information shown.
- It must support calculations within the program and additional calculations at total and subtotal level.
- It must be able to select, using a wide range of selection criteria, so that the user can focus on specific data.
- It must have a large number of functions available including full arithmetic functions, Boolean logic, statistical calculations, various string manipulation functions, date and time functions, and format conversions.
- The totalling and subtotalling must be flexible, have their own headings, and accommodate their own formats.
- It must be able to print on various paper sizes and on various printers, to optionally suppress lines and headings, to produce multiple copies, and so forth.

Programs written by the report writer need to be able to be stored within the system and run easily. They must be able to be incorporated into the standard screens and menus of the primary system so that these reports become a part of the system and not something added onto it.

When a fourth generation report writer is designed, a balance must be struck between ease-of-use and functionality. As a rule of thumb, the more functionality that is incorporated into a program, the more difficult the program is for the users. The skill required in the design of a balanced report writer is to provide a wide range of choice and flexibility without making the tool appear complex and difficult to understand. Some of the more sophisticated report writers have achieved this trick; they provide wide flexibility to the user and yet are simple to use and are very "transparent."

Other Useful Features of a Fourth Generation Report Writer

Many fourth generation report writers have other features that provide additional power to the user. One feature that is pertinent to performance measurement is the ability to upload and download data between machines. When the primary data is held on a mainframe or minicomputer, to be able to extract data from the system on the central computer and to bring it down onto a personal computer for additional analysis and presentation is often a useful feature.

Programs such as spreadsheets and graphics packages provide the individual manager, supervisor, and analyst with powerful tools for analyzing and presenting performance measurement information. Performance measurement data can also be extracted from the central systems into word processing packages for dissemination of the information. These word processing packages can be on the central machine or on personal computers. Many of the reports, charts, and examples contained within this book have been created on a central DEC VAX machine and downloaded onto an Apple Macintosh or IBM PC for final presentation.

Some fourth generation tools provide functionality that takes them beyond the realm of a report writer; they are subsystem development tools. These aspects of a 4GL are not normally made available to people outside of the MIS department because they require a more specialized knowledge of the systems to use them effectively. Also they have the power to change the data on the system's files, thus posing the danger of file corruption if use of the tools is not carefully controlled.

These 4GL features include within the system the establishment of new files that are defined within the 4GL's data dictionary, the ability to update these files through screens on the terminal, the definition of customized screens to update the 4GL files and the primary files within the system, and the ability to write programs that perform mass updates of data contained within the system files and the 4GL files. The use of these tools can quickly and easily provide powerful new features that can be added to the primary system.

An example of the use of a 4GL subsystem for performance measurement purposes is the development of the distance-travelled reports discussed in Chapter 5. A shop floor control and planning system is unlikely to contain the information required to calculate the distance moved from one work cell to another, yet this information is essential to the production of the report. A 4GL can be used to define a new file to contain the distance-moved information and a screen defined to update this information. (A program could be written to establish the distances between each work cell based upon the grid reference of the cells within the factory if this information is available and relevant.)

The reports now can be developed by extracting data from the master schedule to determine which products are to be made, by extracting data from the manufacturing routings for those products to determine where the products are moved, and by accessing the new distance-moved file to calculate the actual distances.

Problems with the use of fourth generation tools Fourth generation tools are computer programs designed to present in simple form the complexity of programming reports and other programs required by managers, supervisors, and analysts. These 4GL programs themselves are large and complex programs that can take up considerable computing resources. One disadvantage of these systems is that they can slow down the computer because of the resources required to run them, and this process in turn makes the primary systems less useful because they are also slowed down.

Another aspect of this problem is often that reports written using 4GL tools are not as efficient to run as programs written using conventional programming languages. When there are a large number of 4GL reports in use, the system performance can be impaired because computer resources are not being used efficiently. This problem is exacerbated when there are many people using the 4GL tools at the same time.

A related problem is that providing this level of flexibility to the users can result in a large number of programs and subsystems being written, a situation that results in procedures being developed in an unplanned, ad-hoc manner. This difficulty, of course, can be overcome by having the use of these tools strictly controlled; but this control can defeat the objective of providing flexible and easy-to-use tools. In reality, companies using 4GL report writers are able to find an appropriate balance between the accessibility of useful information and the efficient use of the machine. As a result, some of the performance measurement reports that have been written using the report writer occasionally will need to be rewritten in COBOL or other more efficient programming languages and incorporated into the company's standard systems.

Example of a Fourth Generation Report Writer

Several excellent report writers are available that run on different machines and employ different technologies. An example of a good report writer is the product PRAXVU, which is marketed by the Unitronix Corporation as a part of their PRAXA manufacturing and distribution system. The same product, which runs on the Digital Equipment Corporation's VAX range of machines, is also available from Park Software and marketed under the name XENTIS.

Figure 11-2 shows an example of the screen used within PRAXVU to develop a report. The central section of the screen shows the selection of data elements that are available to the user from the system files. The user can select a particular data element by putting the cursor on that data element and pressing the "select" key on the keyboard; no entry of data element names is required.

The lower part of the screen shows the user's choices of where to print the data, what the heading should be, what the length of the data field should be, and what kind of totalling or subtotalling is needed on that element. All these choices will be filled by default values if the user does not need to change them.

The central band gives a brief explanation of what action is required by the user at this time, and more detailed instructions can be obtained by pressing the "help" key. There are two levels of help available to the user: (1) a brief paragraph of instructions or (2) a full multi-page explanation of the feature and its valid values.

The top section of the screen shows what the report looks like. Every data element added to the report will be shown on the format at the top of the screen. The same is true of headings, totals, and subtotals. This provides the user with a "what you see is what you get" method of designing and developing reports.

PRAXVU also has an inquiry mode that produces reports in the same way as shown in the example except that the user is not asked so many questions and is able to quickly and easily produce a simple report in a standard format. Most of the work — except selection of the data required — is performed by PRAXVU.

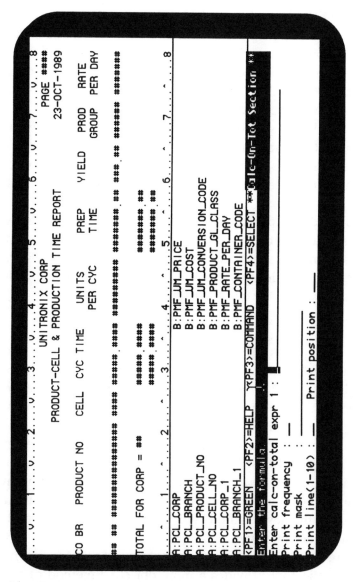

Source: Used by permission of Park Software.

Figure 11-2. Sample Screen From PRAXVU Report Writer

PRAXVU has a feature, helpful to more experienced users of the system, where the "user friendliness" can be switched off and programs written or modified using the more complex codes underlying the programs. A user more knowledgeable of the PRAXVU product can program reports more quickly using this "expert" mode.

PRAXVU has its own data dictionary, which allows users to predefine such things as column headings. This data dictionary is compatible with the data dictionaries supplied by Digital Equipment Corporation, yet provides additional flexibility for the user.

Upload and download features are provided by PRAXVU for spreadsheet, database, and word processing files. Full subsystem development can be achieved through PRAXVU by using the file updating and edit features, which include the ability to easily create customized screens.

Summary

It is important to discontinue the old methods of performance measurement when new techniques are introduced. It is also essential to educate operators, supervisors, and managers in the use of the new methods and in the reasons why they have been introduced.

Financial reports will continue to be produced for external reporting and cost control purposes, but the performance measures that really control and monitor the company's business will be primarily nonfinancial. The importance and status of the new methods will be determined by the attitude of the senior managers.

The Boston University Performance Measurement Diagnostic Tool provides a more objective method of assessing the effectiveness of a performance measurement system and can point to areas where changes need to be made.

While charts, graphs, and signals are useful ways of reporting many kinds of performance measures, most performance measurement reports are produced by accessing data from the company's computer system. A fourth generation report writer can be used to make this information readily accessible and to provide the flexibility required for world class performance measurement.

CHAPTER TWELVE

Alternative Cost and Management Accounting Techniques

THIS CHAPTER IS NOT intended to be a thorough examination and explanation of all the new approaches to cost and management accounting being employed by world class manufacturers; that would take another book. The intention is to provide the reader with an overview of the techniques currently being used and considered in the world class manufacturing arena.

Two important points must be addressed at the outset: (1) the lack of new management accounting standards and (2) the relationship between cost and management accounting and financial accounting.

Lack of New Management Accounting Standards

There is no such thing as world class manufacturing accounting. There is not at this time a definitive, industry-wide set of accounting standards that can be applied. While the time-honored accounting standards (Federal Accounting Standards Board, Statement of Standard Accounting Practice, and others) taught to and used by management accountants worldwide are no longer applicable to world class manufacturing (see Chapter 3), no standard practices have been established to overcome these problems.

Further to the lack of standards, there is a lack of consensus among management accounting professionals and academics about what methods should be employed to replace the traditional approaches. There is a raging debate going on in the universities and colleges, company boardrooms and offices, and within the professional institutions. Although there is considerable debate concerning the importance of these problems, the problems to be addressed are largely understood but, for many companies, the solutions are still in the experimental stage.

The "left wing" of this debate declares that management accounting is so irrelevant and misleading to the running of a business that it should be abandoned completely. The "right wing" feels that gradual and constructive modification of current techniques will lead to an orderly change that will bring management accounting back into the forefront of decision-making tools. These divergent opinions have led to sharp exchanges and heated discussion in print and at conferences around the country. To some it has been amusing to watch otherwise sober accounting ladies and gentlemen locked in conflict over the issues of overhead absorption, standard costing, variances, and the like.

In the office and on the shop floor, management accountants are facing the same issues in a more pragmatic environment. Many financial people within companies, particularly those moving toward world class manufacturing, are aware of the shortcomings of traditional management accounting methods but are uncertain how to resolve these issues. Factory accountants frequently are finding themselves under attack from their nonfinancial colleagues, yet without a clear picture of the way to proceed.

Many new techniques being employed by progressive companies are aimed at providing relevant and simplified accounting methods. This chapter will outline some of these techniques and assess their relevance and usefulness.

Financial Accounting and Cost Accounting

The changes being made to cost and management accounting do *not* significantly impact the financial accounts. The methods of collection and presentation of financial accounting information is largely prescribed by law, securities regulations, and standard accounting practice. Reporting of financial accounts does not change substantially when world class manufacturing techniques are introduced because financial accounts must continue to report the company's situation in a consistent manner according to accepted standards.

Note that there may be different methods employed to gather the information that goes into the financial accounts. The valuation of inventory, both raw material and work-in-process, may change if cost accounting techniques change. The integration between cost accounting and financial accounting may be different. The traditional approach is to treat cost accounts as a subledger of financial accounts so that there is a consistent method of viewing the financial information across both sets of accounts.

World class manufacturers frequently employ different methods within the cost accounts than within the financial accounts, and new methods have to be devised to obtain the information required by the financial accounts. A good example of a new method is the one used by the Harley-Davidson production plant in York, Pennsylvania.

Prior to the implementation of just-in-time manufacturing techniques and a new approach to costing, Harley-Davidson used traditional work order-based cost collection techniques, which valued work-in-process inventory using the standard costs of materials, actual hours worked, and overheads apportioned by labor costs. This WIP inventory valuation was integrated faithfully into the financial accounts. With the implementation of new manufacturing techniques resulting in very much lower WIP inventories and consistent levels of WIP materials, Harley-Davidson was able to eliminate the pedantic cost collection techniques of the previous system and estimate the work-in-process inventory annually, or whenever significant changes occurred in the production mix or methods. These estimates are now used to report WIP inventory values on the balance sheet.

Similarly, world class manufacturing companies frequently have different ways of handling direct labor costs. Many do not keep track of direct labor in a detailed way but fold these costs into their overheads. This simplification in cost accounting results in the balance sheet and profit-and-loss statements showing different figures than the traditional approach shows. The financial reports are the same, but the information contained within the reports is derived differently and often uses different assumptions.

The following discussion deals with management accounting for world class manufacturers, not financial accounting. Although the financial accounts may be impacted by changes in the management accounting techniques, the financial reports will continue to be present in much the same way as before.

New approaches to management accounting The new approaches to cost and management accounting being used by world class manufacturers include:

- abandonment of management accounting
- process costing
- direct costing
- actual costs

- activity-based costing
- throughput accounting
- life cycle costing
- Japanese approaches to cost and management accounting

Abandoning Management Accounting

All world class manufacturers find that traditional management accounting is no longer as useful and important to them as before; some world class manufacturers stop using cost and management accounting completely. The reasoning is that if the traditional cost and management accounting methods are misleading and irrelevant, and if company operations can be successfully controlled and monitored using nonfinancial measures, then using management accounting is not at all necessary.

The concepts inherent within world class manufacturing techniques are so sound that their introduction will reduce production costs significantly even if the company does not record and track production costs. WCM methods address the real issues which cause the costs, including long cycle times, high inventory, low quality, poor customer service, and poor management. If these issues are improved — and especially if they are improved radically — then costs will fall radically and productivity will rise. If you take care of the real issues, the costs will take care of themselves.

Complete abandonment of cost and management accounting is unusual, but significantly limiting its use is quite common. All world class manufacturers simplify their costing systems because the production processes have been simplified and tracking costs in the traditional way is no longer necessary.

Often, this costing simplification takes place after operational changes have taken effect. Management accountants usually do not take a leading role in the introduction of world class manufacturing techniques. This lack of involvement is disappointing because the education, training, experience, and analytical skills of management accounting personnel could be invaluable to a company embarking on world class manufacturing methods. Unfortunately, management accountants are frequently a hindrance to progress rather than instigators. Universities and colleges teaching management accounting and the professional bodies representing management accountants should educate and prepare members of this profession to become leaders in the quest for world class manufacturing status.

Abandoning Labor Reporting

The first thing to change in the costing system is the importance of collecting labor costs. The proportion of labor costs to the total cost of a product is fast reducing; the average for American manufacturers is currently 7 to 8 percent of total cost and in some industries as low as 2 percent or less. Complex and detailed systems to collect, track, and report this information are not necessary.

Detailed labor reporting either is eliminated all together, or it is collected in total and added into production overhead costs. The detailed tracking of labor and reporting of labor variances is meaningless, expensive, and unnecessary.

In a traditional production control system, keeping track of labor hours was easy because detailed labor information was required by the shop floor control system. In order to keep track of the progress of the planned production schedule, it was necessary to report the completion of each detailed job step with the product routing. The labor costs, machine costs, and setup costs could be entered at that time.

The simplification of the production process, however, with the introduction of production cells and synchronized manufacturing techniques makes this kind of detailed shop floor control unnecessary, making it also unnecessary to engage in the wasteful and fruitless activity of tracking and recording all that detailed information.

If tracking the production steps and detailed labor hours on the shop floor is unnecessary, then it is further unnecessary to maintain a work order-style of production control. Most world class manufacturers abandon the traditional MRPII style of shop floor control in favor of planning using flow techniques and rate-based production schedules. These new techniques are entirely compatible with an MRPII approach to manufacturing, providing the software has been designed to integrate synchronized manufacturing into the shop floor planning and control systems.[1]

The abandonment of labor reporting and work order control goes a long way toward significant reductions in overheads within the production plant. Traditional manufacturers spend enormous amounts of time and effort keeping the production systems going. The detailed planning, tracking, recording, correcting, rerouting, rescheduling, and monitoring that goes into a traditional production planning system is not required for world class manufacturers.

Another area frequently abandoned by world class manufacturers is incentive payroll schemes. The idea that individuals are paid according to the amount of product they produce runs contrary to world class manufacturing philosophy. There are two primary problems; the first is that a scheme of this sort places the emphasis on speed rather than quality. The second is that it does not encourage teamwork and problem-solving. The operator who is clamped into an incentive payment scheme and wishes to earn high wages is forced to just keep on producing product at the fastest possible rate. Most incentive payment schemes also have an element of quality built into them in that the operator is paid only for manufactured products that pass inspection; there is no concept of continuous improvement.

These methods of payment have to be replaced with methods that encourage and enhance world class ideas of quality, teamwork, continuous improvement, cross-training, and so forth. This change requires that the managers negotiate new payment methods with their employees or the union representing them, and this situation frequently results in production personnel becoming exempt, salaried employees. When this occurs, there is no need to have the payroll system and the cost accounting systems working together because the people are not being paid according to production quotas or hours worked.

Abandoning Inventory Reporting

The reason most cost accounting systems keep track of the detailed use of inventory — components, raw material, and subassemblies — is that the variation in usage of parts is traditionally high. A high variation of usage necessitates keeping track of what has been used where and of how much it is costing the company to make something. World class manufacturing continuously eliminates that variability by the application of quality improvement, product simplification, better design, and a more detailed understanding of the production process.

Another reason companies keep track of parts issued to jobs is that they have to maintain a detailed measure of work-in-process inventory value. When cycle times and inventory are reduced, keeping track of the cost of inventory is not necessary, because WIP is low and is no longer a prime cost factor. The time and effort that most companies put into the detailed tracking of inventory transactions is clearly wasteful and should be eliminated.

When cycle times are short and material usage consistent, keeping detailed records of what has been issued to which job on which production cell is also no longer required. World class manufacturers make use of backflushing to report component part usage.

Backflushing is a system that reports component issue transactions at the time the assembly or subassembly is completed. When the completion is reported to the production planning system, the quantity of components, raw material, and subassemblies that must have been used to make the assembly is calculated. The amount of components issued is calculated from the quantity completed and the quantities on bills of materials for the assembly. These quantities are then used to reduce the on-hand balance quantities of the components on the inventory system.

When the physical quantities are updated on the inventory system, the material costs used in the manufacture of that product can be posted. The result is that the reporting of a single transaction — the completion of the product and its quantity — results in four separate kinds of transactions being reported in the system: the completion itself, an update of the production schedule, an update of the component on-hand stock quantities, and a posting of the material costs.

This backflushing technique enables world class manufacturers to reduce significantly the work involved in keeping inventory planning and control systems up to date. Backflushing, of course, does require that the bills of materials are accurate and that the levels of work-in-process inventory are low. There is a "happy circle" here; backflushing enhances inventory accuracy because mistakes made in inventory reporting are predominantly human error when entering transactions. With backflushing, the human transactions are reduced enormously and the accuracy of the inventory records is correspondingly improved.

When all inventory reporting is done through backflushing, there must be simple and accurate methods of recording scrap and rejects. A world class manufacturer will have reduced the incidence of scrap, rejects, and rework, but when these elements do occur, procedures need to be in place to account for them. Keeping track of scrap and rejects is, of course, very much part of the continuous improvement process. All scrap and rejects must be analyzed to determine the cause, and the cause must be eliminated from the process.

Variances

What is the place of variance reporting within world class manufacturing? There is no place for variance reporting. If the company ceases to report labor hours on a job-by-job basis, then there are no data to produce labor variance reports. If inventory usage is reported using backflushing then, by definition, there is no variance in material costs other than those reported through the scrap and reject system. The scrap should be reported in nonfinancial terms, and variance reports offer no help with this.

Overhead variances have always been a misunderstood part of cost accounting and serve little or no purpose within world class manufacturing, particularly when there are no work orders to report the variances against. Variances are, by definition, the variation of the actual production process from the "standard" production process. The quest of world class manufacturers is to eliminate that variation; therefore, the concept of variance reporting becomes redundant. During the continuous process of variance reduction (or quality improvement), nonfinancial reports serve as a better guide than do cost accounting variance reports.

Process Costing

The changes that take place within the production plants of a company moving into world class manufacturing have the effect of making them operate more like a repetitive manufacturing facility. The introduction of production cells, reorganization of the shop floor, and synchronized manufacturing techniques result in the plant changing from a job shop orientation to flow line production. The cost accounting needs thus become more like that of a process production plant.

A process production plant, a factory that makes a limited number of products in a continuous flow process, uses accounting techniques that are different from those of a more discrete manufacturing environment. Such a plant is scheduled using rate-based scheduling, and the costing cannot be associated with a work order because there are no work orders.

The techniques of process costing are tried, tested, and well understood by cost accountants. These techniques, or variations of them, can be adapted to meet the needs of world class manufacturers.

Attributes of Process Costing

Management accounting in a process plant is centered around the process itself. The company makes money by optimizing the flow of material through the process; the more product that flows, the more money the company makes (assuming there is demand in the market for the product). The costing focus within process plants is also on the process.

Work orders are not used because the plant is scheduled entirely in terms of the rate of flow a product can make through the plant, and these rates are expressed in quantity per hour or per day — sometimes in tons, gallons, or cubic feet. Production costs are collected by process and product, not by individual job or batch being made. These costs include materials, labor, and overhead applied using a rate per hour (or similar factor). When the process consists of several subprocesses or cells, the costs can be collected for that product at that cell.

The analysis of these costs is not done by job or batch. By their nature, processed products have some uncontrollable variations caused by the physics and chemistry of the process;

and the results of an individual batch or job costs would not be relevant in themselves. Costs are analyzed on a period-to-date and year-to-date basis. The costs are collected by the product (or product group) and the cell or process, and this information is kept in detail for each day and consolidated into the period-to-date and year-to-date figures.

Analysis of these costs is concerned primarily with identifying trends (good or bad) in the process and with using these trends to identify changes in the process that need to be corrected or enhanced. Because there are no batch standards to derive variances from and therefore no variances as such, the trends over time become more significant indicators of progress.

Variance reports are used within process costing systems but are shown in terms of totals over time of actual costs against standard costs and in terms of actual costs against budgeted costs, period-to-date and year-to-date. The value of the variance reports increases as production volumes increase. Only when the inherent variations of the process begin to average out can the true trend and budgetary variances be identified.

Other aspects of process costing do not readily apply to world class manufacturing of discrete products. These include the algorithms used to value work-in-process inventory, the methods that have been developed to handle by-products in the process, and the unpredictable nature of the bills of materials (or recipes) used in the process.

For a company to change its cost accounting system from the traditional work order, batch-based costing and variance reporting is a big step. But moving into a process-style costing system is not as radical as some other alternatives because the techniques are well understood and have been in use for years in other types of industries.

Direct Costing

Some world class manufacturers take the view that the distortions caused by the incorrect application of overhead costs render useless any kind of costing that involves overhead application. The solution is to use direct costs only.

The purpose here is to collect only the costs that are direct and relevant to the production of the product. These costs, of course, include material costs and labor costs, but labor costs would be included only if they are significant. In addition, costs would include as many of the currently indirect costs that can be made into direct costs. This change can be achieved by making organizational changes so that hitherto support departments (perhaps shared by many direct departments) are rearranged so that their services can be identified to a specific direct department. In this way, the costs of the "indirect" department are now direct and can be included in the direct costing system.

Other direct costs that can be included are direct machine costs and outside processing costs. Such intangibles as depreciations, amortization, technology costs, as well as the traditional overheads from indirect departments, are not included in product costing calculations. The advantage of direct costing is that it is simple and clearly understood by all the people who use it; the costs are real.

Overhead costs are not ignored by a direct costing system, they simply are tracked differently. Overhead costs assigned to the indirect departments are based on their budgets, and the variance reports are shown against budgets instead of against standard costs. These budgets may have elements of variable budgeting in them so that the budgets are adjusted automatically for the production volumes occurring in the plant.

The principle idea is that mixing indirect costs and direct costs in the same reporting mechanism is confusing and misleading; therefore, split the two kinds of costs and analyze them differently in ways that are more sensible for the kind of costs involved.

The financial accounts, of course, will never use direct costing because legal, tax, and securities regulations require full absorption costing for financial reporting. Nonetheless, direct costing can be used for cost and management accounting purposes.

Actual Costs

Many world class manufacturers are unhappy with the use of standard costs as tools for measuring the success of production plants. Their arguments are all the traditional ones against standard costing:

- Standard costs are theoretical and do not apply to the realities on the shop floor.
- Should the standards be "ideal," "pragmatic," or reflect the actual current situations?
- When a product can be made in more than one way, the standard is not relevant for the alternate methods.
- Variance reports frequently are available too late to be of any value in resolving production problems.
- When standards are recalculated periodically (every year), they cannot be used to compare one year's results with the next.

In addition, world class manufacturers are unhappy with standard costs because they do not support the ideas of continuous improvement. A supervisor can see a report showing that all his or her variances are positive and be satisfied with the results. In fact, the supervisor should be spurred on to more improvement, but the variance reports create complacency and do not drive people toward continuous improvement.

Another complaint world class manufacturers have about standard costing methods is that, for standard cost variances to work correctly, a work order style of cost collection is necessary. Most world class manufacturers abandon work order systems in favor of rate-based schedules, and standard costs become less meaningful.

An actual costing system collects the actual costs incurred during the production process and reports them directly. These costs may include actual material costs, actual labor costs, actual machine costs, and actual outside processing costs. As with direct costing, making as many as possible of the currently indirect costs into direct cost centers is advantageous.

Actual costs can be reported each day on each shift in total or in terms of the actual cost per unit produced or per pound, gallon, ton, and so on. Alternatively, the direct costs can be expressed in terms of the financial contribution obtained from selling the products manufactured that day.

Actual costing is easy to use and understand and provides a clear-cut and directly relevant method of communicating productivity information to the people on the shop floor. It does not attempt to deal with overhead burdens to finished products, but actual overhead costs can be reported against budgets for the indirect departments whose "product" is a service within the company rather than a saleable item.

Activity-based Costing

The ideas of activity-based costing were developed in the late 1980s by Professors Robert Kaplan and Robin Cooper of the Harvard Business School in an attempt to resolve some of the fundamental inadequacies of traditional cost accounting. Several major companies have been experimenting with the use of activity-based costing, and early indications are that this approach can be of practical value for product pricing, production decision making (mix, volume, and others), overhead cost reduction, and continuous improvement approaches.

Activity-based costing seeks to address some of the short-comings of traditional management accounting discussed in Chapter 3, in particular:

1. Traditional management accounting is driven by the needs of the financial accounts (specifically the need to value inventory) and does not address the development of meaningful product cost information for other purposes. According to Professor Kaplan, "Systems designed mainly to value inventory for financial and tax statements are not giving managers the accurate and timely information they need to promote operating efficiencies and measure product costs."[2]

2. Labor costs are now a small part of total product costs for most manufacturing companies, yet labor cost is still the most popular method of allocating overheads to products through the production process. The average product manufactured in the United States has a labor content of less than 8 percent and for companies using just-in-time techniques as low as 4 percent (as at Tektronix[3]) or 2 percent (as at Hewlett-Packard[4]). Some companies use other overhead allocation factors including machine time and material costs, but these are limited allocation factors and introduce significant distortions into the product costing results.

3. As the marketplace becomes more competitive and production processes more complex and technologically sophisticated, a clearer understanding is needed of the source of product costs. Using only the traditional cost elements of material, labor, outside process, and overhead burdens is no longer meaningful. Being able to understand where the costs are coming from and what activities generate these costs is not of prime importance.

The Concepts of Activity-based Costing

Activity-based costing primarily is concerned about the cost of indirect activities within a company and their relationships to the manufacture of specific products. This understanding can then provide a basis for product costing and profitability analysis. Inventory valuation for financial reporting purposes is recognized as a separate issue and may require a different (and simpler) approach to overhead allocation.

The basic technique of activity-based costing is to analyze the indirect costs within a production plant and to discover the activities that cause those costs. These activities, known as *cost drivers*, can be used to apply those overheads to specific products. For example, if a significant amount of money is spent by a company on the introduction, processing, and control of engineering changes on the shop floor, then it would be possible to gather all the costs associated with engineering change control into a single cost pool. From this total cost, calculating the cost per engineering change note (ECN) processed is now possible. These costs can then be assigned to individual products by simply counting how many ECNs have been processed for the product (or product group) and by multiplying this number by the cost per ECN. This method allows the ECN costs, which previously were lumped into overhead burden, to be applied directly to the product cost.

Similar analysis can be done for all the different aspects of indirect costs and cost drivers identified. The analysis of the sources of costs and their application to specific products will result in the use of multiple cost drivers. The following is a list of cost drivers used by some of the companies using activity-based costing. This list is not exhaustive, but is intended to provide an indication of the diverse cost drivers that can be employed:

- number of production batches
- number of goods-received batches

- number of purchase orders
- number of customer orders
- number of suppliers
- number of engineering changes
- number of component parts
- number of component part numbers
- number of unique parts in the assembly
- number of steps in the routing
- number of material moves
- distance moved through the plant
- number of setups
- total change over time
- production cycle time
- specific production operations (for example, in the printed circuit board process, the number of component insertions, the number of manual soldering tasks, wave soldering cycle time, etc. For a press machine, the number of strikes performed may be used.)
- number of rejects
- number of returns
- number of line stops
- number of cases shipped
- weight of product shipped
- number of trucks loaded
- number of tools issued to the shop floor

The diversity of cost drivers chosen by a production plant is what enables the activity-based costing technique to be flexible and to recognize the complexity of the production process. However, as the case studies given below will demonstrate, activity-based costing, to be helpful, does not have to have all overhead costs allocated by unconventional cost drivers. Some companies carefully choose just a handful of cost drivers that enable them to allocate 50 percent (for example) of their indirect costs based on activities and continue to apply the remaining 50 percent by conventional methods. By the use of multiple cost drivers and an analysis of the activities that can be attributed to each product or product family, costs that were previously considered indirect can be applied in a similar way to direct costs.

There is an 80/20 rule that applies to the use of cost drivers. If there is a potential of 50 cost drivers and 80 percent of the production costs can be accounted for by 10 of those drivers, then it will often be sufficient to use just the 10 drivers. The cost of collecting and processing the data for the other 40 drivers is not matched by the usefulness of the information. In reality, all companies implementing activity-based costing find that there are costs that have no meaningful cost driver at all. These costs have to be applied in conventional ways or by simply dividing these costs by the number of products manufactured, and thus an additional burden amount to be applied to each product is derived.

Another view of this process is to consider activity-based costing as making more of the production costs into direct costs. In reality, many of the costs that traditionally are considered fixed costs are, in fact, variable costs but over a longer time frame. For example, purchasing costs are considered fixed costs in most traditional costing systems, but if the volume or mix of production changes over time, the number of people, equipment, and expenses needed by the purchasing department (and other related departments) will change. Purchasing costs are variable over the longer term, not the short term. Activity-based costing takes account of these changes by charging items like purchasing costs to the product in proportion to the amount of activity generated by the product.

How Hewlett-Packard Uses Activity-based Costing

Hewlett-Packard has been a leader in the quest for world class manufacturing and has implemented many innovative techniques in its production plants over the last ten to 15 years. Several HP plants have established new costing systems to complement the changes taking place in the production technologies of the plant. There are two case studies of particular note: one relates to an HP plant in England[5] and the other to the Roseville Networks Division (RND) plant in the United States.[6]

The English plant manufactures three different product lines each consisting of a range of individual products and makes its own printed circuit board assemblies, which are used in all three products (Figure 12-1 shows a schematic diagram of the plant). The RND plant makes major subassemblies, primarily printed circuit board assemblies and mechanical devices used in the HP central processors. RND has 250 different products with up to 1,100 different variations.

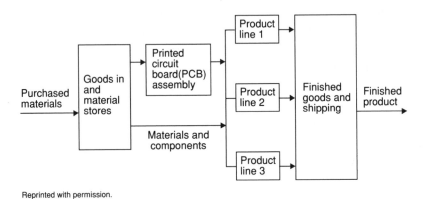

Reprinted with permission.

Figure 12-1. Hewlett-Packard UK Plant

Costing system in the English plant The UK plant needed a new costing approach so as to provide better information for strategic decision making, for accurately calculating individual product costs, and for valuing inventory for financial accounting purposes. The first step taken was to directly allocate more indirect expenses. This phase was achieved by reorganizing some of the support departments so that they could be associated directly with a particular product line and the costs applied directly to the product line.

Another step was to separate the calculation of inventory valuation for financial accounting purposes from that used for operational decision making. The inventory valuation used in the financial reports has a simple overhead burden rate based on the material cost of the product. This method of overhead application is suitable for financial accounts because it is simple, consistent, and accurate enough in total for each product line. This method is unsuitable for cost analysis and decision-making purposes because it distorts the costs of individual products and assemblies and does not provide any insight into the source of indirect costs. Again, according to Professor Kaplan, "I have no argument with the use of financial accounting for external reporting to shareholders, tax authorities, creditors, and the like. My complaint is that managers are using the same figures to make important decisions for which the data is unsuitable. Entirely different methods are required to give managers the information they need for operational control of the business and for accurately assessing the costs of producing and marketing a product."[7]

The next step was to implement an activity-based costing system. The analysis of what really drives indirect costs in the plant was thorough and pragmatic, with department managers very much involved with the selection of cost drivers. A limited number of cost drivers was selected, including product part count, number of schedule calls, number of component insertions, and the number of boxes shipped.

The primary purpose of the introduction of activity-based costing was to improve cost information, but the spin-off benefit has been the understanding gained by company managers into the source and control of costs. "Managers have been effectively educated in the principles of activity-based costing and these principles are considered in assessing the resources consumed by each product line and product."[8]

Costing system in the U.S. plant The use of new costing methods stemmed from two different needs. One need was the conflict that existed between the manufacturing managers and the management accounting personnel; the other was the introduction of world class manufacturing techniques. Initially, WCM was perceived as a change in the focus of the plant from individual products to manufacturing processes. As a result, different accounting techniques became required for process manufacturing rather than for discrete manufacturing.

A project team established to develop a new approach to management accounting soon discovered that the source of much of the conflict between operational managers and the accountants was caused by the operational managers using different methods to calculate product costs. These methods were essentially an activity-based approach, and the new accounting system was developed using the same concepts already being used by the operational managers. The ideas had been refined and adapted over time, but the concepts were essentially the same.

The indirect costs are now divided into three primary areas: procurement overhead, production overhead, and support overhead. All labor, both direct and indirect, are included in overhead; the labor reporting system has been abandoned. The support overhead, which includes production engineering, process engineering, data processing, and manufacturing management, is allocated into the procurement and production overheads using a simple allocation method. Procurement overheads are applied to individual products using the cost driver of the number of parts per product. It was determined that the number of parts per product was the best cost driver for the application of procurement, incoming inspection, warehousing, documentation, production planning, and logistics expenses.

The production overheads are applied differently; a cost driver has been identified for each of the eight major production departments, and the costs of these departments are applied to the products that pass through the department using that department's cost driver. The drivers are:

- start station (number of PC boards)
- axial insertion (number of axial insertions)
- dip insertion (number of dip insertions)
- manual insertion (number of manual insertions)
- wave soldering (number of boards soldered)
- backload (number of backload insertions)
- test (standard time board in test)
- defect analysis (yielded standard time)

The RND methods differ significantly from those of the Hewlett-Packard plant in England. The cost drivers are very different, the cost pools are organized differently, and the U.S. plant does not have a separate method of inventory valuation for financial reporting purposes. The two systems are different primarily because their operations are different. The techniques of activity-based costing are the same but the outcome is different. This difference shows the flexibility of activity-based costing to different production environments.

Three More Case Studies of Activity-based Costing

Siemens Electric Motor Works once had a thriving business manufacturing standard electric motors — 200 different styles and a volume of 230,000 motors each year. During the 1980s

Siemens found their market for standard motors diminishing owing to severe competition, and in 1988 the company invested in new facilities to expand its business in the customized motor marketplace.

The cost characteristics of customized motors differ widely from those of standard motors. The production order sizes are much smaller and the engineering design costs are significant. An extensive study revealed that there were only two primary cost drivers: the number of production orders and the number of special components required to make the motor.

The cost accountants at Siemens decided to implement a combination of activity-based costing and traditional costing. They established cost pools related to each of these cost drivers and calculated the cost per production order and the cost per special component. Rather than using a labor value rate, other overhead costs (unrelated to the two cost drivers) continued to be applied using a material value overhead rate and a machine hours overhead rate. The customized motors have a reasonably high labor content, and Siemens decided to continue tracking direct labor.

The production costs are calculated by summing the following factors (the numbers are not actual):

Material cost	*12.00*
Direct labor cost	*6.00*
Material value overhead @ 50%	*6.00*
Machine hours overhead @ $3.20/hours	*9.60*
Cost per order (1 order @ $12.25)	*12.25*
Cost per special component (6 @ $2.95)	*17.70*
TOTAL COST	45.85

John Deere Component Works also implemented new production methods as a result of severe competition in an already soft market for agricultural equipment in the 1980s.

The component division is a supplier to other John Deere plants but has to compete for its business with outside vendors; the component division did not win business just by being an in-house supplier. Increasingly, company plants were looking to outside suppliers rather than the components division because they could get better prices and service. John Deere's management accountants studied the problem and determined that in some of their major product lines the cost distortions generated by the traditional cost accounting system were causing the division to quote too high on some of their products and lose money on others.

The gear and special products department was the first area of the company to implement activity-based costing. Seven cost pools were derived:

1. direct labor support
2. machine operation
3. setup hours
4. production order processing
5. material handling
6. parts administration
7. general overhead

Cost drivers and allocation rates were established for each of the cost pools, resulting in a much clearer understanding of the costs and profitability of their products. Forty-one percent of the overhead shifted away from labor and machine rates to the newer cost drivers, significantly changing the product costs and favoring high volume items.

A simple estimating system was established based on this analysis, and John Deere Component Works achieved significantly more profitable business in the following round of bidding for internal orders. In addition, the analysis highlighted several areas where operation improvement would reduce costs. The activity-based costing system has been continuously adjusted as these and other improvements have been gradually implemented.

Tektronix Portable Instruments Division (PID) built a successful business on the design and manufacture of electronic laboratory equipment and gained a reputation for innovation and engineering excellence. As is often the case, PID embarked on a thorough implementation of world class manufacturing techniques as a result of their market share falling when Japanese competitors introduced similar products at 25-percent lower prices.

Although PID made great strides in product quality, just-in-time, and innovative management styles, the cost and management accounting systems were not changed. In addition, there was sharp conflict within the company between the accountants, the designers, the production personnel, and the sales staff. Informal costing and pricing systems appeared in various departments of the company as the managers began to seriously distrust the financial results.

The company instituted a review of their cost accounting methods. Reporting of labor hours was abandoned and an activity-based costing approach adopted. It was determined that 50 percent of the total product cost could be related to materials. These costs included procurement, material planning, inspection, warehousing, and material movement. Three possible cost drivers were suggested:

1. material cost
2. number of components per product
3. number of component part numbers

The third approach was adopted because findings revealed that it was the number of different parts handled — rather than their value or quantity — that generated the costs. In addition, this cost driver sends a clear message to the design engineers that additional unique or low volume parts significantly add cost.

Implementing Activity-based Costing

Activity-based costing is still in its infancy and no proven path has been established for the implementation of these ideas. On the contrary, one of the aspects of activity-based costing is its flexibility, which results in different companies applying these ideas differently. Some guidelines, however, are emerging:

1. Do not attempt to include all, or even the majority, of overhead costs into activity-based cost drivers. Concentrate on overhead costs that are directly related to the supply of your product or service to your customers. These include procurement, warehousing, material handling, indirect production activities, sales order processing, production engineering, and delivery costs. These costs lend themselves more readily to clearly defined cost drivers. Other costs like the accounting department, technical library, and personnel services do not have straightforward cost drivers.

2. Limit the number of cost drivers. A few well chosen, thoroughly understood cost drivers are of far more value than a large number of drivers yielding a more "correct" result. Use an 80/20 approach in the early stages, select a handful of drivers, and then allow the refinements to come as a result of experience with use of the system.

3. Education in the concepts and practical use of activity-based costing is essential. This education should be widespread. Anyone using the results of the costing system must have a thorough understanding of activity-based costing and how the cost figures are derived. Gaining this understanding is not difficult because the ideas of activity-

based costing are not complex; and the cost drivers, if they have been selected well, will make sense to the people using the system.

4. Use the experience and common sense of the managers and supervisors in the plant and offices when selecting cost drivers. The analysis done to identify the cost drivers should be pragmatic, not academic. The people doing the work are the ones that really understand where the costs are coming from; use their experience. Robert Kaplan has suggested this approach: "Find out from each support department what creates the work for them. Do something unusual for accountants; ask people what they do. At first they will say, 'I can't tell you because every week is different.' 'Well sure, every week is different but over the last six months, or over last year, approximately how much time do you spend on this activity versus that activity?' 'Oh I can't tell you.' We say, 'Is it 80 percent?' 'Oh no, that is much too high.' '10 percent?' 'Too low.' Well, we are making progress. Pretty soon we have at least a ball park estimate."[9]

5. Determine the level at which the costs should be applied; they do not have to be applied to individual products. Some costs make sense to apply at the individual product level, others at batch level (for example, setup costs), others at the product family level (for example, machine depreciation, technology, engineering costs), and others at the plant level. Applying costs at each of these levels would usually be confusing, but it is important to understand the most appropriate method of presenting this cost information.

6. Consider the use of a different, simpler method of calculating inventory values for financial accounting purposes. The management accounts used for decision making, pricing, and analysis need not be integrated with the finan-

cial accounts. There is great advantage in splitting financial and management accounting. While this is a big step, in many cases it is the right thing to do.

7. Above all, keep the activity-based accounting system simple. This approach is to be useful to the supervisors and managers in the plant. Do not make it so complicated that only an MBA can understand it and that three days are needed to analyze the results. Design the system so that it is readily understandable and easy to use.

Throughput Accounting

Throughput accounting is not yet as widely used but does provide some insight into aspects of production costs that fit well within a world class manufacturing environment. While activity-based costing is concerned with the application of indirect costs, throughput accounting is concerned with optimizing the flow of materials through the plant.

For many years, management accountants have been using the idea of a product's contribution when making decisions about product volumes and mix. Contribution is calculated by subtracting a product's total direct costs to make from its selling price. If you have the capacity to make just one product today and the contribution of Product X is $1,000 and the contribution of Product Y is $350, then it makes sense to produce X, providing you have a buyer for it.

Contribution theory, however, does not take into account anything relating to the flow of product through the plant. Throughput accounting is a method of considering not only the contribution the product can make but also the effect that its manufacture has on the plant as a whole. Throughput accounting looks at the flow through the plant in addition to the individual contribution of each product.

Consider the following simple illustration: A factory manufactures two machined products with the same material content and sells both for the same price. There are six production steps and the timings of these steps (in minutes) are:

Steps	1	2	3	4	5	6	TOTAL
Product A	0.20	0.30	0.15	0.25	0.20	0.15	1.25
Product B	0.20	0.15	0.25	0.35	0.15	0.20	1.30
Capacity (minutes)	6000	5000	6000	7000	6000	6000	

The selling price of both products is $2.25 and the material content is $1.30. The direct labor rate is $6.00 per hour.

The direct costs of Product A are $1.425 and of Product B are $1.430, which yield a contribution for Product A of $0.825 and for Product B of $0.820. Traditional management accounting would conclude that it is more profitable to make A than B. However, the bottleneck work center is job step 2 and Product A spends twice as long in step 2 as Product B. From this it is clear that by making Product B the factory can generate more money more quickly than by making Product A. The number of Product A that can be manufactured is 16,666 per day and of Product B 33,333 per day. The daily contribution from manufacturing Product B is $27,333.06, whereas Product A contributes only $13,749.45.

This concentration not only on the costs and profitability of the products but also on the flow of those products through the production plant is very much in line with the concepts popularized in Eli Goldratt and Jeff Cox's book *The Goal*, which demonstrated the importance of understanding the bottleneck operations within a plant and the synchronized flow of material through these bottlenecks in order to optimize the flow of production.[10]

These concepts of throughput accounting can be expanded into a complete theory of costing and product profitability.[11] The most straightforward aspect of this theory is the development of what is known as the throughput accounting ratio. The ratio is calculated:

ratio = return per factory hour ÷ cost per factory hour

Return per factory hour is the price less the material costs divided by the time the product spends in the bottleneck work center. Cost per factory hour is the total factory costs divided by the total amount of time available in the bottleneck work center.

The throughput accounting ratio can then be used to gauge the actual costs and the "real" opportunity costs of a particular mix of production.

Life-cycle Costing

The need for life-cycle costing has developed as a result of the shortening life cycles of modern products and the high cost of research and product development. In the days when cost and management accounting were in their infancy, products were typically inexpensive to design because they rarely broke new ground in technology; and once they were designed, the owner could plan to manufacture the product profitably (hopefully) for many years.

A notable aspect of modern industrial life is the high cost of technology and the rapid rate of change. A major challenge for any modern manufacturer is to bring innovative new products to market quickly. Traditional cost accounting is concerned primarily with the cost of manufacturing a product. It has little to say about the costs of research and development, and it does not concern itself with the end-of-life issues relating to products.

The concept of life-cycle costing is that of a product's life cycle (perhaps as short as three to five years in the consumer electronic industry), the manufacturing period is relatively short in comparison to the design period, distribution, and end-of-life period. The concentration of management accounting involvement needs to encompass every stage in the product life cycle, not just to concentrate on manufacturing.

There are a number of aspects involved with this new way of thinking. One is that the management accountants must be very much involved with the design of the product, working with the engineers and assisting them with cost estimates and targets costs (see Chapter 10), helping with the development of cost reduction programs, and understanding the production process so that when production does start the manufacturing costs are very predictable. This aspect of management accounting has been proven by some of the best Japanese companies in recent years.

Another aspect of life-cycle costing is the application of research and development costs and others to the product during the manufacturing stage of its life cycle. R & D costs can outweigh the material and production costs several times over, and an understanding of these cost patterns is essential if the company is to realize the kind of return it requires on its investment.

The area of end-of-life for a product can be important. The management accountant can assist the product managers by assessing the impact of new products (both one's own products and one's competitors) on the products in current manufacture and can thus provide an assessment of how and when to end the life of an existing product.

Management accountants have been performing these roles for many years now. What is different among world class manufacturers is the degree of importance that these ideas have in the broader success of the company. The increasing speed with which new products are brought to market requires a level of sophistication in these processes that was not previously needed. The emphasis of the role of management accountants is different within world class manufacturing plants, and life-cycle accounting and analysis is an increasingly important aspect of this new role.

Japanese Approach to Cost and Management Accounting

The astonishing success of Japanese manufacturers during the last decade has led to some considerable interest among finance professionals in the techniques employed by Japanese management accountants. There are some differences between traditional Western-style management accounting and the Japanese approach, and most of these differences stem from a fundamentally different attitude toward the art of accounting. This fundamental difference has led some commentators to seek for sociological and ethnic explanations, quoting from Marco Polo and ancient samurai texts and even crediting Western management accountants (who are not noted for their philosophical turn of mind) with an ontological view of the perception of truth.[12]

In reality, however, the differences between the two approaches derive from a different approach to the use and importance of cost and management accounting within Japanese and Western companies. The decision-making process employed by most of the more successful Japanese companies takes into consideration the needs of many aspects of the business — of which management accounting is only one. The techniques of cost and management accounting in Western companies usually is afforded a more dominant role than in Japanese companies. Consequently, Japanese management accounting tends to vary considerably from one company to the next and is viewed with more flexibility than in the West.

Japanese management accountants view their craft as one of influencing and assisting the management of the company. So the question is not, "What is the most accurate method of accounting for costs?" but "Which cost accounting method will provide information to support the company's manufacturing strategy?" The Western management accountant is trained to consider his or her role (and this is where the ontological argument comes in) to be one of providing accurate, complete, and unbiased information for the company's managers. The practical outworking of these differences and the extensive use of world class manufacturing ideas have led to some significantly different techniques being used by Japanese management accountants.

Japanese Management Accounting Techniques

While the management accounting techniques used by different Japanese manufacturers vary widely, the following eight observations serve to illustrate some of the more important differences between Japanese and Western accounting techniques.[13][14][15][16]

1. Japanese tax and business laws require the valuation of inventory to be shown on the balance sheet in the same way as is required for Western accounting practice. Japanese companies provide this valuation using simple and consistent techniques, but there is no attempt to integrate this financial accounting need into the cost and management accounting used for decision-making purposes.

   This same approach is advocated by Robert Kaplan and others involved in the use of activity-based costing. The purpose of inventory valuation should determine the method of calculation; if this results in multiple calculations — so be it.

2. Simple methods are used to allocate overhead burdens to products and product families. The more complex techniques being proposed by Western accounting theorists have not been accepted or used in Japanese companies.

3. Management accounting in Japan is specifically used to support and reinforce the manufacturing strategy. A more direct link exists between corporate goals and management accounting practices. This emphasis is shown by the involvement of management accountants through the entire business planning, product design, manufacturing, and marketing aspects of the business. Management accounting is seen as a part of the company's corporate control mechanism.

4. Management accounting plays an influencing role in the company's continuous improvement programs. The choice of management accounting methods is very much determined by the changes in the manufacturing process the company is trying to make. Mr. Hiromoto cites the methods of overhead allocation used by the Hitachi Corporation, which employs labor hours as the only factor used to apply overhead — quite contrary to the activity-based costing ideas.[17] The reason for this is that Hitachi has a policy of automation and actively and systematically wants to remove labor from their production operations. If labor hours are used as the method of applying overheads, then this will mitigate toward the reduction of labor in the production process.

It is important to remember that this method is chosen specifically for this purpose and that questions of cost distortion are not pertinent. In fact, the costs are being distorted deliberately so as to influence the decision making of the engineers and production managers.

5. There is extensive use made of target costs. In many companies, target costs are derived as a breakdown from the target prices the marketing people feel can be achieved in the marketplace. Thus, Japanese management accountants are very focused on the needs of the marketplace and their role in the continuous improvement processes within the

company. In fact, the process of calculating target costs for individual assemblies and fabricated and purchased parts frequently spawns continuous improvement and value engineering programs itself (see Chapter 10). The gap between the allowable cost and actual cost during the design phase often requires considerable improvements to be made in the design and the production process.

6. Japanese management accountants make significantly much more use of nonfinancial measures. The management accountant sees his or her role in a wider context than do most Western accountants, and the preparation of financial data and analysis is not viewed as the primary purpose of the job. Consequently, the Japanese management accountant is always looking for the most appropriate measurement methods to achieve company goals and strategy. This quest frequently results in the extensive use of nonfinancial measures.

7. Standard costing is not used very much by Japanese manufacturers. When it is used, it is primarily for the purpose of estimating the costs of new products, budgeting, and inventory valuation. It is not used for cost control. There is very little use of traditional financial variance reporting by Japanese companies.

8. Japanese management accounting emphasizes cost reduction rather than cost control. This facet is exemplified by the use of management accounting techniques in the product design process (discussed in Chapter 10) where the reduction of cost prior to commencing manufacture is the prime objective. Western management accounting emphasizes cost control, where the detailed tracking and analysis of costs throughout the manufacturing stage of the product's life cycle is of primary importance.

Summary

While there is no consensus or widely accepted standards for cost and management accounting in a world class manufacturing environment, many companies are experimenting with new approaches aimed at overcoming the problems and irrelevance of traditional management accounting techniques.

Financial accounting does not need to change when new methods of cost and management accounting are introduced because the financial accounts must continue to be presented using the methods laid down by law, securities regulations, and accepted accounting standards.

Very few world class manufacturers eliminate cost and management accounting entirely, but their roles and importance diminish. Detailed labor reporting is usually eliminated, and direct labor costs are added into production overheads. The detailed reporting of shop floor activities through a work order system is often eliminated and replaced with rate-based, synchronized manufacturing systems. Detailed inventory transaction reporting is eliminated and replaced by backflushing materials when the products are completed. The reporting of cost variances is irrelevant when labor and material costs are not tracked in detail, and these reports are also eliminated.

As world class manufacturing techniques are implemented within a manufacturing site, the characteristics of production become more like those of a process manufacturer. Some of the techniques of process costing can be applied readily once the plant is operating in a flow environment. These include collecting costs by product and cell (or line), reporting year-to-date and period-to-date costs, and showing variances against period-to-date and year-to-date budgets and targets. The inadequacies of standard costing and the allocation of overhead costs can be eliminated by using direct costing and actual costing techniques. Direct costing takes account only of costs that can be directly identified with the manufacture of a product; overheads are not included in the product costing but are reported as variances against budgets for indirect departments. Actual costing reports the actual costs applied to the manufacture of the products and does not attempt to show variances against standards. The actual costs are reported in terms of trends and cost per unit sold, which clearly show the improvements occurring within the plant and can motivate people to further improvement.

Activity-based costing provides a technique for allocating indirect costs to a product or product group according to the activities required to make the product. The indirect costs are summed into a number of "cost pools" related to specific activities (cost drivers) and are then applied to the products by calculating how many of each cost driver activity has been required by the product. Activity-based costing provides a better understanding of the true manufacturing costs of a product and can be used for decision making, cost reduction programs, and product pricing.

Some innovative new techniques are creating some interest and may prove to be useful additions to the management accountant's toolbox. Throughput accounting is one of these new approaches. It attempts to assist managers in deciding on product profitability and production mix by taking account not only of the contribution a product makes but also of the total flow of production through the plant based upon a selected mix and volume. Life-cycle costing is not a new idea but its importance is increased very much by world class manufacturing techniques. Life-cycle costing is concerned with more than just production costs; it takes account of the entire costs of designing, marketing, making, servicing, and withdrawal of a product (or product family). The fast introduction of new products and the high cost of research and development make some aspects of life-cycle costing imperative for world class manufacturers.

Japanese management accounting supports and reinforces the manufacturing strategy of the company rather than merely reporting the information. The methods used are more flexible than Western management accounting because their primary goal is to influence the behavior of the company's employees. The emphasis of Japanese management accounting is the reduction of costs (often prior to the commencement of manufacturing) rather than controlling costs during the production part of the product's life cycle.

References

Chapter 1

1. Jeffrey G. Miller, Jinichiro Nakane, and Arnoud De Meyer, *Flexibility: The Next Competitive Battle* (Report of the International Manufacturing Futures Survey) (Boston: Boston University, 1988).

Chapter 5

1. Ritzman, King, and Krajewski, "Pulling the Right Levers," *Harvard Business Review* (March 1984).

Chapter 6

1. Jinichiro Nakane, *Japan 2001* (Boston University Manufacturing Roundtable, September 1988).
2. James Mellas, "Making it Happen — JIT and World Class Manufacturing," *Manufacturing Systems* (February 1990).
3. Isao Shinohara, *NPS: New Production System: JIT Crossing Industry Boundaries* (Cambridge, Massachusetts: Productivity Press, 1988), 43.
4. Hal Mather, *Competitive Manufacturing* (Englewood Cliffs, New Jersey: Prentice-Hall, 1988).

5. James W. Dean and Gerald I. Susman, "Organizing for Manufacturable Design," *Harvard Business Review* (January 1989).
6. Ibid.
7. Isao Shinohara, op. cit., 181.
8. Brian Maskell, "Bills of Material for Manufacturing, Engineering, and Accounting," *Product and Inventory Management Review* (June 1988).

Chapter 7
1. Philip B. Crosby, *Quality Is Free* (New York: New American Library, 1979).
2. J. M. Juran, *Quality Planning and Analysis* (New York: McGraw-Hill, 1980).
3. Robert W. Grenier, *Customer Satisfaction Through Total Quality Assurance* (Carol Stream, Illinois: Hitchcock Publishing, 1988).
4. K. Theodor Krantz, "How Velcro Got Hooked on Quality," *Harvard Business Review* (September 1989).
5. A. Hald, *Statistical Theory of Sampling Inspection by Attributes* (New York: Academic Press, 1981).
   Walter A. Shewhart, *Statistical Method from the Viewpoint of Quality Control* (New York: Dover, 1981).
   W. Edwards Deming, *Some Theories of Sampling* (New York: Dover, 1981).
6. Allen F. Scott, *SPC for Continuous Quality Improvement* (International Conference Proceedings) (Falls Church, Virginia: American Production and Inventory Control Society, 1989).
7. Jerry Roth, "An Alternative to SPC," *Manufacturing Systems* (March 1990).
8. Irwin Bross, *Design for Decision* (New York: Macmillan, 1953).
9. George J. Miller, "Inventory Accuracy: How We Did It in 60 Days," (1990 LA-ADSIG Conference Proceedings).

10. Isao Shinohara, op. cit.
11. Philip B. Crosby, op. cit., 178.

Chapter 8

1. Shigeo Shingo, *A Study of the Toyota Production System from an IE Viewpoint* (Cambridge, Massachusetts: Productivity Press, English transl., 1989).
2. McNair, Mosconi, and Norris, *Beyond the Bottom Line* (Homewood, Illinois: Dow-Jones Irwin, 1989), 87.
3. Yasuhiro Monden and Michiharu Sakurai, Eds., *Japanese Management Accounting* (Cambridge, Massachusetts: Productivity Press, 1989), 197.
4. Ph.D. Thesis. Carlene M. Crawford, "Analysis of Performance Measurement Systems in JIT Operations," (University of Georgia, 1988), 165.

Chapter 9

1. W. Edwards Deming, *Out of the Crisis* (Cambridge, Massachusetts: Massachusetts Institute of Technology, 1982), 54.
2. Rudolf H. Moos, *Work Environment Scale* (Palo Alto California: Consulting Psychologists Press, 1981).

Chapter 10

1. W. Edwards Deming, op. cit., Chapter 2.
2. Ibid., 71.
3. Philip B. Crosby, op. cit.
4. Joseph M. Juran, *Planning for Quality* (Wilton, Connecticut: Juran Institute, 1988).
5. Gary Jacobson and John Hillkirk, *Xerox: American Samurai* (New York: Macmillan, 1986).
6. Nico Timmer, "The Factory of the Future — Today," (BPICS Internation Conference Proceedings) (Bishops Stortford, England: British Production and Inventory Control Society, 1985).

7. Yasuhiro Monden and Michiharu Sakurai, op. cit., 22.
8. Roy Merrills, "How Northern Telecom Competes on Time," *Harvard Business Review* (July 1989).
9. Arthur M. Schneiderman, "Setting Quality Goals," *Quality Progress* (April 1981), 51.
10. Roy Merrills, op. cit.
11. Kelvin F. Cross and Richard L. Lynch, "The SMART Way to Define and Sustain Success," *National Productivity Review* (Vol. 8, No. 1, Winter 1988).

Chapter 11

1. Robert S. Kaplan, "Relevance Regained," *Management Accounting* (UK: September 1988).
2. S. Robb Dixon, Alfred J. Nanni, and Thomas E. Vollman, "Using the Diagnostic Tool," (Manufacturing Executive Forum, April 1989).

Chapter 12

1. Brian Maskell, *Just-in-Time: Implementing the New Strategy* (Carol Stream, Illinois: Hitchcock Publishing, 1989), 134.
2. Robert S. Kaplan, "One Cost System Isn't Enough," *Harvard Business Review* (January 1988).
3. Michael Jeans and Michael Morrow, "The Practicalities of Activity-based Costing," *Management Accounting* (UK: November 1988).
4. Debbie Berlant, Reese Browning, and George Foster, "How Hewlett-Packard Gets Numbers It Can Trust," *Harvard Business Review* (January 1990).
5. David Dugdale and Sue Shrimpton, "Product Costing in a JIT Environment," *Management Accounting* (UK: March 1990).
6. Debbie Berlant et al, op. cit.
7. Robert S. Kaplan, "Relevance Regained."
8. David Dugdale and Sue Shrimpton, op. cit.

9. William J. Bruns, Jr., and Robert S. Kaplan, *Accounting and Management: Field Study Perspectives* (Cambridge, Massachusetts: Harvard Business School, 1987).

10. Eliyahu M. Goldratt and Jeff Cox, *The Goal* (Croton-on-Hudson, New York: North River Press, 1984).

11. David Galloway and David Waldron, "Throughput Accounting," *Management Accounting* (UK: December 1988; January, February, March 1989).

12. Jusuf Harriman, "Influencing rather than Informing," *Management Accounting* (UK: March 1990).

13. Yasuhiro Monden and Michiharu Sakurai, op. cit.

14. Toshimo Hiromoto, "Another Hidden Edge — Japanese Management Accounting," *Harvard Business Review* (July 1988).

15. Michiharu Sakurai, "Influence of Factory Automation on Management Accounting Practices of Japanese Companies," (Harvard Colloquium on Measuring Manufacturing Performance, January 1989).

16. Michael Morgan and Prasanna Weerakoon, "Japanese Management Accounting — Its Contribution to the Japanese Economic Miracle," *Management Accounting* (UK: June 1989).

17. Toshimo Hiromoto, op. cit.

About the Author

A WIDELY REGARDED author and speaker, Brian Maskell brings 18 years of practical experience within manufacturing and distribution industries. He has served both as a manager and a consultant in Britain, Europe, and the United States. Mr. Maskell is currently vice president of product development and customer support with the Unitronix Corporation, a supplier of advanced software for the manufacturing and distribution industries. Prior to joining Unitronix, he held various positions with the Xerox Corporation, including materials manager for European spare parts, implementation manager for the Xerox manufacturing systems, and the design of advanced distribution systems. Mr. Maskell has provided consulting services to a wide range of companies including Xerox, Volvo Cars, Schlumberger, SmithKline Beecham, the Eaton Corporation, and Stanley Tools.

He is certified as a Fellow of the American Production and Inventory Control Society, is a member of the Chartered Institute of Management Accountants, and holds degrees in both engineering and management accounting. His published books include *Just-in-Time: Implementing the New Strategy* (Hitchcock, 1989) and *Performance Measurement for World Class Manufacturing: A Model for American Companies* (Productivity Press, 1991).

Index

ABC class, 234, 241, 252-53
Absenteeism, 288
Activity-based costing
    concepts of, 367-69
    development of, 51, 365
    implementing, 377-79
    problems addressed by, 366
    used by Hewlett-Packard, 366,
        369-73
    used by John Deere Component
        Works, 374-76
    used by Siemens Electric Motor
        Works, 373-74
    used by Tektronix Portable
        Instruments, 366, 376-77
Actual/standard costing, 364-65
Amoeba System, 277

Backflushing, 232, 359-60
Bar codes, 132
Batch sizes
    machine and labor efficiencies
        and, 60-61
    overhead absorption variance
        report and, 62-64
    reduction of, 9

L. L. Bean, 310
Bhopal, India, 286
Bills of materials
    definition of, 189
    engineering, 192
    measuring, 192, 194-95
    phantom assemblies and, 190-92
    reasons for limiting, 190
    routing accuracy and, 236, 238-39
Blake, William, 286
Bloomington Seating Co., 171
Bodek, Norman, xii
Boston University, Performance
        Measurement Diagnostic
        Tool, 335
Bottleneck/limiting operations,
        10-11, 128-29
Bross, Irwin, 230
Budgeting, use of, 43, 44
Business Week, 123-24

Capacity versus output, 201-2
Capital investment analysis
    early use of, 43
    impact of, on world class
        manufacturing, 57

Capital investment analysis *(cont.)*
  problems with traditional
    methods of, 56
Cell completions report, 93-95
Cell layout systems, 8, 157
Certification, vendor, 12-13, 79, 212,
  215
Charts
  bar, 81, 83
  customer survey, 120
  Demos control, 220-26
  limitations of, 338
  manual, 84
  past-due products, 97-99
  snake, 228-30
  statistical process control, 218-19
  use of, 77, 337
Checkbook accounting, 276-78
Chrysler Corp., 171, 198
COGS. *See* Cost of goods sold
Commonality
  definition of, 179-80
  process, 181-82
  reporting, 180
Competitive benchmarking, 145,
  309-12
Complexity, system, 280-82
Cooper, Robin, 365
Cost accounting. *See* Management
  accounting
Costing systems
  activity-based, 51, 365-79
  actual/standard, 364-65
  direct, 363-64
  full-absorption, 69-70
  life-cycle, 381-83
  process, 360-62
  standard, 44, 364-65
  throughput accounting, 379-81
Cost of goods sold (COGS),
  valuation of, 257-58
Costs
  of adding value per unit, 271-72

direct versus indirect, 50
distortion of, 45-46, 49-54
drivers of, 51, 367, 368-69
fixed versus variable, 50-51, 54
/output ratio, 272-73
overhead absorption rates and,
  53-54
overhead apportionment of,
  51-53
production/potential, 313
of productivity per unit, 270-71
of quality, 244-45
target/allowable, 313
Cox, Jeff, 380
Crosby, Philip B., 204, 245, 308
Cross-training. *See* Training
Customer requirements
  changes in, 2-3
  world class manufacturing and
    flexibility and, 16-18
Customer satisfaction, production
  quality and, 227-30
Customer service level
  delivery performance and,
    107-16
  importance of, 106
  inventory levels and, 108-9
  measuring, 30-31, 109-11
  qualitative approach to, 106,
    116-20
  quantitative approach to, 106,
    107-16
  reports, 109
Customer service time (CST),
  process time and, 166, 168
Customer survey of service, 116-20
Cycle counting, 233-34
Cycle times
  how to shorten, 126-29
  importance of, 123-24
  problems caused by long, 124-26
  production flexibility and, 174
  value-added analysis and, 264

Cycle times, measuring
  analysis of engineering routings,
    132-33
  detailed recording of cycle times,
    129-32
  lot sizes and, 126-27, 140-41
  pragmatic methods, 138-39
  sampling, 133, 135-38

Data quality
  bills of materials and routing
    accuracy, 236, 238-39
  forecast accuracy, 239-42
  importance of, 231-32
  measuring inventory accuracy,
    232-34
  purpose of checking inventory
    accuracy, 235-36
  reporting inventory accuracy,
    236
John Deere Component Works, 374-
  76
Delivery lead time, 141, 142-44
Delivery performance
  customer service and, 107-16
  description of, 77-78
  on-time, 78-79, 111-13
   receipt versus dispatch, 113, 115
  scheduling and, 85-102
  vendor, 78-85
del Rio, Carlos, 280
Demand
  capacity versus, 201-2
  matching output to, 59-60
Deming, W. Edwards, 203, 209, 297,
  306, 307
Deming Circle, 209
Demos control charts
  examples of, 221-23
  for multi-variation processes,
    224-26
  purpose of, 220-21
Department of Trade and Industry
  (England), 286

Design
  flexibility, 17-18, 186-87
  quality through, 205
Design for Decision (Bross), 230
Digital Equipment Corp. (DEC),
  346, 348
Direct costing, 363-64
Direct labor productivity (DLP),
  265-68
Discounted cash flow (DCF), 56
Distance moved. *See* Material
  movement
Double-entry bookkeeping, 42
Down time of machines, 166, 244
D:P ratio, 141-45

Economic order quantity (EOQ),
  127
Education of employees, 294-97
Efficiency reports, problems with,
  61-62
Electronic data interchange (EDI),
  115
Employees, involvement of, 290-97
Engineering, value, 312-15
Engineering change note (ECN),
  367
Engineering routings, analysis of,
  132-33
Enhancements, measuring, 198-99
Environmental issues, 286, 301-3

Federal Accounting Standards
  Board, 351
Feedback, providing fast, 35-37
Financial accounting
  integration of, 44-45
  management accounting and, 47,
    67-72
  purpose of, 43
  versus cost accounting, 353-54
Financial measures
  abandoning, 332-33
  checkbook accounting, 276-78

Financial measures *(cont.)*
   cost productivity, 270-73
   direct labor productivity, 265-68
   inventory turns and work-in-
       process turns, 252-58
   overhead efficiency, 273-76
   reasons for, 22-23, 247-49
   system complexity, 280-82
   value-added analysis, 258-65
   waste rate and, 249-52
Fishbone chart, use of, 35
Flexibility
   capital project evaluation and,
       57-59
   design, 17-18, 186-87
Flexibility, production. *See*
   Production flexibility
Forecast accuracy, 239-42
Fourth generation languages (4GL).
   See Report writers/fourth
   generation languages (4GL)
France, 4
Full-absorption costing, 69-70

General Electric Corp. (GE), 176,
   310
General Motors Corp. (GM), 206,
   276, 289
Goal-setting. *See* Performance
   targets
Goal, The (Goldratt and Cox), 380
Goldratt, Eli, 380
Graph(s)
   limitations of, 338
   past-due products, 97-99
   Green movement, 286
Grenier, Robert W., 204

Half-life concept, 315-20
Harley-Davidson, 248, 266, 353-54
Harvard Business Review, 132
Hewlett-Packard, 366, 369-73
Hiromoto, Toshimo, 385
Hitachi Corp., 385

Honda Motor, 173

IBM, 176, 276, 298
Improvement
   continuous, 28-29, 205, 219
   fostering rather than monitoring,
       37-40
   half-life concept of continuous,
       315-20
   role of employees in, 292-94
Incentive payroll schemes, 357
In Search of Excellence (Peters and
   Waterman), 26
Inter-plant comparisons, 39-40
Inventory
   abandoning reporting of, 358-60
   accuracy report, 236
   customer service and levels of,
       108-9
   measuring accuracy of, 232-34
   pull method, 11
   purpose of checking accuracy of,
       235-36
   turns and financial measures,
       252-58
   valuation, 44-45, 69-72
Investment analysis, 45

Japanese companies
   Amoeba System in, 277
   approach to management
       accounting, 383-86
   automobile manufacturers,
       186-87, 292-93
   flexibility and customer needs
       and, 16-18
   kanban system in, 11
   preventive maintenance in, 242-
       43
   pricing and, 48-49
   value engineering and, 312
Johnson Controls, 302-3
Juran, Joseph M., 204, 308

Just-in-time (JIT) manufacturing.
See also Delivery performance
purpose of, 6-7
setup times and, 8-10
shop floor layout and, 7-8
synchronized manufacturing
and, 10-11
vendor relationships and, 11-14
world class manufacturing and,
6-14

Kaizen. *See* Improvement
Kanban system
cycle times and, 135, 141
description of, 11
material movement and, 162
synchronized production and,
128
Kaplan, Robert S., 332, 365, 366, 371,
378, 384
Kawasaki, 173
Korea, 4
Kyocera Corp., 277

Labor efficiencies, batch size and,
60-61
Labor reporting, abandoning,
356-58
Leadership, 297-98
Life-cycle costing, 381-83
Lost sales, assessing, 121
Lot sizes, cycle times and, 126-27,
140-41
Love Canal, 286

Machine
batch size and efficiency of,
60-61
down time of, 166, 244
up time of, 165-66
McLuhan, Marshall, 3
Maintenance, preventive, 208,
242-44
Make-to-order, 172

Make-to-stock, 125
Management accounting
abandoning, 355-60
areas of, 44
development of standard, 1-2, 41
financial accounting versus cost
accounting, 353-54
history of, 41-43
Japanese approach to, 383-86
manufacturing strategy and, 47-
48
monthly cycle, 71
new approaches to, 354-55
operational control and, 48
pricing and, 44, 48-49
purpose of, 43-45
Management accounting, problems
with
cost distortion, 45-46, 49-54
financial accounting and, 47, 67-
72
impediment to progress, 46,
55-67
inflexibility, 46, 54-55
lack of new standards, 351-53
lack of relevance, 45, 47-49
Management information systems
(MIS), 339
Management techniques, changes
in, 3
Manufacturing resource planning
(MRPII) system, 144, 154, 238,
357
Manufacturing strategy
elements of, 21-22
establishing a, 20-21
management accounting and,
47-48
relating performance measures
to, 21
Material availability, measuring,
154-55
Material movement
cell styles and, 157

Material movement *(cont.)*
  manual methods of tracking,
    162-63
  measuring distance moved,
    158-61
  next work center report, 163
  problems with, 155, 157
Material requirements planning
  (MRP), 144
Merrills, Roy, 323
Miller, Jeffrey G., 17
MMAS standards, 233, 236
Moos, Rudolf H., 298
Morale, 286-90
MRP. *See* Material requirements
  planning
MRPII. *See* Manufacturing resource
  planning

Nakane, Jinichiro, 17
Net-present-value (NPV), 45
New products, introducing, 173-74,
  196-99
Nissan Motor, 17, 29, 49, 292-93
Nonfinancial reports, abandoning,
  333-34
Non-value-added activities, 211,
  251, 260-61
Normalized schedule variance,
  99-101
Northern Telecom (NT), 24-25, 314,
  322-23

Occupational Safety and Health
  Administration (OSHA), 286
Ohno, Taiichi, 180
One-touch changeover (OTC), 9
Operational control, management
  accounting and, 48
Optical scanners, 132
Order(s)
  changes in orders and changes
    in scheduling, 102-5
  past-due, 115-16

types of, 102
Output
  cost/output ratio, 272-73
  matching demand and, 59-60
  versus capacity, 201-2
Overhead absorption rates,
  calculating, 53-54, 63
Overhead absorption variance
  report, batch size and, 62-64
Overhead apportionment, 51-53
Overhead efficiency, measuring,
  273-76

Pareto analysis, 180, 224, 253
Park Software, 346
Participation groups. *See* Quality
  circles
Part reduction, 177-78
Parts, production flexibility and
  number of different, 175-78
  percentage of standard,
    common, and unique, 178-80
Past-due orders, measuring, 115-16
Past-due products graph, 97-99
Payback period, 56
Performance measures. *See* also
  Delivery performance
  direct reporting methods, 32-35
  establishing need for new,
    334-36
  methods used to present
    information, 76-77, 337-38
  problems caused by different,
    27-28
  reasons for, 1
Performance measures,
  characteristics of
  changes over time, 28-29
  feedback, 35-37
  fostering rather than monitoring
    improvement, 37-40
  nonfinancial measures, 22-25
  relationship to manufacturing
    strategy, 20-22

Performance measures,
    characteristics of *(cont.)*
    simplicity and ease of use, 30-35
    variation among locations, 25-28
Performance targets
    common sense goal-setting,
        320-22
    competitive benchmarking, 145,
        309-12
    half-life concept, 315-20
    interdepartmental, 322-28
    price targeting, 312-15
    should targets be set, 306-9
Personnel management
    education and cross-training,
        15-16
    involvement of employees,
        290-97
    morale and teamwork, 286-90
    transfer of responsibility, 14-15
Peters, Tom, 26
PRAXA, 346
PRAXVU, 345-48
Preventive maintenance, 208,
    242-44
Price targeting, 312-15
Pricing, management accounting
    and, 44, 48-49
Process commonality, 181-82
Process costing, 360-62
Process time, measuring
    customer service time and, 166,
        168
    D:P ratio and, 141-45
    machine up time and, 165-66
    manufacturing cycle time and,
        123-41
    material availability and, 154-55
    material movement and, 155-64
    setup times and, 145-54
Product
    completions report, 88-89
    completions summary report, 89
    enrichment, 186-87

Production
    completions, 266-68
    commonality, 174
    lead time, 141-42
    rate, 275-76
Production flexibility
    capacity versus demand, 201-2
    changes in production mix and,
        171-72
    changes in production volume
        and, 172-73
    cross-training and, 199-201
    definition of, 17
    factors that affect, 174-75
    introduction of new products
        196-99
    levels in the bills of materials
        and, 189-95
    number of different parts and,
        175-78
    number of different processes
        and, 181-82
    percentage of standard,
        common, and unique parts
        and, 178-80
    product variability and, 182-89
Production quality
    customer satisfaction and,
        227-30
    Demos control charts and,
        220-26
    quality improvement boards
        and, 227
    snake charts and, 228-30
    statistical process control and,
        208, 211, 215, 217-20, 226-27
    time between service calls and,
        231
    workplace organization and, 207
    works first time and, 230
Productivity per unit, cost, 270-71
Product variability, production
    flexibility and, 182-89

Qualitative approach to customer
service
definition of, 106
description of, 116-20
Quality
cost of, 244-45
data, 231-42
definition of, 204
goal of, 205
how to implement and measure,
209
improvement boards, 227
measuring incoming, 211-15
preventive maintenance and,
208, 242-44
production, 206-8, 216-31
reporting methods, 34-35
through design, 205
vendor, 206, 210-15
world class manufacturing
approach to, 4-6
Quality circles
implementing, 291-92
purpose of, 208
setup times and, 147
world class manufacturing and,
16
Quality Is Free (Crosby), 204, 308
Quantitative approach to customer
service
definition of, 106
description of, 107-16
Questionnaires, use of, 116-17

Rate of return, internal, 56
Receiving operation, importance of,
85
*Relevance Lost: The Rise and Fall of
Management Accounting*
(Kaplan), 332
Reply cards, use of, 115
Report(s)
cell completions, 93-95
checkbook accounting, 278

customer service level, 109
detailed cycle time, 129-31
distance moved, 159
incoming quality, 212
inventory accuracy, 236
next work center, 163
product completions, 88-89, 268
product completions summary,
89
use of, 76-77
vendor summary, 81, 212-13
for waste, 250-52
work order completions, 95-97
Report writers/fourth generation
languages (4GL)
criteria for, 340-43
definitions, 339-40
example of, 345-48
problems with, 344-45
purpose of, 339
useful features of, 343-44
Return-on-investment (ROI), 45, 56
Routing accuracy, bills of materials
and, 236, 238-39

Safety index, calculation of, 303
Safety issues, 286, 301-3
Safety stock, use of, 36
J. Sainsbury, 200-201
Sampling
cycle times and, 133, 135-38
material movement and, 162
Scheduling
cell completions report, 93-95
completions schedule table, 99
established by operators, 87-88
importance of, 85, 87
normalized variance, 99-101
order changes and changes in,
102-5
past-due products graph, 97-99
product completions report, 88-89
product completions summary,
89

Scheduling *(cont.)*
  work order completions report,
    95-97
Schneiderman, Arthur M., 315-17
Schonberger, Richard, 3
Scientific Management movement,
  285
Sellafield (England), 286
Selling price, standard, 266, 268
Service calls, time between, 231
Setup times
  average, 148, 150, 152
  importance of, 145, 147
  just-in-time manufacturing and,
    8-10
  measuring, 147-48
  pragmatic methods for
    measuring, 152, 154
  quality circles and, 147
Shingo, Shigeo, 259
Shop floor layouts, 7-8, 157, 207
Short-term thinking, problems
  with, 71-72
Siemens Electric Motor Works,
  373-74
Signals
  limitations of, 338
  use of, 77, 337
  use of visual, 34, 36-37
Single-minute exchange of dies
  (SMED), 9
Single sourcing, 12, 210
SMART. *See* Strategic Measurement
  and Reporting Technique
SmithKline Beecham
  Pharmaceuticals, 280-82, 298
Snake charts, 228-30
Social issues
  environmental issues, 286, 301-3
  involvement of employees,
    290-97
  leadership and working
    environment, 297-301
  morale and teamwork, 286-90

safety issues, 286, 301-3
SPC. *See* Statistical process control
Spreadsheets, use of, 102, 135-36
Statement of Standard Accounting
  Practice, 351
Statistical process control (SPC)
    continuous improvement
      and, 219
  determining sample sizes and
    upper/lower limits and,
    219-20
  purpose of, 208, 217-18
  uses for, 226-27
  vendor quality and, 211, 215
Stock turns, 252, 256-58
Strategic Measurement and
  Reporting Technique
  (SMART), 323-28
Study of the Toyota Production System
  (Shingo), 259
Suzuki Motor, 17-18
Synchronized manufacturing
  cycle times and, 128-29
  just-in-time manufacturing and,
    10-11
System complexity, 280-82

Table, completions schedule, 99
Taiwan, 4
Targets. *See* Performance targets
Taylor, Frederick, 285, 287
Teamwork, 286-90
Tektronix Portable Instruments,
  366, 376-77
Telephone survey, use of, 117, 119
Throughput accounting, 379-81
Time between service calls, 231
Time-to-market, 197-98
Toyota Motor, 173, 259, 312
Training
  cross-, 15-16
  importance of, 294-97
  production flexibility and cross-,
    174

Turnover rates, 288-89

United Auto Workers, 289
Unitronix Corp., 345

Valuation
  of cost of goods sold, 257-58
  of production completions,
    266-68
Value-added activities/analysis
  cycle time and, 264
  determining, 259-60
  in non-manufacturing activities,
    264-65
  purpose of, 258-59
  vendor quality and, 211
Value engineering, 312-15
Value per unit, cost of adding,
    271-72
Variability, production flexibility
  and product, 182-89
Variance
  normalized schedule, 99-101
  overhead absorption variance
    report, 62-64
  reporting, 360
Velcro Co., 206
Vendor
  certification, 12-13, 79, 212, 215
  quality, 206, 210-15
Vendor delivery performance
  detail report, 79-81
  importance of, 78-79
  importance of receiving
    operation, 85
  manual charts for, 84
  summary report, 81-83, 212-13
Vendor relationships, just-in-time
  manufacturing and, 11-14
Videotaping, 138
Visual signals. *See* Signals
Vollmann, Thomas E., 132, 334

Wang Laboratories, 323-28, 338
Waste
  definition of, 6
  management accounting and,
    64-65, 66-67
  rate, 249-52
Waterman, Robert, 26
West Germany, 4
Wilson Sporting Goods, 221, 223
Work environment scale, 298-301
Work-in-process (WIP)
  financial measures and, 252-58
  long cycle times and high, 124
  setup time reduction and, 10
Work order completions report,
    95-97
Workplace organization, 207
Works first time, 230
World class manufacturing (WCM)
  approach to quality, 4-6
  customer requirements and
    flexibility and, 16-18
  definition of, 3, 4
  just-in-time manufacturing and,
    6-14
  people management and, 14-16
  quality circles and, 16
  World Co., 242

XENTIS, 346
Xerox Corp., 12, 298, 309-12, 322

Yokogawa Electric, 175

Zero defects, 5

ALSO FROM
PRODUCTIVITY PRESS

Productivity Press publishes and distributes materials on continuous improvement in productivity, quality, customer service, and the creative involvement of all employees. Many of our products are direct source materials from Japan that have been translated into English for the first time and are available exclusively from Productivity. Supplemental products and services include newsletters, conferences, seminars, in-house training and consulting, audio-visual training programs, and industrial study missions. Call 1-800-274-9911 for our free book catalog.

Championship Management
An Action Model for High Performance
by James A. Belohlav

Many current books extol the values of being an excellent company. This book goes beyond that to explain how excellence can be achieved and why it is so critically important. A model for action demonstrates how any company can become a "championship" caliber company. Further, it explains why some excellent companies lose their edge while others remain excellent, and why still others appear to be excellent but are not.
ISBN 0-915299-76-3 / 272 pages / $29.95 / Order code CHAMPS-BK

Productivity Measurement Handbook
by William F. Christopher

A compilation of practical, detailed methods for measuring productivity company-wide that has become a standard reference book. Measurement makes productivity performance visible and provides a feedback system that helps everyone do a better job. This book explains standard economic formulas and includes query forms for assessing measurement, case studies, charts for overhead projection, and an extensive bibliography.
ISBN 0-915299-05-4 / 680 pages / 3-ring binder / $137.95 / Order code PMH-BK

Productivity Press, Inc., Dept. BK, P.O. Box 3007, Cambridge, MA 02140 1-800-274-9911

Managerial Engineering
Techniques for Improving Quality and Productivity in the Workplace (rev.)
by Ryuji Fukuda

A proven path to managerial success, based on reliable methods developed by one of Japan's leading productivity experts and winner of the coveted Deming Prize for quality. Dr. W. Edwards Deming, world-famous consultant on quality, says that the book "provides an excellent and clear description of the devotion and methods of Japanese management to continual improvement of quality." (CEDAC training programs also available.)
ISBN 0-915299-09-7 / 208 pages / $39.95 / Order code ME-BK

Manager Revolution!
A Guide to Survival in Today's Changing Workplace
by Yoshio Hatakeyama

An extraordinary blueprint for effective management, here is a step-by-step guide to improving your skills, both in everyday performance and in long-term planning. *Manager Revolution!* explores in detail the basics of the Japanese success story and proves that it is readily transferable to other settings. Written by the president of the Japan Management Association and a bestseller in Japan, here is a survival kit for beginning and seasoned managers alike. Each chapter includes case studies, checklists, and self-tests.
ISBN 0-915299-10-0 / 208 pages / $24.95 / MREV-BK

The Best of TEI
Current Perspectives on Total Employee Involvement
edited by Karen Jones

An outstanding compilation of the 29 best presentations from the first three International Total Employee Involvement (TEI) conferences sponsored by Productivity. You'll find sections on management strategy, case studies, training and retraining, *kaizen* (continuous improvement), and high quality teamwork. Here's the cutting edge in implemented TEI strategies doubly valuable to you because it comprises both theory and practice. It's also amply illustrated with presentation charts. Whether you're a manager, a team member, or in HR development, you'll find The Best of TEI a rich and stimulating source of information. Comes in handy 3-ring binder.
ISBN 0-915299-63-1 / 502 pages / $175.00 / Order code TEI-BK

Productivity Press, Inc., Dept. BK, P.O. Box 3007, Cambridge, MA 02140 1-800-274-9911

TQC for Accounting
A New Role in Companywide Improvement
by Takashi Kanatsu

TQC for accounting means more than streamlining office procedures or upgrading financial analyses. It requires, instead, a linking of the basics of marketing with the fundamentals of accounting through the medium of TQC. This book is a guide for top and middle managers who wish to turn their companies around by redesigning the roles played by the accounting, sales, and marketing departments. The book's format offers detailed examinations of accounting TQC in relation to a company's business plan, accounting department, and specific statistical methods. Its use will help to create the "awareness revolution" that is imperative in turning around a factory or any type of company.

ISBN 0-915299-73-9 / 176 pages / $45.00 / Order code TQCA-BK

Japanese Management Accounting
A World Class Approach to Profit Management
edited by Yasuhiro Monden

Just as the Japanese redefined manufacturing excellence, so they have transformed management accounting in world class companies. Here is a comprehensive overview of the Japanese approach to management accounting, especially helpful for companies that have adopted Just-In-Time manufacturing. More than thirty chapters discuss how to account for, and reduce, costs in every area of a company, from the plant and warehouse to design and planning. This unprecedented inside view reveals different strategic approaches to profit planning in Japan and shows how they can be adapted to American needs.

ISBN 0-915299-50-X / 568 pages / $59.95 / Order code JMACT-BK

Measuring, Managing, and Maximizing Performance
by Will Kaydos

You do not need to be an exceptionally skilled technician or inspirational leader to improve your company's quality and productivity. In non-technical, jargon-free, practical terms this books details the entire process of improving performance, from "why" and "how" the improvement process works to "what" must be done to begin and to sustain continuous improvement of performance. Special emphasis is given to the role that performance measurement plays in identifying problems and opportunities.

ISBN 0-915299-98-4 / 208 pages / $34.95 / Order MMMP-BK

Productivity Press, Inc., Dept. BK, P.O. Box 3007, Cambridge, MA 02140 1-800-274-9911

Workplace Management

by Taiichi Ohno

An in-depth view of how one of this century's leading industrial thinkers approaches problem solving and continuous improvement. Gleaned from Ohno's forty years of experimentation and innovation at Toyota Motor Co., where he created JIT, this book explains the concepts Ohno considers most important to successful management, with an emphasis on quality.

ISBN 0-915299-19-4 / 165 pages / $34.95 / Order code WPM-BK

Achieving Total Quality Management
A Program for Action

by Michel Perigord

This is an outstanding book on total quality management (TQM) a compact guide to the concepts, methods, and techniques involved in achieving total quality. It shows you how to make TQM a company-wide strategy, not just in technical areas, but in marketing and administration as well. Written in an accessible, instructive style by a top European quality expert, it is methodical, logical, and thorough. A historical outline and discussion of the quality-price relationship, is followed by an investigation of the five quality imperatives (conformity, prevention, excellence, measurement, and responsibility). Major methods and tools for total quality are spelled out and implementation strategies are reviewed.

ISBN 0-915299-60-7 / 384 pages / $45.00 / Order Code ACHTQM-BK

The Quality and Productivity Equation
American Corporate Strategies for the 1990s

edited by Ross E. Robson

How well will your business succeed in the next decade? What challenges are in store, and how are you planning to meet them? Here's what over thirty of America's most forward-thinking business and academic leaders (including John Diebold, Malcolm Forbes, Donald Ephlin, Alan Magazine, and Wickham Skinner) are already thinking about and doing. Based on presentations made at Utah State University's College of Business "Partners in Business" seminars for 1989. Take advantage of their expertise to shape your own strategy.

ISBN 0-915299-71-2 / 558 pages / $29.95 / Order code QPE-BK

Productivity Press, Inc., Dept. BK, P.O. Box 3007, Cambridge, MA 02140 1-800-274-9911

Competing Through Productivity and Quality

edited by Y.K. Shetty and Vernon M. Buehler

Fifty authorities from American industry, labor, and higher education share their most up-to-date strategies and policies for productivity and quality improvement. Inspiring, insightful, and practical guidance from such people as David Halberstam, Shigeo Shingo, C. Jackson Grayson, Lynn Williams, and John Young. This book provides the information necessary to ensure the long-term economic health of the U.S.

ISBN 0-915299-43-7 / 576 pages / $39.95 / Order code COMP-BK

Productivity Newsletter

Productivity has been helping America's most effective companies improve quality, lower costs, and increase their competitive power since 1979. Productivity has direct, immediate access to a unique netwok of internationl information you can't find anywhere else. Every month, you'll read about dozens of specific strategies and techniques that can make a dramatic diffeence in your career and in your company's future.

• Learn exactly which productivity strategies work and which do not from detailed case studies
• Discover the latest international developments and future trends
• Read about important innovations, new books, and the people and companies responsible for them
• Save money on Productivity conferences and seminars with special subscriber discounts.

To subscribe, or for more information, call 1-800-899-5009. Please state order code "BA" when ordering.

The Profit Management Institute (PMI)

Unless an accounting system shared the values of the new manufacturing strategies, it will not reflect what is really going on within an organization. In a Just-In-Time environment, operating performance can no longer be measured by antiquated notions of labor, machine utilization and overhead absorption, because it results in inconsistent and unreliable data. The "World Class Management Accounting" course presents a simplified accounting system that supports the elimination of waste in all segments of the company. This two-day intense and interactive workshop is a revolutionary new way to approach a business's need for information. You'll acquire new tools that marketing, sales, production, finance, and executive managers can use to make day-to-day decisions.

For more information about PMI's course in "World Class Management Accounting," please call 1-800-888-6485.

Productivity Press, Inc., Dept. BK, P.O. Box 3007, Cambridge, MA 02140 1-800-274-9911

COMPLETE LIST OF TITLES FROM PRODUCTIVITY PRESS

Akao, Yoji (ed.). **Quality Function Deployment: Integrating Customer Requirements into Product Design**
ISBN 0-915299-41-0 / 1990 / 387 pages / $ 75.00 / order code QFD

Asaka, Tetsuichi and Kazuo Ozeki (eds.). **Handbook of Quality Tools: The Japanese Approach**
ISBN 0-915299-45-3 / 1990 / 336 pages / $59.95 / order code HQT

Belohlav, James A. **Championship Management: An Action Model for High Performance**
ISBN 0-915299-76-3 / 1990 / 265 pages / $29.95 / order code CHAMPS

Birkholz, Charles and Jim Villella. **The Battle to Stay Competitive: Changing the Traditional Workplace**
ISBN 0-915-299-96-8 / 1991 / 110 pages / $9.95 /order code BATTLE

Christopher, William F. **Productivity Measurement Handbook**
ISBN 0-915299-05-4 / 1985 / 680 pages / $137.95 / order code PMH

D'Egidio, Franco. **The Service Era: Leadership in a Global Environment**
ISBN 0-915299-68-2 / 1990 / 165 pages / $29.95 / order code SERA

Ford, Henry. **Today and Tomorrow**
ISBN 0-915299-36-4 / 1988 / 286 pages / $24.95 / order code FORD

Fukuda, Ryuji. **CEDAC: A Tool for Continuous Systematic Improvement**
ISBN 0-915299-26-7 / 1990 / 144 pages / $49.95 / order code CEDAC

Fukuda, Ryuji. **Managerial Engineering: Techniques for Improving Quality and Productivity in the Workplace** (rev.)
ISBN 0-915299-09-7 / 1986 / 208 pages / $39.95 / order code ME

Grief, Michel. **The Visual Factory: Building Participation Through Shared Information**
ISBN 0-915299-67-4 / 1991 / 320 pages / $49.95 / order code VFAC

Hatakeyama, Yoshio. **Manager Revolution! A Guide to Survival in Today's Changing Workplace**
ISBN 0-915299-10-0 / 1986 / 208 pages / $24.95 / order code MREV

Hirano, Hiroyuki. **JIT Factory Revolution: A Pictorial Guide to Factory Design of the Future**
ISBN 0-915299-44-5 / 1989 / 227 pages / $49.95 / order code JITFAC

Hirano, Hiroyuki. **JIT Implementation Manual: The Complete Guide to Just-In-Time Manufacturing**
ISBN 0-915299-66-6 / 1990 / 1006 pages / $2500.00 / order code HIRANO

Horovitz, Jacques. **Winning Ways: Achieving Zero-Defect Service**
ISBN 0-915299-78-X / 1990 / 165 pages / $24.95 / order code WWAYS

Japan Human Relations Association (ed.). **The Idea Book: Improvement Through TEI (Total Employee Involvement)**
ISBN 0-915299-22-4 / 1988 / 232 pages / $49.95 / order code IDEA

Japan Human Relations Association (ed.). **The Service Industry Idea Book: Employee Involvement in Retail and Office Improvement**
ISBN 0-915299-65-8 / 1990 / 294 pages / $49.95 / order code SIDEA

Japan Management Association (ed.). **Kanban and Just-In-Time at Toyota: Management Begins at the Workplace** (rev.), Translated by David J. Lu
ISBN 0-915299-48-8 / 1989 / 224 pages / $36.50 / order code KAN

Japan Management Association and Constance E. Dyer. **The Canon Production System: Creative Involvement of the Total Workforce**
ISBN 0-915299-06-2 / 1987 / 251 pages / $36.95 / order code CAN

Jones, Karen (ed.). **The Best of TEI: Current Perspectives on Total Employee Involvement**
ISBN 0-915299-63-1 / 1989 / 502 pages / $175.00 / order code TEI

JUSE. **TQC Solutions: The 14-Step Process**
ISBN 0-915299-79-8 / 1991 / 416 pages / 2 volumes / $120.00 / order code TQCS

Kanatsu, Takashi. **TQC for Accounting: A New Role in Companywide Improvement**
ISBN 0-915299-73-9 / 1991 / 244 pages / $45.00 / order code TQCA

Karatsu, Hajime. **Tough Words For American Industry**
ISBN 0-915299-25-9 / 1988 / 178 pages / $24.95 / order code TOUGH

Karatsu, Hajime. **TQC Wisdom of Japan: Managing for Total Quality Control**, Translated by David J. Lu
ISBN 0-915299-18-6 / 1988 / 136 pages / $34.95 / order code WISD

Kaydos, Will. **Measuring, Managing, and Maximizing Performance**
ISBN 0-915299- 98-4 / 1991 / 208 pages / $34.95 / order code MMMP

Kobayashi, Iwao. **20 Keys to Workplace Improvement**
ISBN 0-915299-61-5 / 1990 / 264 pages / $34.95 / order code 20KEYS

Lu, David J. **Inside Corporate Japan: The Art of Fumble-Free Management**
ISBN 0-915299-16-X / 1987 / 278 pages / $24.95 / order code ICJ

Merli, Giorgio. **Total Manufacturing Management: Production Organization for the 1990s**
ISBN 0-915299-58-5 / 1990 / 224 pages / $39.95 / order code TMM

Mizuno, Shigeru (ed.). **Management for Quality Improvement: The 7 New QC Tools**
ISBN 0-915299-29-1 / 1988 / 324 pages / $59.95 / order code 7QC

Monden, Yasuhiro and Michiharu Sakurai (eds.). **Japanese Management Accounting: A World Class Approach to Profit Management**
ISBN 0-915299-50-X / 1990 / 568 pages / $59.95 / order code JMACT

Nachi-Fujikoshi (ed.). **Training for TPM: A Manufacturing Success Story**
ISBN 0-915299-34-8 / 1990 / 272 pages / $59.95 / order code CTPM

Nakajima, Seiichi. **Introduction to TPM: Total Productive Maintenance**
ISBN 0-915299-23-2 / 1988 / 149 pages / $39.95 / order code ITPM

Nakajima, Seiichi. **TPM Development Program: Implementing Total Productive Maintenance**
ISBN 0-915299-37-2 / 1989 / 428 pages / $85.00 / order code DTPM

Nikkan Kogyo Shimbun, Ltd./Factory Magazine (ed.). **Poka-yoke: Improving Product Quality by Preventing Defects**
ISBN 0-915299-31-3 / 1989 / 288 pages / $59.95 / order code IPOKA

Ohno, Taiichi. **Toyota Production System: Beyond Large-Scale Production**
ISBN 0-915299-14-3 / 1988 / 162 pages / $39.95 / order code OTPS

Productivity Press, Inc., Dept. BK, P.O. Box 3007, Cambridge, MA 02140 1-800-274-9911

Ohno, Taiichi. **Workplace Management**
ISBN 0-915299-19-4 / 1988 / 165 pages / $34.95 / order code WPM

Ohno, Taiichi and Setsuo Mito. **Just-In-Time for Today and Tomorrow**
ISBN 0-915299-20-8 / 1988 / 208 pages / $34.95 / order code OMJIT

Perigord, Michel. **Achieving Total Quality Management: A Program for Action**
ISBN 0-915299-60-7 / 1991 / 384 pages / $45.00 / order code ACHTQM

Psarouthakis, John. **Better Makes Us Best**
ISBN 0-915299-56-9 / 1989 / 112 pages / $16.95 / order code BMUB

Robinson, Alan. **Continuous Improvement in Operations: A Systematic Approach to Waste Reduction**
ISBN 0-915299-51-8 / 1991 / 416 pages / $34.95 / order code ROB2-C

Robson, Ross (ed.). **The Quality and Productivity Equation: American Corporate Strategies for the 1990s**
ISBN 0-915299-71-2 / 1990 / 558 pages / $29.95 / order code QPE

Shetty, Y.K and Vernon M. Buehler (eds.). **Competing Through Productivity and Quality**
ISBN 0-915299-43-7 / 1989 / 576 pages / $39.95 / order code COMP

Shingo, Shigeo. **Non-Stock Production: The Shingo System for Continuous Improvement**
ISBN 0-915299-30-5 / 1988 / 480 pages / $75.00 / order code NON

Shingo, Shigeo. **A Revolution In Manufacturing: The SMED System**, Translated by Andrew P. Dillon
ISBN 0-915299-03-8 / 1985 / 383 pages / $70.00 / order code SMED

Shingo, Shigeo. **The Sayings of Shigeo Shingo: Key Strategies for Plant Improvement**, Translated by Andrew P. Dillon
ISBN 0-915299-15-1 / 1987 / 208 pages / $39.95 / order code SAY

Shingo, Shigeo. **A Study of the Toyota Production System from an Industrial Engineering Viewpoint** (rev.)
ISBN 0-915299-17-8 / 1989 / 293 pages / $39.95 / order code STREV

Shingo, Shigeo. **Zero Quality Control: Source Inspection and the Poka-yoke System**,Translated by Andrew P. Dillon
ISBN 0-915299-07-0 / 1986 / 328 pages / $70.00 / order code ZQC

Shinohara, Isao (ed.). **New Production System: JIT Crossing Industry Boundaries**
ISBN 0-915299-21-6 / 1988 / 224 pages / $34.95 / order code NPS

Sugiyama, Tomo. **The Improvement Book: Creating the Problem-Free Workplace**
ISBN 0-915299-47-X / 1989 / 236 pages / $49.95 / order code IB

Suzue, Toshio and Akira Kohdate. **Variety Reduction Program (VRP): A Production Strategy for Product Diversification**
ISBN 0-915299-32-1 / 1990 / 164 pages / $59.95 / order code VRP

Tateisi, Kazuma. **The Eternal Venture Spirit: An Executive's Practical Philosophy**
ISBN 0-915299-55-0 / 1989 / 208 pages/ $19.95 / order code EVS

Yasuda, Yuzo. **40 Years, 20 Million Ideas: The Toyota Suggestion System**
ISBN 0-915299-74-7 / 1991 / 210 pages / $39.95 / order code 4020

Productivity Press, Inc., Dept. BK, P.O. Box 3007, Cambridge, MA 02140 1-800-274-9911

Audio-Visual Programs

Japan Management Association. **Total Productive Maintenance: Maximizing Productivity and Quality**
ISBN 0-915299-46-1 / 167 slides / 1989 / $749.00 / order code STPM
ISBN 0-915299-49-6 / 2 videos / 1989 / $749.00 / order code VTPM

Shingo, Shigeo. **The SMED System**, Translated by Andrew P. Dillon
ISBN 0-915299-11-9 / 181 slides / 1986 / $749.00 / order code S5
ISBN 0-915299-27-5 / 2 videos / 1987 / $749.00 / order code V5

Shingo, Shigeo. **The Poka-yoke System**, Translated by Andrew P. Dillon
ISBN 0-915299-13-5 / 235 slides / 1987 / $749.00 / order code S6
ISBN 0-915299-28-3 / 2 videos / 1987 / $749.00 / order code V6

Returns of AV programs willl be accepted for incorrect or damaged shipments only.

TO ORDER: Write, phone, or fax Productivity Press, Dept. BK, P.O. Box 3007, Cambridge, MA 02140, phone 1-800-274-9911, fax 617-864-6286. Send check or charge to your credit card (American Express, Visa, MasterCard accepted).

U.S. ORDERS: Add $5 shipping for first book, $2 each additional for UPS surface delivery. CT residents add 8% and MA residents 5% sales tax. For each AV program that you order, add $5 for programs with 1 or 2 tapes, and $12 for programs with 3 or more tapes.

INTERNATIONAL ORDERS: Write, phone, or fax for quote and indicate shipping method desired. Pre-payment in U.S. dollars must accompany your order (checks must be drawn on U.S. banks). When quote is returned with payment, your order will be shipped promptly by the method requested.

NOTE: Prices subject to change without notice.